Saral Jyotish

Part IV

Author

V.P.Goel

Published by

Performonks Education and Consulting Services LLP

44, Tatvam Villas, Sector 48, Sohna Road,Gurugram, Haryana 122018
E-Mail: rashi@performonks.com

First published in 2021

Revised & Reprinted 2024

ISBN: 978 - 81- 973347- 5- 7

Published by

Performonks Education and Consulting Services LLP

Books by the Author

हिंदी में	**In English**	**In Russian**
वर्ग कुंडलियों से सटीक पफलित	Comprehensive Prediction by Divisional Charts	Comprehensive Prediction by Divisional Charts
योगिनी दशा से पफलित	Snapshot Prediction using Yogini Dasha	Snapshot Prediction using Yogini Dasha
शोडाषोत्तरी दशा से पफलित	Predict Through Shodashottary Dasha	
आयु रहस्य	Unravelling Puzzle of longevity	
	Predict Through Shasti Hayani Dasha	
	Locate Disease Astrologically	Locate Disease Astrologically
जैमिनी ज्योतिष से पफलित	Predicting through Jaimini Astrology	Predicting through Jaimini Astrology
नवांश से पफलित	Predict with Navamsha	Predict with Navamsha
सप्तांश से पफलित	Predict with Saptamsha	Predict with Saptamsha
दशमांश से पफलित	Predict with Dashamsha	Predict with Dashamsha
	Predict with Trishamsha	
सरल ज्योतिष 1	Saral Jyotish 1	Saral Jyotish 1
	Saral Jyotish 2	Saral Jyotish 2
	Saral Jyotish 3	Saral Jyotish 3
	Saral Jyotish 4	Saral Jyotish 4
	Saral Jyotish 5	
	Saral Jyotish 6	
सरल षड्बल		

Preface

I take great pleasure in writing Part 4 of Saral Jyotish and thanks all Astrology lovers for their encouragement and good wishes to continue writing this series.

This part of Saral Jyotish deals with two important features of Hindu Astrology. One is exaltation of planets and the other is Panch Maha Purush Yoga. These features, when present in a horoscope, bring smile and happiness. A planet is exalted in 9 percent of time of its movement in twelve signs. A good number of horoscopes will have at least one planet in its exaltation sign. Some horoscopes can have more planets in exaltation but we do not find many highly placed people with this feature. The percentage of successful people is lower than the percentage of horoscopes having exalted planets. Sage Garg has opined that in Kaliyuga debilitated planets are desired even when there are three planets in exaltation. The effects of debilitation have been discussed in part 2 of Saral Jyotish.

Panch Maha Purush Yoga is the second topic of this part. This yoga is also found in a large number of horoscopes. There are 56 possible ways by which this yoga is formed. The presence of Panch Maha Purush Yoga is not a rare feature. This yoga is praised by sages. All persons having this yoga do not experience the praiseworthy effects as described in classics.

The results of these yoga are given in simple and easy to understand explanation. Formation of these yoga for each Ascendant is given and will help practithe readers to apply them on a horoscope. This is equally useful for practising Astrologers and for learners.

A chapter on modifications of these yoga is also included which will be helpful to gauge the potential of the yoga.

My sincere thanks to all Astrology lovers and readers of Saral Jyotish series for their encouragement and comments.

Vinod Prakash Goel
Email: vpgoel2019@gmail.com
Subscribe to my YouTube channel: saraljyotishbyvpgoe

Contents

Chapter 01

Exaltation

Exaltation is one of the five dignities of a planet. The dictionary meaning of exaltation is elation, raised or elevated in rank or character or to powerful position.

Every planet is assigned a sign in which he gets exalted. The planet gets at the peak of exaltation at some longitude in the sign of its exaltation. This is called the deep exaltation point of the planet. We can tabulate the sign and the longitude of peak or deep exaltation for each planet. Generally, we take the full sign as the exaltation sign.

Planet	**Sign of Exaltation**	**Longitude of deep exaltation**
Sun	Aries	10 degrees
Moon	Taurus	3 degrees
Mars	Capricorn	28 degrees
Mercury	Virgo	15 degrees
Jupiter	Cancer	5 degrees
Venus	Pisces	27 degrees
Saturn	Libra	20 degrees
Rahu	Gemini	3 degrees
Ketu	Sagittarius	3 degrees

1. As per Al – Baruni, the deep exaltation longitude is 19 degrees for Sun, 5 degrees for Jupiter and 20 degrees for Saturn.
2. In some other view the exaltation of Rahu is 20-degree Taurus and of Ketu is 20-degree Scorpio.

Discussion

We will discuss each planet in exaltation for every Ascendant. This is based on the principles of Laghu Parasari. We follow a simple rule that exaltation of auspicious planet is good and the exaltation of inauspicious planet is bad. This way we can identify the effects of exaltation for each Ascendant. This is not the final word. The final results depend on the complete horoscope and not on one planet only. These results are still subjected to modifications.

Aries – Sun is lord of fifth house and is a benefic. Sun gets exalted in Ascendant and improves the results of fifth house like intelligence but will not improve the Jeeva of fifth house especially when associated with trik or trishadaya house. Any association of trik lord will damage Sun but will improve the trik lord. Moon is lord of fourth house and is a neutral. Moon is exalted in second house which is also a neutral house. Thus, Moon will impart result of its association. Mars is lagna and eighth lord. In its exaltation it will aspect lagna and lagna becomes very strong. Mars with benefic will behave as a benefic. Mercury is third and sixth lord. Mercury is a malefic for Aries. Exalted Mercury will boost the effects of third house and the person will be very courageous and can be army chief. Malefic relation with Mercury will make Mercury a bitter malefic. Jupiter is lord of ninth and twelfth house. Exaltation of Jupiter in fourth house will improve ninth and twelfth house. Venus is second and seventh lord and exalts in twelfth house. Venus can be treated as neutral and maraca. Second house will be greatly benefitted and seventh house is harmed. Saturn is lord of tenth and is neutral. Being eleventh lord, it is now a malefic. It will exalt in seventh house and can damage the marriage but will improve tenth and eleventh house. Saturn is Dig Bali when exalted.

Taurus – Sun is fourth lord and is neutral. Sun is exalted in twelfth house which is also a neutral house. Sun will give effects according to its association. Moon is third lord and is exalted in lagna. Third house is a trishadaya house. Third lord exalted may not be fully beneficial but will be malefic and gives success after hard work. Mars is lord of seventh and twelfth house. Mars is neutral and gives results according to its association. Mercury is lord of second and fifth house. It exalts in fifth house and is a benefic. Any malefic association will spoil the fifth house. Jupiter is lord of a trik and a trishadaya house. Its exaltation is not good. Venus is lagna and sixth lord. The mooltrikona sign is in sixth house and he exalts in eleventh house. It will promote the sixth house and lagna. Saturn is the lord of ninth and tenth house and is a benefic. The exaltation of Saturn will be considered good.

Gemini – Sun is a trishadaya lord. Its exaltation is eleventh house. Benefic association is desired to get good results of Sun. A trishadaya lord when placed in trishadaya house generally gives good results but after efforts and hard work. Moon is second lord and exalts in twelfth house. It will promote second house effects. Mars is not a benefic planet for Gemini. If Mars is with trine lord, then Mars will be good but will spoil the trine lord. Mercury is lagna and fourth lord and is a benefic. Jupiter is lord of two Kendra house and is neutral. With trishadaya lords it will give bad results but with trine lords it will give good results. Venus is a trine lord. The other house owned by Venus is neutral house as such Venus is auspicious. Saturn is lord of neutral eighth house and a lord of a trine. It will give good results.

Cancer – Sun is a neutral lord of second house. In exaltation, it is in tenth house and is Dig Bali. Sun will give good results. Moon is lagna lord and in exaltation will be in eleventh house and is very auspicious. Mars is a lord of a Kendra and a trikona and is a yoga karaka. Mars exalts in seventh house. Mercury is not a benefic as it is lord of third and twelfth house. Exalted Mercury is not welcome. Jupiter is lord of a trine and a trik house. Mooltrikona of Jupiter is in trine and Jupiter is auspicious. Venus is lord of fourth and eleventh house. Venus is not a benefic planet for Cancer. Saturn is the lord of seventh and eighth house and behaves as neutral.

Leo – Sun is lagna lord getting exalted in ninth house. It is a benefic. Moon is lord of neutral twelfth house and exalts in tenth house. Mars is lord of a trine and a Kendra and is yoga Karaka. Mercury is lord of second and eleventh house. Eleventh house is trishadaya and Mercury exalts in second house. It can create problems for second house. Jupiter is lord of a trine and of neutral eighth house. Jupiter is benefic. Venus is tenth and third lord. As tenth lord, he is neutral and becomes malefic as owner of third house. Venus is not considered benefic. Saturn is lord of sixth and seventh house. Saturn is considered malefic.

Virgo – Sun is lord of neutral twelfth house and exalts in eighth house. He is not a benefic but at best it can behave as neutral. Moon is lord of strongest trishadaya, eleventh house and is a malefic. Moon exalts in ninth house and may not give good results. Mars is lord of third and eighth house and is a malefic. Mercury is lord of lagna and tenth house. Mercury is very beneficial. Jupiter is the lord of two Kendra and is neutral. It is exalted in eleventh house and gives above average results. Venus is ninth and second lord. Second house is neutral and Venus is a benefic. Saturn is the lord of fifth and sixth house. He can give good results.

Libra – Sun is the lord of trishadaya house and is exalted in seventh house. Sun remains a malefic. Moon is tenth lord and is exalted in eighth house. Moon is neutral and gives results as per its association. Mars is maraca lord. As seventh lord it is neutral and remains so. Mars exalts in fourth house and give results depending on its conjunction. Mercury is lord of twelfth and ninth house and is treated as benefic. Jupiter is lord of two trishadaya houses and is a malefic. Jupiter exalts in tenth house and will promote sixth house effects. Venus is lagna lord and of neutral eighth house. Generally, it will give good results but it depends on the association with Venus. Saturn is a benefic and yoga Karaka. Saturn exalts in lagna and is no longer Dig Bali.

Scorpio – Sun is neutral being tenth lord. The results of Sun depend on its association. Moon is trine lord and is benefic. Mars is lagna and sixth lord. Sixth house is a trik and trishadaya house and is the mooltrikona sign of Mars. Mars associated with benefic will act as a benefic. Mercury is lord of eighth and eleventh house and is a malefic. Jupiter is the lord of trine and neutral second house. Jupiter is a benefic. Jupiter exalts in ninth house and his benefic results are increased manifold. Venus is seventh and twelfth house. Venus can be taken as neutral. Saturn is the lord of third and fourth house. As fourth lord, he is neutral but acquire malefic nature by lordship of third house.

Sagittarius – Sun is trine lord and is a benefic. Sun exalts in the other trine and become more benefic. Moon is neutral eighth lord. Moon exalts in sixth house. Mars is twelfth and trine lord and is a benefic. Mars exalts in second house of wealth. Mercury is the lord of two Kendra and is neutral. Jupiter is also lord of two Kendra. One of the Kendra is lagna and Jupiter now behave as a benefic but the association is also important. Venus is lord of sixth and eleventh house and is a malefic. Venus exalts in fourth house and can be harmful to fourth house. Saturn is a malefic lord of third house. Saturn exalts in eleventh house, which is other trishadaya house and it will give good results.

Capricorn – Sun is the lord of neutral eighth house. Sun is exalted in fourth house and can cause problems to fourth house effects. It may not harm tenth house. Moon is seventh lord and exalts in fifth house. Moon should give very good results. Mars is lord of fourth and eleventh house. Mars is malefic and will exalt in lagna and will aspect fourth house and promotes it. Mercury is the lord of sixth and ninth house. Mercury is a benefic and exalts in ninth house. Jupiter is lord of twelfth and third house and is a malefic. Jupiter is exalted in seventh house. Venus is a lord of a Kendra and a trine. Venus is a benefic and yoga Karaka. Saturn is lord of lagna and second house. Saturn will give maraca results as well.

Aquarius – Sun is lord of seventh house and its results will depend on its association. Moon is the lord of malefic sixth house. Moon exalts in fourth house and carry effects of sixth house to fourth house. Mars is third lord and tenth lord. Mars becomes a malefic and is exalted in twelfth house. This can give displacement for job. Mercury is fifth and eighth house and can be a benefic if he is well associated with benefic. Jupiter is eleventh lord and is a malefic. Exaltation of Jupiter in sixth house is good for second house. Venus is the lord of a Kendra and a trikona and is a benefic yoga Karaka. Venus will exalt in second house and promote it. Saturn is lagna and twelfth lord and is a benefic. Saturn will be in exaltation in ninth house and will give good results.

Pisces – Sun is lord of malefic sixth house getting exalted in second house and promotes the second house. Moon is fifth lord and is a benefic. Moon is exalted in third house and promotes both the houses. Mars is second and ninth lord. Mars is benefic and is exalted in eleventh house giving all gains. Mercury is lord of two Kendra and is neutral. The results of Mercury are according to its association. Jupiter is also lord of two Kendra including lagna. Jupiter will give good results. Jupiter is exalted in a trine and gives big strength to lagna. Venus is lord of third and eighth house and is a malefic. The exaltation of Venus is in lagna which may not prove good until it has association with trine lord. Saturn is the lord of eleventh and twelfth house. Saturn is a malefic and exalts in eighth house. Saturn is not good.

Special important rules

1. It is important to check "who is this planet". Exaltation of a functional malefic is bad. Exaltation of functional benefic is good.
2. The dispositors play an important role in deciding the result of a planet. These should not be ignored. This is discussed in Saral Jyotish part 3.
3. A planet in exaltation is in Deepta state. It means that the planet is bright and is in full awakened state. He will give its results in abundance and knowingly.
4. Mars in exaltation will aspect Aries. Mars will boost Aries sign. The results will depend on the house significations occupied by Aries. Mars gets exalted in third house from Scorpio. The house containing Scorpio has to in put extra efforts.
5. Jupiter in exaltation will always aspect its sign Pisces and will promote the effects of the house. Jupiter is exalted in eighth house from Sagittarius. The house containing Sagittarius will face problems.
6. Venus is exalted in sixth house from Libra. The house containing libra can face problems. From Taurus, Venus is exalted in eleventh house and Taurus stand to gain.
7. Sagittarius sign gains strength from exaltation of Saturn if Saturn is a benefic for lagna.
8. Sun is exalted in a trine from Leo and will boost the significations of the house containing Leo.
9. Moon gets exaltation in eleventh from Cancer. The significations of house containing Cancer will get boosted.
10. Three sets of planets get their exaltation in the signs opposite to each. They are Jupiter and Mars, Sun and Saturn, Venus and Mercury. In exaltation they will be opposite to each other and will also aspect mutually. Two exalted planets in mutual aspect are not good as they both exert their influence on the other.

11. Classic has not given any rules for cancellation of exaltation. The rules for cancellation of debilitation are given. Can the same apply for cancellation of exaltation?
12. The results of a horoscope are not decided by a single planet. it is the combined effect of planets, signs, houses and the finer divisions.

Very special rule

This rule is given to decide the support to the exalted planet. every planet is exalted in a sign. We will call the lord of this sign as exaltation dispositor of the planet. now note the lord of exaltation and debilitation sign of this exaltation dispositor. If the planet is associated with this exaltation lord, then the planet gets support. If it is associated with debilitation lord then effects of exaltation are weakened.

Sun – Sun is exalted in sign of Mars. Mars is exalted in the sign of Saturn and is debilitated in the sign of Moon. If Sun is associated with Saturn, the exaltation of Sun gets support. If Sun is associated with Moon, then the exaltation of Sun is weakened.

Moon - Moon is exalted in sign of Venus. Venus is exalted in the sign of Jupiter and is debilitated in the sign of Mercury. If Moon is associated with Jupiter, the exaltation gets support. If Moon is associated with Mercury, then the exaltation of Moon is weakened.

Mars - Mars is exalted in sign of Saturn. Saturn is exalted in the sign of Venus and is debilitated in the sign of Mars. If Mars is associated with Venus, the exaltation gets support. The exaltation of Mars is not weakened.

Mercury – Mercury is exalted in its own sign. Mercury is debilitated in the sign of Jupiter. If Mercury is associated with

Jupiter, the exaltation gets weakened. Mercury is self-supportive otherwise.

Jupiter – Jupiter is exalted in sign of Moon. Moon is exalted in the sign of Venus and is debilitated in the sign of Mars. If Jupiter is associated with Venus, the exaltation gets support. If Jupiter is associated with Mars, then the exaltation of Jupiter is weakened.

Venus - Venus is exalted in sign of Jupiter. Jupiter is exalted in the sign of Moon and is debilitated in the sign of Saturn. If Venus is associated with Moon, the exaltation gets support. If Venus is associated with Saturn, then the exaltation of Venus is weakened.

Saturn – Saturn is exalted in sign of Venus. Venus is exalted in the sign of Jupiter and is debilitated in the sign of Mercury. If Saturn is associated with Jupiter, the exaltation gets support. If Saturn is associated with Mercury, then the exaltation of Saturn is weakened.

This rule can be applied even when the planet is not exalted.

ARIES

Sun

Saravali – The person will have less hair on head, will be lazy in function, angry, is a prominent personality, honourable, have weak eyesight, has coarse physique, courageous, impatient and unkind.

Saral – Sun is fifth lord. This will give good progeny and intelligence. If Sun is under malefic influence (Mars is not taken malefic as it is lord of Ascendant) then will have perverted intelligence and is worried because of progeny. His younger sibling will be well placed in life. Benefic association with Sun will make him a friend of noble person and he will be benefitted from them.

When Sun is in Virgo or Scorpio Navamsha then the good results will be feeble. If combinations of Sannyasa yoga are present then he will become head of a mutt.

Example Donatella Versace DOB 2 May 1955 TOB 5.00 POB Reggio, Italy

Birth Chart

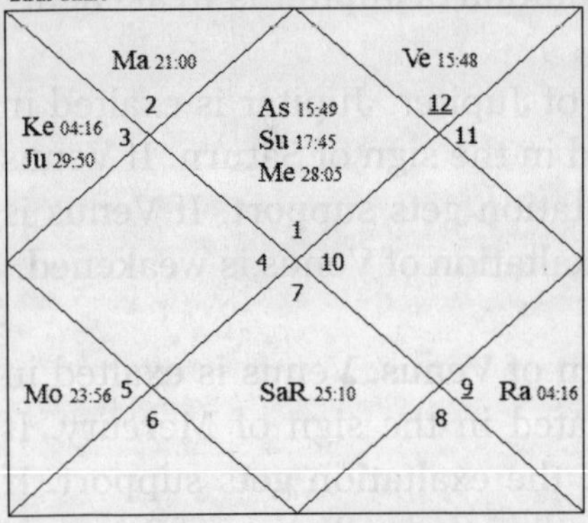

Birth Chart

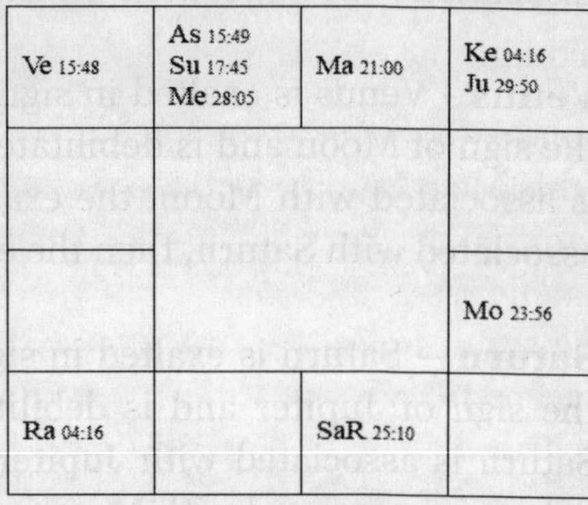

She is a fashion designer and a model. Her elder sister, Gianni Versace, founded a luxury fashion company. After the death of her brother, she inherited a portion of that company in 1997. She sold the company in 2018 but remained the chief creative officer.

She married twice. First marriage took place in 1983 in Rahu/ Rahu. Saturn is the seventh lord of Navamsha placed in tenth house with Rahu. The marriage lasted till the end of Rahu dasha and ended in divorce in 2000. She had two children from the marriage. She married again in 2004 but divorced in 2005.

She had been a heavy cocaine smoker but left it in 2014.

Three planets are exalted. No planet is debilitated and as such the yoga of exalted planets are not experienced. Sun and Saturn are exalted and are in mutual aspect. Sun is fifth lord and Saturn is tenth lord. This causes a raj yoga which enabled her to become head of an organisation. Association of Sun and

Mercury induced her to drug. Mercury is lord of third and sixth house and is a malefic. Association of Mercury with exalted Sun will weaken him. Her Sun is in Virgo in Navamsha.

Moon

Saravali – When Moon is in second house, the person will enjoy incomparable happiness and friends and be wealthy.

Saral – The person will be very happy and has all luxuries of life. If this Moon is a waxing Moon, then the good effects are increased manifold. He will have a good family and is of good character. Malefic association can create problems but will not deny luxuries. The results will depend on paksha Bala and association of Moon. Placement of Moon in Aries or Libra Navamsha will deny the luxuries and will destroy family happiness.

Example Jean Claude Romana DOB 11 February 1954 TOB 10.45 POB Lons Le Saunier, France

Birth Chart

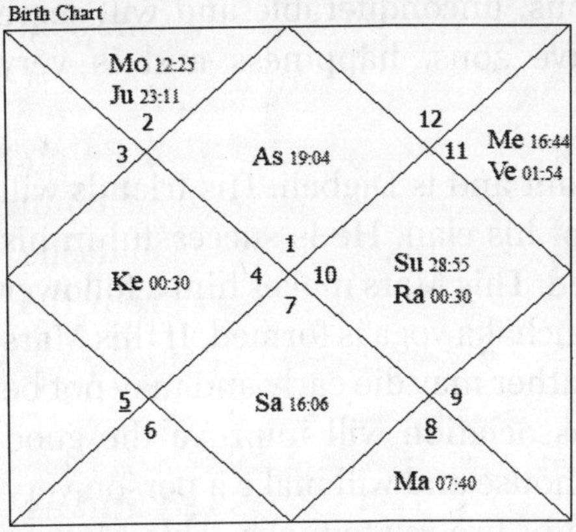

Birth Chart

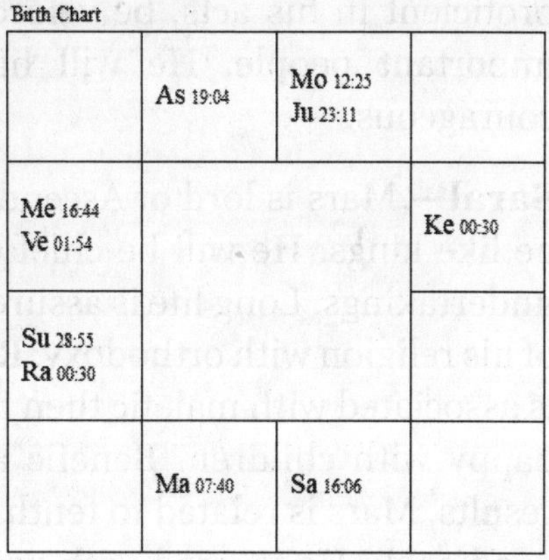

He pretended to be doctor and fooled his family for 18 years. His family thought that he is a researcher with WHO. On 9 January 1993, he borrowed gun of his father. He killed his wife and slept. Next morning, he had breakfast with children and watched cartoons. When children went to sleep, he shot them and travelled to his parent's house and had dinner with them and then shot them also. He called his girlfriend and tried to kill her also but she escaped. After this he returned to his parent's home and set it on fire. Police came but he did not reveal anything. His trial began on 25 June 1996 and was sentenced to life imprisonment on 6 July 1996.

His Moon is exalted. Mars is in seventh house from Moon and is a cause of his violent behaviour. Ketu is in fourth house and is aspected by Saturn. Moon sign is afflicted. But Jupiter with Moon will give support to the nature of Moon. Saturn is a serious malefic. Fourth house and lord are afflicted. His Moon is in Aries Navamsha and is a cause of problems. On 9 January, the dasha was Jupiter/ Mercury /Moon. All are afflicted by Mars. Mars is in Virgo in Navamsha.

Mars

Saravali – If Mars occupy tenth house, the person will be proficient in his acts, be valorous, unconquerable and will serve important people. He will have sons, happiness and is very courageous.

Saral – Mars is lord of Ascendant and is Digbali. His friends will be like kings. He will be chief of his clan. He is successful in his undertakings. Long life is assured. This Mars makes him a follower of his religion with orthodoxy. Ruchaka yoga is formed. If this Mars is associated with malefic then father may die early and may not be happy with children. Benefic association will improve the good results. Mars is related to tenth house and will make a person very good cook. He is good with use of fire related jobs. This Mars is related to fourth and fifth house, his mother may die early and his property is taken away by creditors. Placement of Mars in sixth or eighth Navamsha is not good.

Example Marc Meneau DOB 16 March 1943 TOB 9.00 POB Avallon, France

Birth Chart

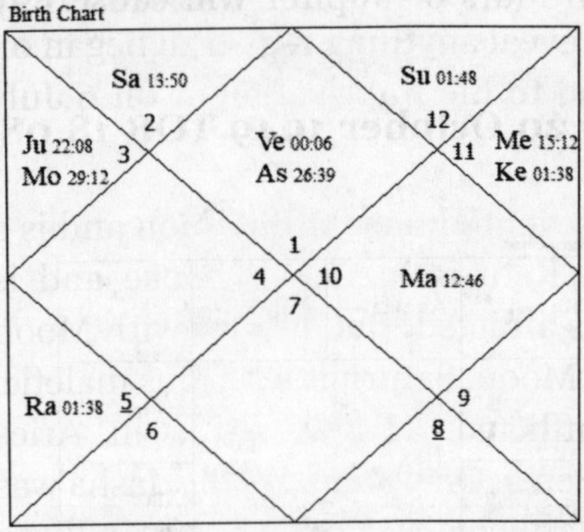

Birth Chart

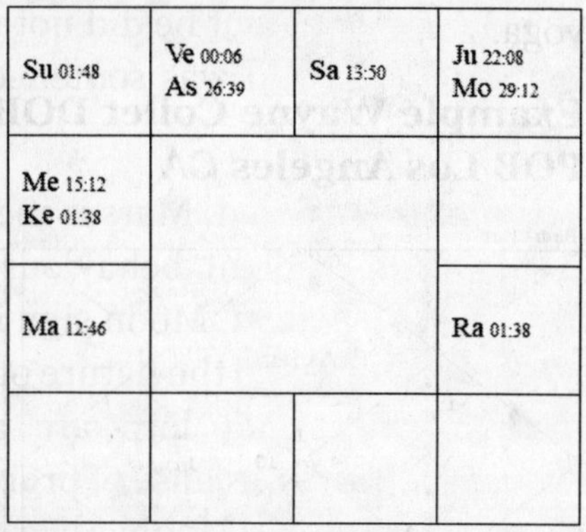

Marc was a chef. He is the three-time winner of star from Guide Michelin for cooking. All these awards came in dasha of Mercury. He married a daughter of a restaurant owner. To impress her, he stared searching old recipes from old cook books and became famous for his cooking. He earned his first star in 1972, second in 1975 and third in 1983. He was adjusted best cook of France in 1983. He started a restaurant with his wife and invented new recipes. He went bankrupt in 2007 in the dasha of Venus/ Mercury. It is Mercury who gave him honour in his MD. He died of Covid on 9 December 2020 in the dasha of Moon/ Jupiter/ Sun.

Mercury

Saravali – The person will be successful in litigations and disputes. He can contract disease, harsh in speech but not angry. He gets insulted.

Saral – He is capable in winning in any arguments. This possibly will make him a successful lawyer or a diplomate. His maternal uncles will be well placed in life but will not be helpful to him. His younger Coborn will outshine him in prosperity and position. This can lead to unhealthy relation with Coborn. This Mercury can give a strong sense of competition. When it is associated with malefic then he can be an army officer. He will get benefit from his maternal uncle. Association with Mars or Jupiter will cause Raj yoga.

Example Wayne Collet DOB 20 October 1949 TOB 18.08 POB Los Angeles CA

Birth Chart

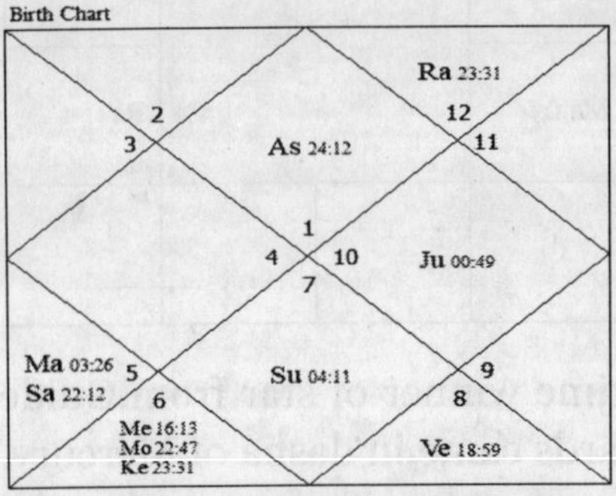

Birth Chart

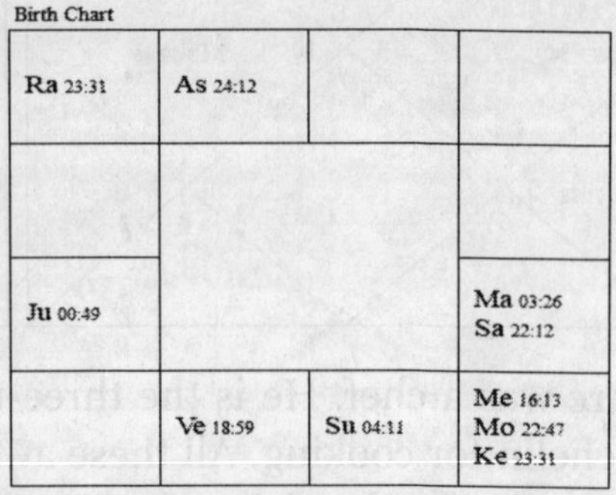

He is a silver medallist of 1972 Olympic games. He won it in 400-meter race. The dasha was Rahu/ Moon. He is an MBA and practice law. He also works as real estate agent and mortgage finance. He was inducted in the UCLA athletics hall of fame in 1992 in Saturn / Saturn. He died of cancer on 17 March 2010 at the age of 60. His Mercury dasha started on the day of his death. Mercury is aspected by debilitated Jupiter.

Jupiter

Saravali – The person will be endowed with relatives, conveyance, happiness, intelligence, pleasures and wealth. He will be great and is a source of misery to his enemy.

Saral – The ninth and twelfth lord is exalted. He will earn from foreign countries and will inherit the wealth of his father and Maternal Grandfather (Nana). He can have secret enemies in his family or will leave the house of father. Jupiter is ninth lord and is aspecting twelfth house. Placement of Jupiter in Sagittarius or Aquarius Navamsha will give separation from father and will not be very fortunate. Jupiter will aspect twelfth house. If malefic is in twelfth house then he will do wasteful expenditure. With benefic in twelfth house, he gets honours from the world. Exalted Jupiter in Kendra forms Hansa yoga.

Example James Mitchell DOB 29 February 1920 TOB 8.50 POB Sacramento CA

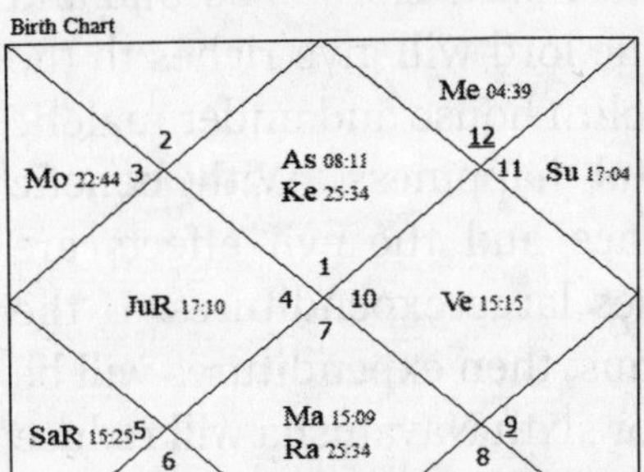

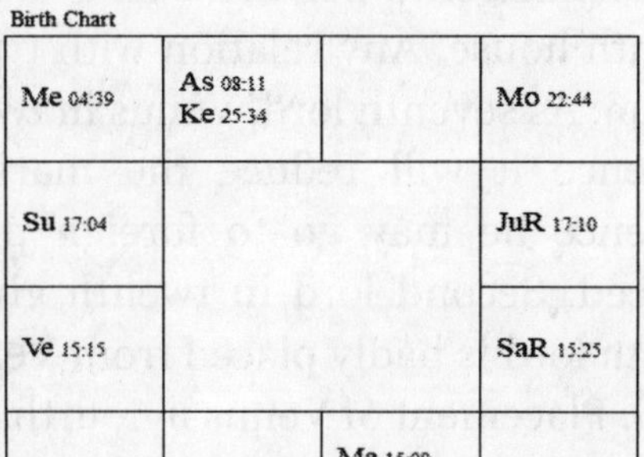

He was an actor and a dancer. His parents had migrated from England to USA. After the birth of James, his mother left for England in 1923 and never returned. His father could not handle the farm and young child. He gave James to foster father. After the death of his mother, his father married again but James remained close to his foster father. At the age of 17 years, he left for Los Angeles and started his career. He was judged best dancer of the year in the dasha of Saturn / Rahu. He was nominated for Emmy award for seven times. He got married in 1970 in Venus/ Ketu. He died on 22 January 2010 due to chronic obstructive pulmonary disease. The dasha was Moon/ Venus. Venus is maraca lord placed in Kendra. Mutual aspect of Jupiter and Venus gives strength to Jupiter.

Venus

Saravali – The person will be indolent, happy, corpulent and fallen in moral sense. He will eat clean food, be skilful in providing sleeping comforts and attendants. He will be won over by women.

Saral – He is wealthy and spendthrift. If Venus has malefic association, then he spends his wealth on luxuries and on women of questionable character. This Venus will provide wealth when he is associated with benefic. Venus is the maraca lord of second and seventh house. Any relation with trine lord will give riches to the person. As seventh lord, Venus in twelfth house and under malefic influence it will reduce the marital happiness. With benefic influence he may go to foreign place and the evil effects are reduced. Second lord in twelfth gives large expenditures. If the twelfth lord is badly placed from Venus, then expenditures will be small. Placement of Venus in fourth or sixth Navamsha will reduce the happiness of marriage.

Example Mia Farrow DOB 9 February 1945 TOB 11.27 POB Los Angeles CA

Birth Chart

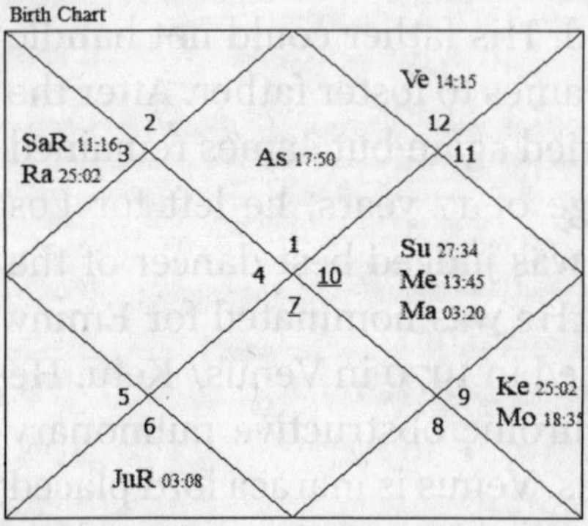

Birth Chart

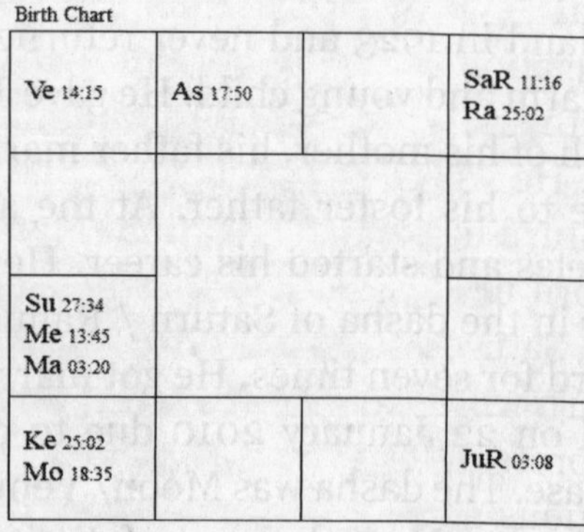

Mia Farrow is famous actress of Hollywood. She acted in more than 50 films. Her award list is very long. She was named as most influential people in the world by Times Magazine. She married Frank Sinatra on 19 July 1966. At the time of marriage, she was 21

years of age and Sinatra was of 50 years old. Marriage happened in Moon/ Jupiter. Marriage did not last long and they separated in August 1968 in dasha of Moon/ Saturn. She married Andre Previn on 10 September 1970. She was 25 and Andre was 41 years of age. The dasha was Moon/ Rahu. They divorced in 1979 in the dasha of Rahu/ Rahu. She has 15 children. Four children are born to her and she has adopted 11 children.

Her Mars is also exalted. Fifth lord is with lagna lord in tenth house and both are Digbali. In Navamsha Jupiter is seventh lord. Jupiter and Saturn are together in fifth house. Saturn is influencing seventh house and seventh lord in Navamsha. Saturn caused big age difference between her and the spouse. Venus is in fifth Navamsha with Ketu in Navamsha. The aspect of Saturn on Venus has diminished the good effects of exalted Venus.

Saturn

Saravali – The person will have ill health, lose his wife, bereft of wealth, ugly, sinful and do many mean acts.

Saral – He will be friend of powerful people. With benefic association with Jupiter, he will occupy high position and be wealthy. His wife will have a dominating nature and can control him. He will be very religious. She will be helpful in his earnings. If Saturn has malefic relation (Mars is not a malefic), then his wife is born in low family or may be separated from him. As eleventh lord, Saturn will give wealth from wife or from foreign country. The Saturn will aspect fourth house and gives involvement of public in his profession. Aspect of Saturn on ninth house will promote his religious activity and more so if Jupiter is influencing Saturn or tenth house. Placement of Saturn in Pisces or Taurus in Navamsha is not good. Saturn is causing Sasha yoga and is Digbali.

Example Rick Warren DOB 28 January 1954 TOB 11.01 POB San Jose CA

Birth Chart

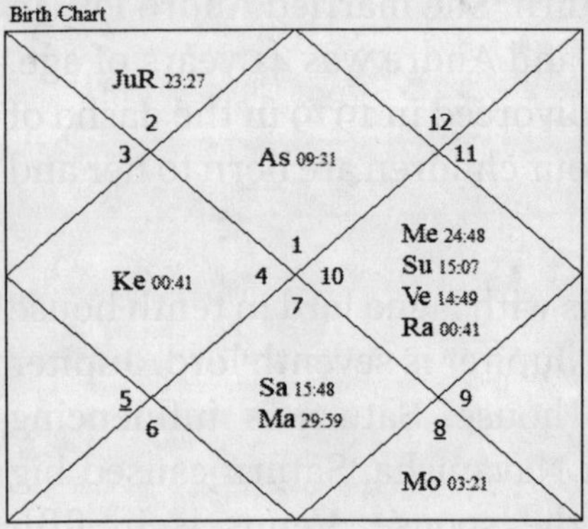

Birth Chart

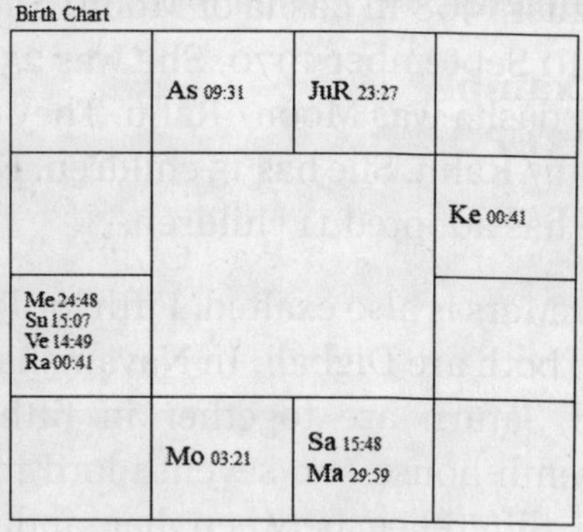

He is the founder of Saddleback Church. This is the sixth largest Church of USA. He is a writer and a Pastor. His book 'The purpose driven life' sold 30 million copies. Relation of third and fifth lord made him a writer. He was married on 21 June 1975 and has three children. The dasha at marriage was Mercury/ Ketu. Saturn is aspecting Sagittarius which is ninth house and gives efforts for religion. The tenth house from tenth lord is Cancer. Cancer and its lord are very strong and the person builds new institutions.

TAURUS

Sun

Saravali – Person will have deformed physique, be one eyed, fallen in moral sense, will marry a barren lady, be inimical to his father, weak and mean.

Saral – Sun is lord of fourth house. If fourth house has malefic then the person will change his place of living. His father is well placed in life. Any association with trine lord will be a yoga. In case Sun is with twelfth lord then the good effects of fourth house are lost. His education, lands, mother and happiness suffer. But if twelfth lord is placed in sixth, eighth or twelfth house from Sun then these effects are not experienced. Placement of Sun in sixth or eighth Navamsha is not good.

Example James Addison Baker DOB 28 April 1930 TOB 7.31 POB Houston Texas

Birth Chart

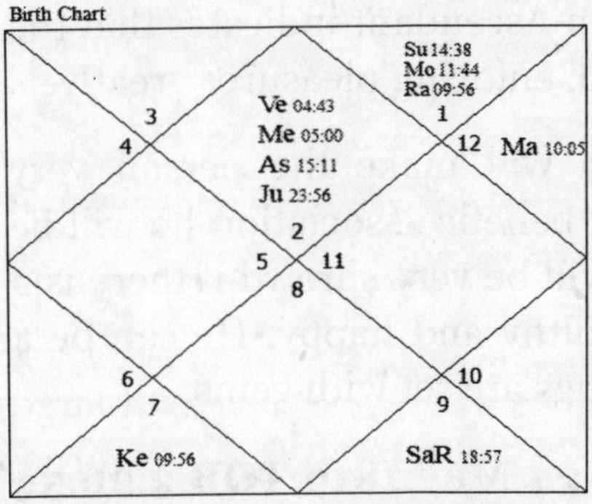

Birth Chart

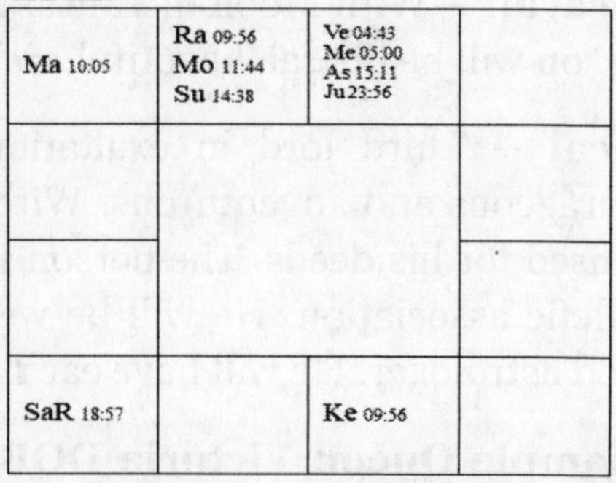

He is an American politician and held important positions in the Government. He served as an Army captain from 1952 to 1954 in the dasha of Sun/ Rahu to Sun/ Saturn. Saturn is ninth and eighth lord placed in lagna and give change for better. He married in 1953 in the dasha of Sun/ `Jupiter. Association of Sun with Moon weakens the strength of exalted Sun. In Navamsha Jupiter and Sun are together in fourth house. His first wife died in 1970 in the dasha of Mars/ Mercury. Mars is seventh lord and Mercury is second lord of Navamsha. He married for second time in 1973 in the dasha of Mars/ Sun. Mars is twelfth lord also and Sun is aspected by Venus in Navamsha. He has three children. He was appointed White house chief of staff on 20 January 1981 in the dasha of Rahu/ Saturn. Rahu is in second house and Saturn is in lagna in D 10. He left this job on 3 February 1985 to take over as US secretary of treasury. The dasha was Rahu/ Ketu. He again left this on 17 August 1988 and took over as Secretary of State on 25 January 1989. The dasha was Rahu/ Sun. Sun is third lord of D 10 and this was a willing change. He held this post till August 1992 and moved to be white house chief. On 20 January 1993, he retired. His retirement came in Jupiter/ Jupiter. Jupiter is in third house and with third lord Sun in D 10. He is 91 years now. The long life is given by three benefic in lagna.

Moon

Saravali – With Moon in Taurus in Ascendant indicates that the person will be liberal, beautiful, rich, enjoying pleasures greatly.

Saral – Third lord in exaltation will make the person very courageous and adventurous. With benefic association he will be praised for his deeds. The person will be very shrewd if there is a malefic association. He will be wealthy and happy. He can be a good astrologer. He will have ear rings are set with gems.

Example Queen Victoria DOB 24 May 1819 TOB 2.26.54 POB London

Birth Chart

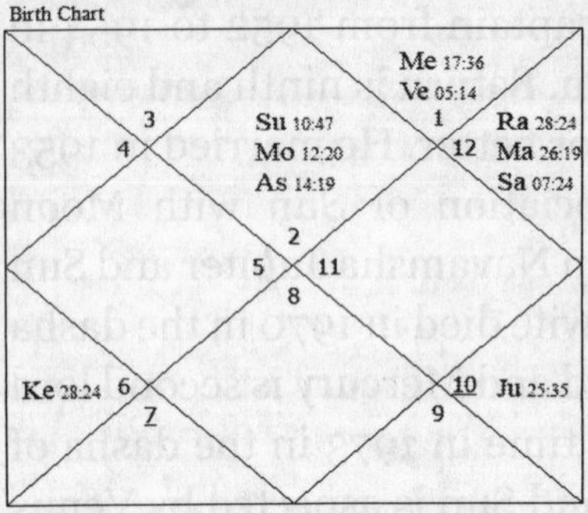

Birth Chart

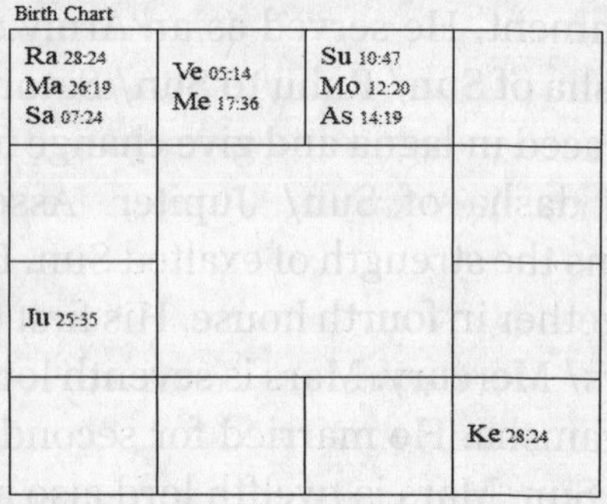

Queen Victoria remained Queen for 72 years. She was fifth in the line of succession. After the death of her father and three brothers of her father died, without a surviving legitimate issue. She became Queen at the age of 18 years. The coronation was on 20 June 1837 in the dasha of Rahu/ Jupiter. Jupiter is a yoga karaka because of its debilitation and support of Saturn to lagna. (Refer to part 2 of Saral Jyotish). She married on 10 February 1840 in the dasha of Rahu/ Saturn. In Navamsha, Saturn is in fifth house and is aspected by seventh lord Mars. She had nine children. Saturn is lagna lord of Saptamsha and is exalted. She died on 22 January 1901.

Mars

Saravali – The person is not skilful in acts, be odious, will kill living being, will not be virtuous, be very sinful and honoured by the king.

Saral – He will spend on religious activity but will be inimical to his father. His wife will be dominating. If there is a malefic in seventh house, he may have second marriage or lead a life of detachment. He has good physique and is free from illness. If Mars is associated with benefic then its dasha will be very fortunate. He may get property of his wife and will be wealthy. Placement of Mars in sixth or eighth Navamsha may deprive him of property. Mars is twelfth lord and is evil for the profession and cause obstacles. Association of Saturn by aspect can remove the hurdles as this will support ninth house. Conjunction of Saturn is not good as ninth lord will now be spoiled by twelfth lord.

Example Richard James De mont DOB 21 April 1956 TOB 6.57 POB San Francisco CA

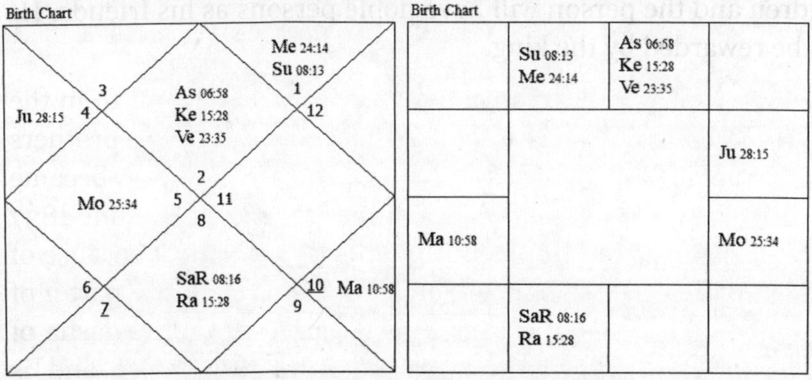

He is a record holder swimmer. He was disqualified in 1972 for use of banned drugs but was given space in the International Swimming Hall of Fame in 1990. The dasha in 1972 was of Moon/ Venus and in 1990 was Rahu/ Mercury. Moon is the third lord and Venus is the fifth lord of D 10 which causes dishonour by actions done by himself. Rahu and Mercury are in tenth house with tenth lord Jupiter in D 10. He was Coach of South Africa team in 2004 in the dasha of Jupiter/ Mercury. In 2014, he was the head coach of Arizona University. The dasha was Saturn/ Saturn. He holds record in 400-meter, 1500 meter and 4x 100 free style.

Mercury

Saravali – The person will be expert in Mantra and Tantra. He will have many sons, be endowed with learning, happiness and be delighted.

Saral – When Mercury is afflicted then it causes humiliation to the person. Mercury gives wealth through the sources of fifth house like art, son, religious institutions, king or officers. If Mercury is having benefic relation, then the person is learned, has good progeny and is born in a reputed family. He earns money from the king or he is a treasurer. Placement of Mercury in second or fourth Navamsha will not be good. As fifth lord, Mercury will give good children and the person will have noble persons as his friends. He will be rewarded by the king.

Example Jennifer Landen DOB 29 August 1983 TOB 23.52 POB Los Angeles CA

Birth Chart

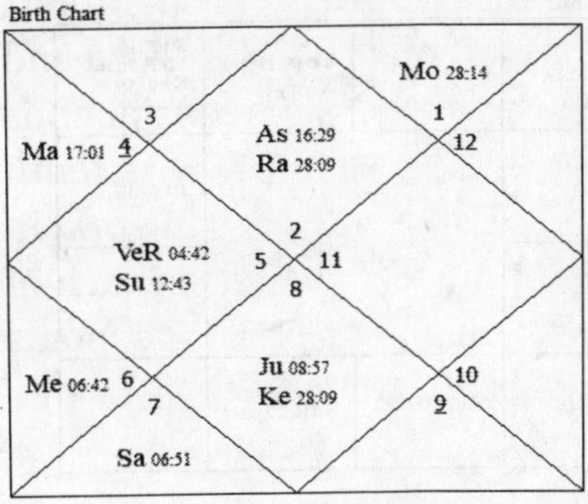

Birth Chart

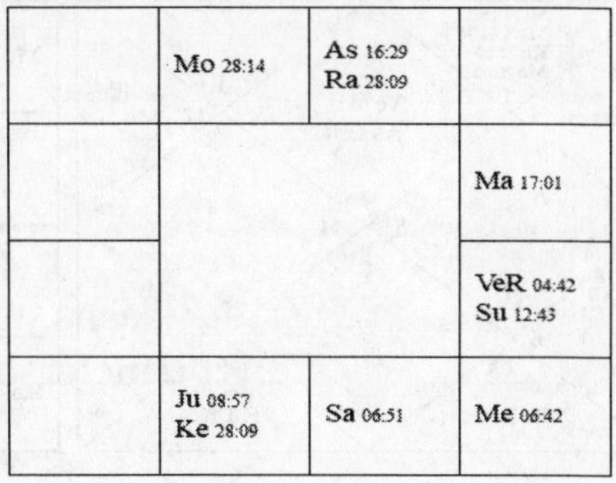

She is an actress. She has won three consecutive Emmy awards for outstanding younger actress in drama series. This came in 2006, 2007 and 2008. The dasha was Rahu/ Rahu. She is active from 1991 till date. The dasha was Moon/ Rahu in 1991. In D 10 Moon is aspected by tenth lord Jupiter. Rahu is in fifth house acting as Venus. In Navamsha, Rahu is in Virgo with Jupiter and aspected by Mercury.

Jupiter

Saravali – The person will be humiliated, be vile, ever successful, will have digestive problem and will be defeated by women and does sinful acts.

Saral – He will have gains in all efforts. He will be rich but he is not involved in the enjoyment of wealth and lead a life of contentment. He will face humiliation if Jupiter has malefic aspect. His immediate younger sibling will have short life if Saturn is aspecting Jupiter. Eighth lord in third house may give quarrels with brothers, ear trouble, fear and loss of courage. Jupiter in third house is a strong Vipreet Raj yoga and gives wealth and status. Placement of Jupiter in sixth or eighth Navamsha will be harmful. Eleventh lord in third house will give gains through self-efforts.

Example Julie Hagerty DOB 15 June 1955 TOB 4.19 POB Cincinnati OH

Birth Chart

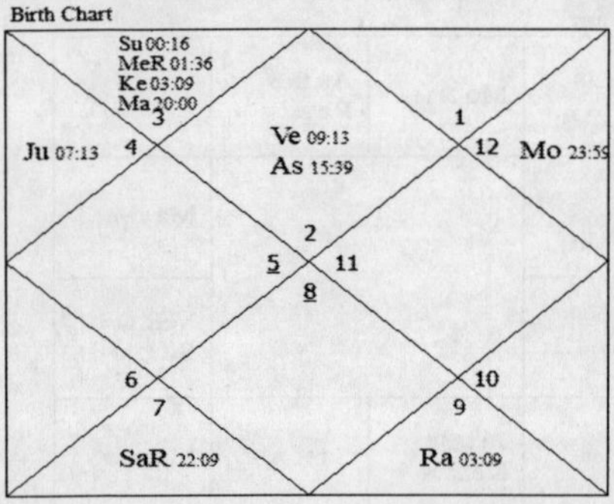

Birth Chart

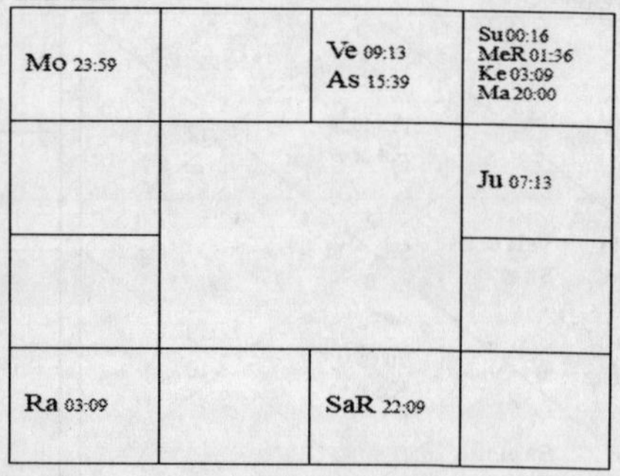

She is an actor working for films and TV shows. She started her career with the film 'Airplane' in 1980. The dasha was Venus/ Jupiter. She has acted in more than 50 films and TV show till 2020. Mercury is the lagna lord of D 10 and is placed in lagna giving long career. Her first marriage was in 1986 in dasha of Venus/ Mercury and ended in divorce in 1991 in the dasha of Sun/ Rahu. She again married in 1999 in dasha of Moon/ Jupiter. Her husband of second marriage is 9-year senior to her. Venus is the lagna lord of Navamsha and is exalted giving multiple marriage or affairs. Lord of third house has exchanged place with lord of eleventh house. This is Khala yoga and the person uses all tricks for gains.

Venus

Saravali – The person has good servants who are liked by him. He has no misery and have abundant gains.

Saral – Ascendant lord in exaltation in eleventh house will give abundant wealth. As sixth lord he will keep the enemies away. He wants to win anyway. Conjunction of Mercury with Venus is first grade wealth yoga and gives good progeny, mostly daughters, who will be very famous.

Example Tony Blair DOB 6 May 1953 TOB 6.10 POB Edinburgh UK

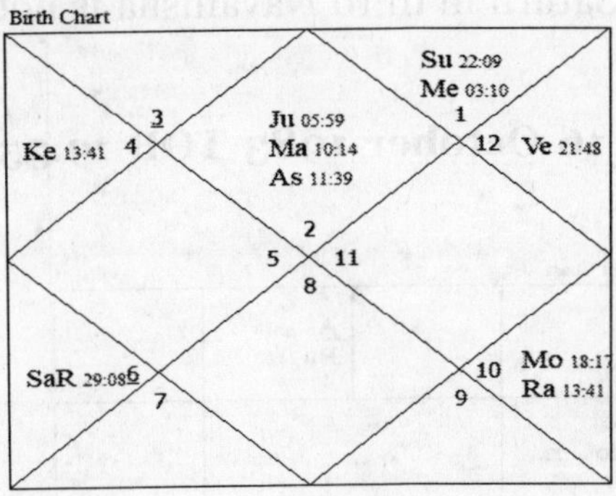

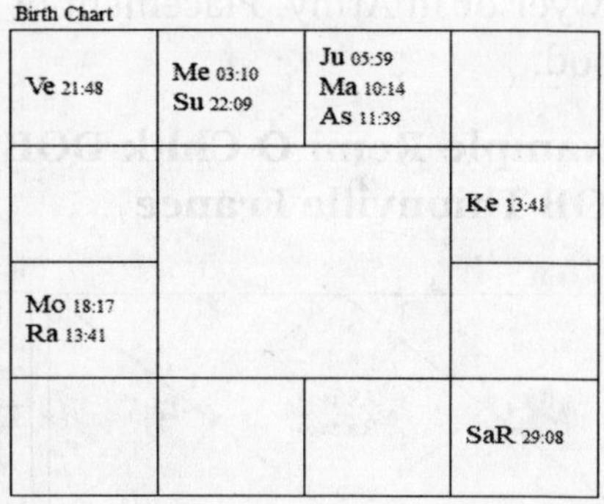

Tony Blair was Prime Minister of UK from 1997 to 2007. He was elected PM in dasha of Jupiter/ Rahu. In D 10, Jupiter is ninth lord forming a Raj yoga with Saturn in eleventh house. Rahu is in tenth house of Dashamsha. He resigned on 27 June 2007 because the casualties mounted in Iraq war. The dasha was Saturn/ Venus/ Mercury. Aspect of Saturn on Venus has weakened the exaltation of Venus. Exchange of Venus and Jupiter is the reason of all round gains. Venus is in third house and Mercury is third lord of Dashamsha. He remained an active Member of Parliament from 9 June 1983 till his resignation. He was married in 1980 in the dasha of Rahu/ Moon. He has four children. Actually, Jupiter gets stronger and Venus becomes weak by placement of eleventh lord in his sign.

Saturn

Saravali – The person will be very licentious, beautiful, courageous, eat abundantly, be crooked and conquer many enemies.

Saral – Saturn is yoga karaka and exalted in sixth house. His father will be highly placed in life but will not keep good health. His wife will not keep good health. As tenth lord, Saturn will make the person to work in the courts. His maternal uncle will be a powerful person and command authority. The person may work as a doctor, lawyer or in Army. Placement of Saturn in third Navamsha is not good.

Example Remi O Chlik DOB 16 October 1983 TOB 19.35 POB Thionville France

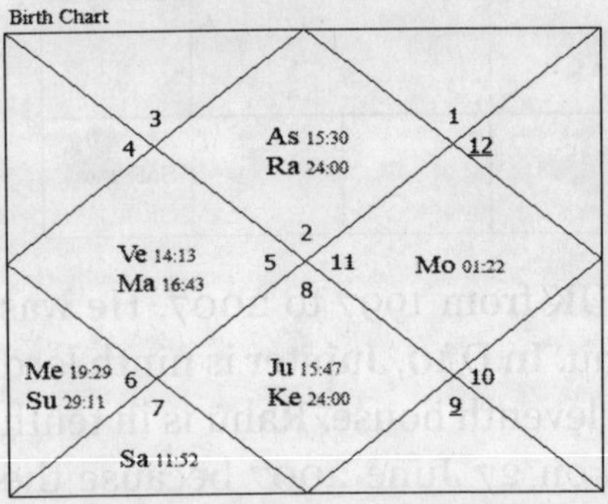

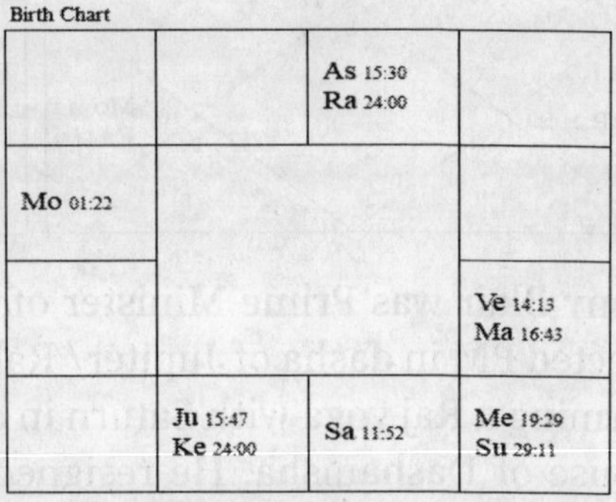

Remi was a photo journalist of France. He reported many wars and was honoured for his work. He was covering war of Haiti and Arab spring revolution. He was reporting on Syrian Civil war and was killed in the bombardment at HOMS along with Marie Colvin on 22 February 2012. The dasha was Jupiter/ Ketu. Jupiter is eighth lord placed in seventh house with Ketu. He was awarded for world press photo in 2012. Jupiter and Ketu are in seventh house and are aspected by maraca Mars. He could not see his Saturn dasha.

GEMINI

Sun

Saravali – He will be interested in gathering money, be strong, will hate others, devoid of servants, be himself a servant, devoid of affection, be modest and successful in his undertakings.

Saral – His efforts are increased manifold. He has to work hard in dasha of Sun and will get success if Sun is associated with a benefic. He has grief because of progeny. Sun is lord of Kama trine placed in a Kama house, if the third Kama trine lord Jupiter also joins Sun, then the person is involved in luxuries. He will be rich by his own efforts. When Mars is placed in third house or Sun is aspected by malefic then the person wants to get success by hook or crook. The person has brothers. Placement of Sun in sixth or eighth Navamsha will be harmful to brothers.

Example Charlotte Elizabeth Diana DOB 2 May 2015 TOB 8.34 POB London

Birth Chart

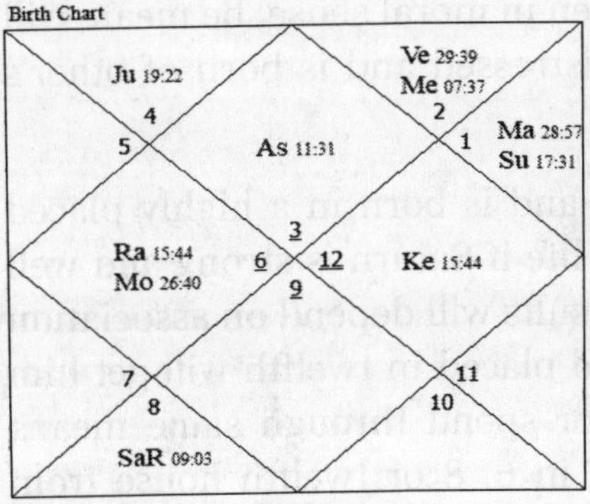

Birth Chart

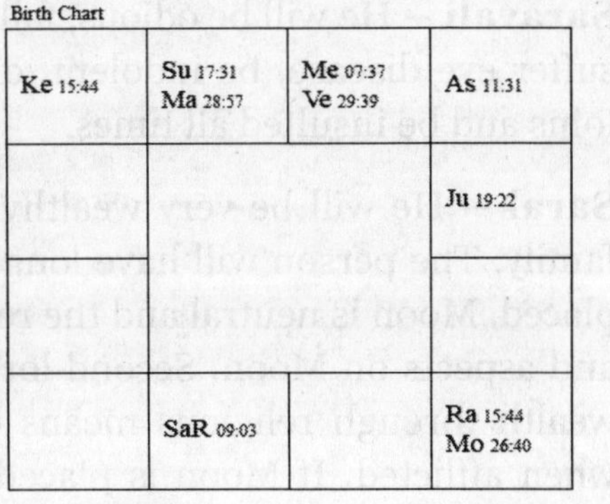

D3 Dreshkana (happiness siblings)

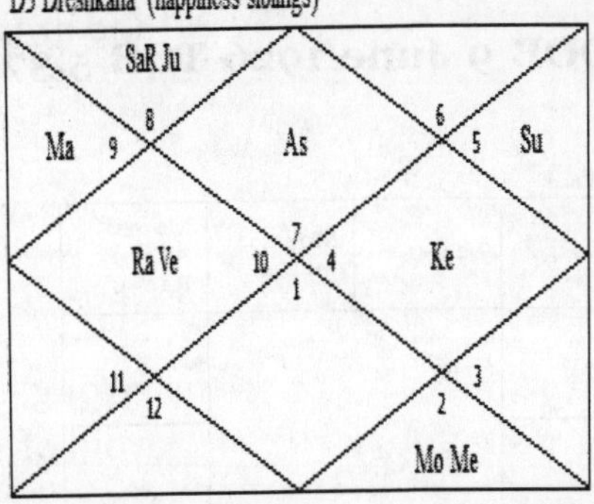

D3 Dreshkana (happiness siblings)

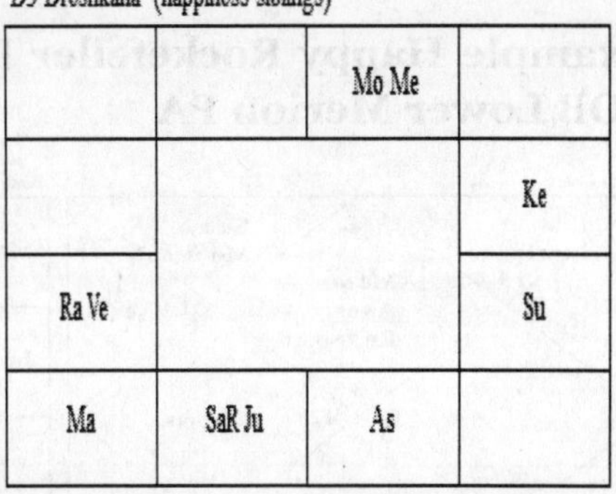

She is the second child of Prince William and Princess Catherin. She is fourth in the line of succession of throne of UK after her grandfather, Father and Elder brother. Her elder brother, Prince

George was born on 22 July 2013. Her dasha would be Moon/ Sun at the time of birth of elder brother. In D 3, Moon is exalted and Sun is in own sign. He is likely to get the throne. For analysis of elder brother, we check Dreshkana. Make eleventh house of D 3 as lagna of elder. Sun is placed in lagna as lagna lord. The tenth house is Taurus which is occupied by exalted Moon. Mercury is with Moon and are aspected by Saturn and Jupiter. The tenth house of elder brother is very strong. She is born in Mars dasha and will not have Sun dasha.

Moon

Saravali – He will be odious, fallen in moral sense, be mean, will suffer eye disease, be indolent, distressed and is born of other's loins and be insulted all times.

Saral – He will be very wealthy and is born in a highly placed family. The person will have long life if Saturn is strong and well placed. Moon is neutral and the results will depend on association and aspects on Moon. Second lord placed in twelfth will get him wealth through religious means or spend through same means when afflicted. If Moon is placed in 6, 8 or twelfth house from Venus in Navamsha then this brings bad expenditure.

Example Happy Rockefeller DOB 9 June 1926 TOB 5.37 POB Lower Merion PA

Birth Chart

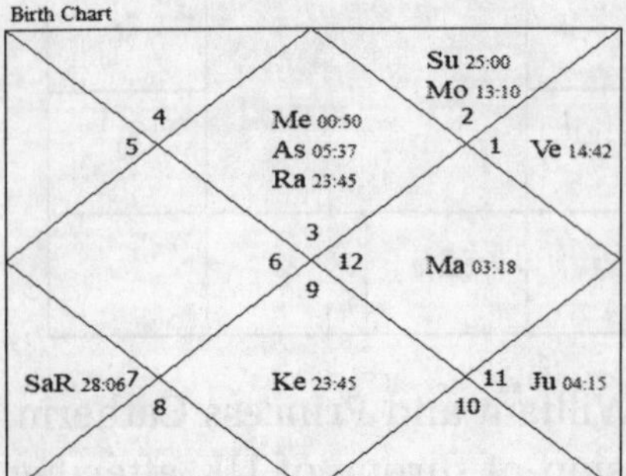

Birth Chart

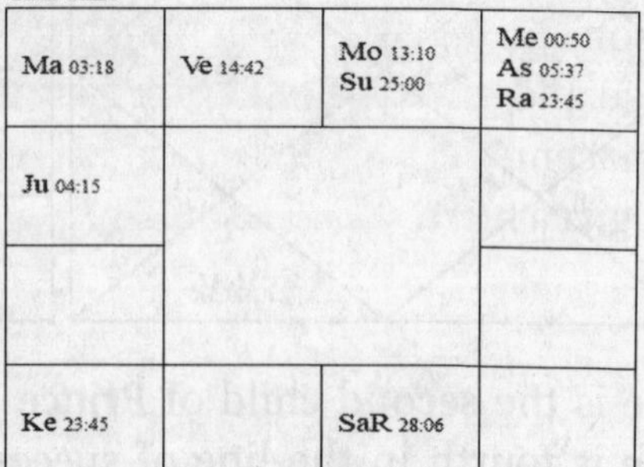

She was named happy by her parents because of her happy nature in child hood. She was first lady of New York from 1963 to 1973 when her second husband, Nelson Rockefeller was Governor of New York. She was second lady of USA from 19 December 1974 to 20 January 1977, when her husband was Vice President of USA. Her first marriage was on 11 December 1949 which ended in Divorce on 1 April 1963. Her first marriage was in Rahu/ Mercury and ended in Jupiter/ Saturn. She had four children from this marriage. She married second time on 4 May 1963 in Jupiter / Saturn and had two children from this marriage. Her second husband died in 1979 in the dasha of Saturn/ Mercury. In Navamsha Saturn is in eighth house and the lagna lord is debilitated. Her death came on 19 May 2015 at the age of 88 years. The cause of death was breast cancer. She had undergone surgery of breast cancer in 1974.

Mars

Saravali – When Mars is in eighth house, the person will suffer from disease, be short lived, will possess an ugly or deformed body, will do base acts and will suffer grief.

Saral – The person will be very rich and famous. He suffers from chronic diseases. He will face very strong enemies and will win over them provided that Mars is placed in trik house from lagna lord in Navamsha. Mars is eleventh lord also and is exalted in eighth house. This can give short life to marriage but gives long life to person. Eleventh lord is a malefic but Mars will aspect eleventh house and gives lot of earning in its dasha. Mars is sixth lord and its placement in eighth house with malefic is a strong Vipreet yoga and gives fame and wealth.

Example David Alan Ladd DOB 5 February 1947 TOB 14.18 POB Hollywood Beach CA

Birth Chart

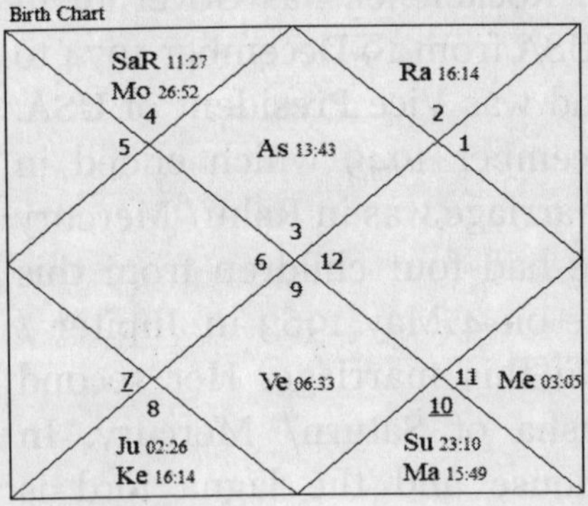

Birth Chart

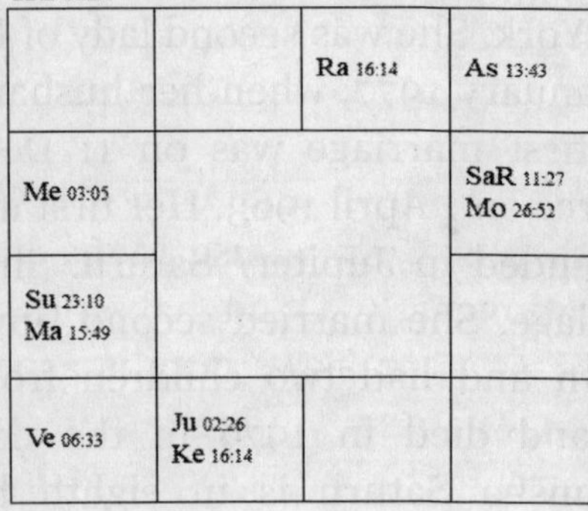

D9 Navamsha (spouse)

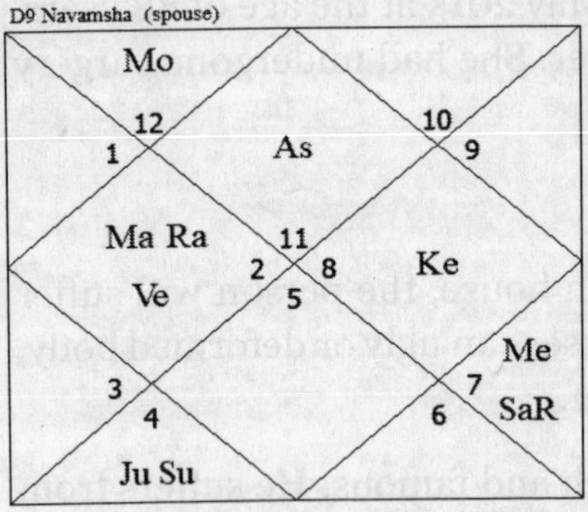

D9 Navamsha (spouse)

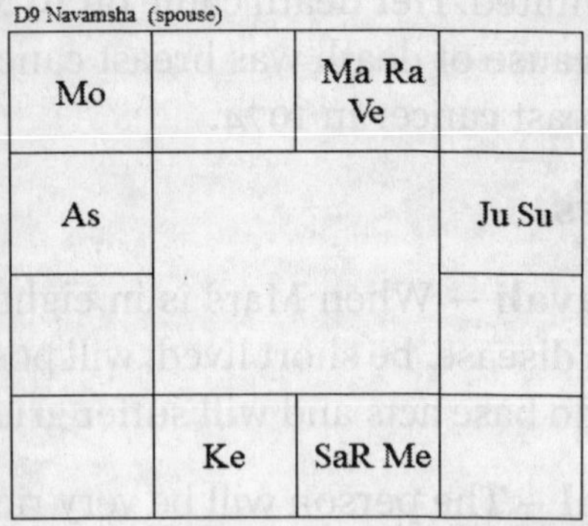

He is a film and TV producer. He married four times. His lagna lord of Navamsha is exalted in ninth house. He has two children. His first marriage was in 1971 which ended in divorce in 1972. Marriage and divorce came in Venus/ Saturn. In the same dasha of Venus/ Saturn, he married for second time in 1973. This ended in 1980 in the dasha of Sun/ Saturn. Third marriage was in 1982 in dasha of Sun/ Ketu. This lasted for 30 years and ended in 2012 in Rahu/ Venus. He married for fourth time in 2017 in Rahu/ Moon and is going on till now.

Mercury

Saravali – The person will have money and relatives, be fortunate, will have conveyance and be very learned.

Saral – He will enjoy all material happiness like house, conveyance, large family and relatives. He is wise and enjoys respect if there is no malefic association with Mercury. Mercury in fourth house will cause Maha Purush yoga. He will get higher education, gain of land, happiness. He will plant fruit trees and do public service. If Mercury is aspected by Triyangmukha planets (Moon, Mercury, Jupiter and Venus), he will come across a hidden treasure. If Mercury is aspected by urdhavamukh planets (Sun and Mars), then he grows crops to get a treasure. Mercury is forming Bhadra yoga.

Example Donald A Glaser DOB 21 September 1926 TOB 23.30 POB Cleveland Ohio

Birth Chart

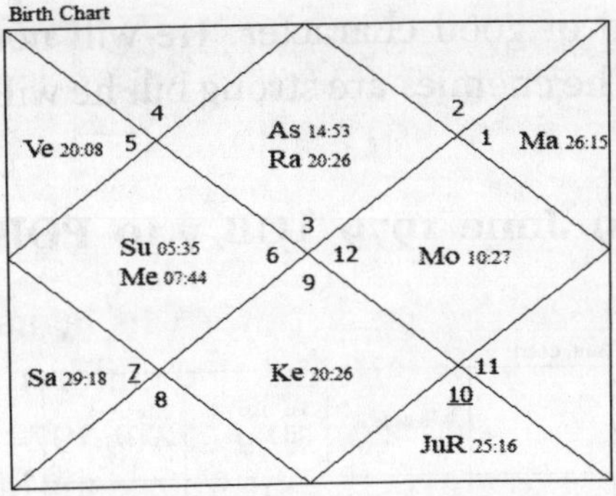

Birth Chart

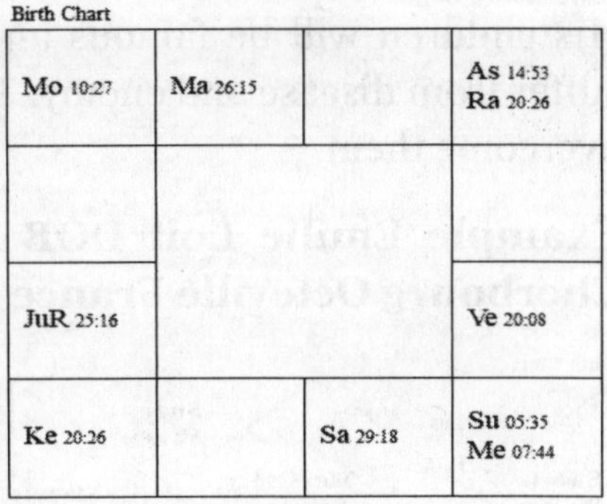

He was a Physicist and a neuro biologist. He was honoured with Noble prize in 1960 for his invention of bubble chamber. He holds a Doctorate degree in Physics from California Institute of Technology. He got his doctorate in 1949. He worked as a professor. Mercury is exalted in birth horoscope but it is debilitated in Navamsha. Mercury is very close to Sun and gives super intelligence. Mercury has the effect of Sun, Moon and Jupiter. Aspect of Jupiter on Mercury will reduce the effect of exaltation of

Mercury. Placement of Mercury in second or fourth Navamsha is not good and can ruin the good effects of Mercury. He had two marriages. The first was in 1960 and second in 1975. He has two children from first marriage. He died on 28 February 2013 in sleep. Dasha was Rahu/ Ketu.

Jupiter

Saravali – The person will be rich, will enjoy good food, be an eloquent speaker, fortunate, charitable and will have beautiful body and face.

Saral – He will hold high position in the Government. His wife may have short life if Jupiter is afflicted by malefic. He will gain money from his wife. Seventh and second house are maraca houses and death may happen in the dasha of Jupiter. This can give separation from wife. As tenth lord, Jupiter will give wealth through profession. He will be held in high esteem in his family. His children will be famous and of good character. He will not suffer from disease and enemy. The enemies are strong but he will overcome them.

Example Emilie Loit DOB 9 June 1979 TOB 7.10 POB Cherbourg Octeville France

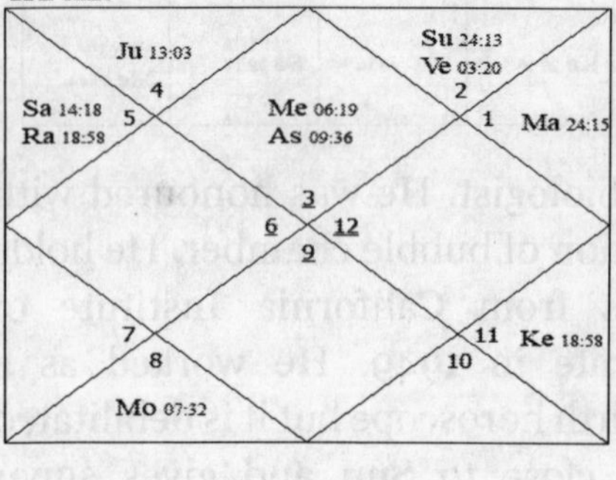

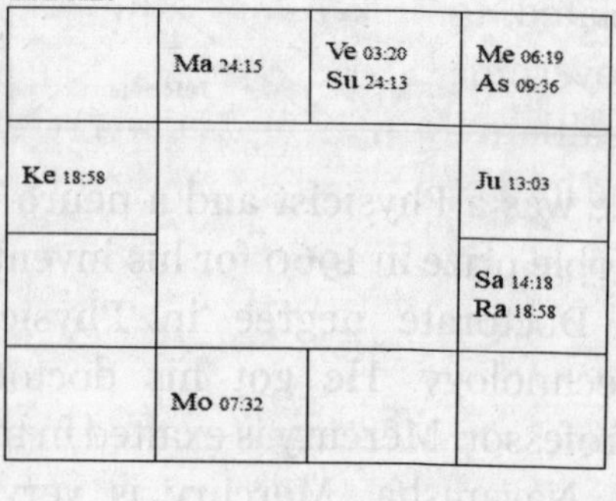

She is a Tennis player from France. She won 3 single and 16 double titles. She became professional in 1994 at the start of Mercury dasha. Her best was in 2003 in Mercury/ Rahu. Her third and sixth house are strong taking her to sports. She earned a prize money of two million Francs. She retired on 24 May 2005 in Mercury/ Saturn after losing her first-round match in French open. Jupiter has given support to her career by its aspect on tenth house but the support is not very effective as Jupiter is aspected by Mars. Mercury is the strongest planet as it is lagna lord and is placed in lagna.

Venus

Saravali – With Venus in tenth house, the person will have success in litigations, be happy, sexual unions, honour, wealth, fame and great wisdom.

Saral – Fifth lord placed in Kendra causes Raj yoga. The person will hold high position. But as twelfth lord in tenth house, he is not able to retain his position and will change jobs frequently. Association with Jupiter or Mercury will increase the yoga. He is wealthy. Fifth lord in sixth from fifth house can give worries in regard to progeny. Fifth lord in tenth will cause Raj yoga and the person will acquire high post during dasha of Venus. When it is related to tenth lord, the person will hold high position in Government. Malavya yoga is caused which give long life of good health to the person. Benefic relation will make him do charities. If the lord of Ascendant is weak the he becomes a saint.

Example Albert Einstein DOB 14 March 1879 TOB 11.28 POB ULM Germany

Birth Chart

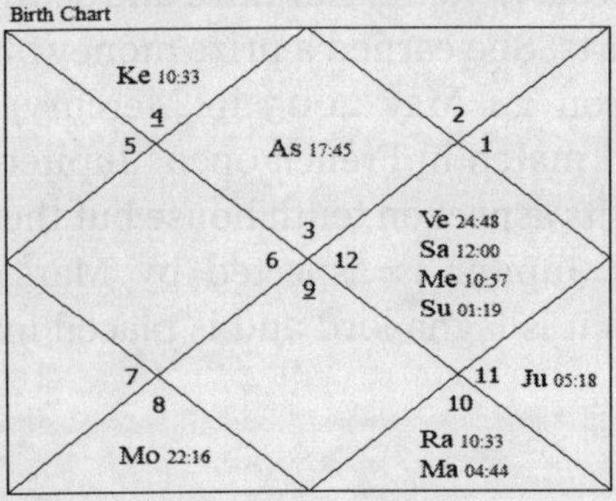

Birth Chart

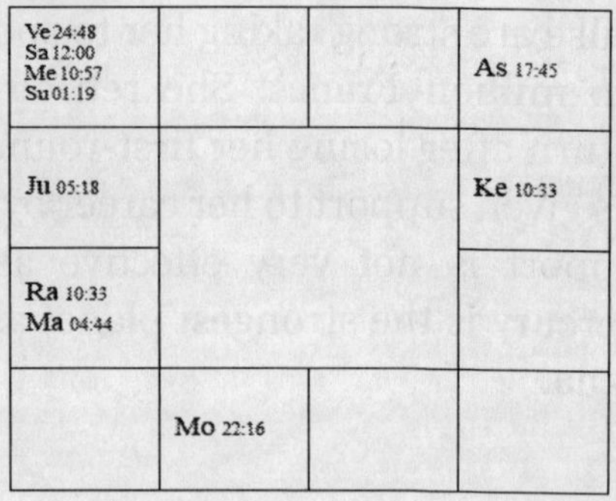

Einstein is a world-famous scientist known for Theory of Relativity. He did his diploma in 1900 in Venus/ Moon and doctorate in 1905 in Venus/ Rahu. He was awarded Noble prize in 1921. He gave this award to his first wife Maric as divorce settlement and she used this money for treatment of her son. He married in 1903 and had a girl child born before the marriage. Marriage was in January 1903 in dasha of Venus/ Rahu. The divorce came in 1919 in Sun/ Mercury after a separation of 5 years. He married again in 1919 and his second wife died in 1936 due to heart and Kidney problems. For long period he remained stateless. In his D 4 chart, fourth lord is in third house, fourth house has Sun aspected by Saturn. This gives no permanent residence. The relation of eighth lord with tenth house promotes new research. Strong raj yoga is forming in tenth house with exalted Venus. The potency of yoga is low as Venus is with Saturn. Mars is sixth lord and is placed in eighth house causing strong Vipreet yoga. The potency of this yoga is increase by association of Rahu with Mars.

Saturn

Saravali – He will be bereft of happiness, sons, friends, intelligence and kindness, will be poor and agitated.

Saral – His father will be a lord. He himself will be in the service of the Government. He will enjoy long and healthy life. If the fifth lord is in Ascendant, then the person will also be a lord. His son will be an intelligent person who will get royal patronage and occupy high rank under the king.

Example Giorgio Napolitano DOB 29 June 1925 TOB 5.30 POB Naples Italy

Birth Chart

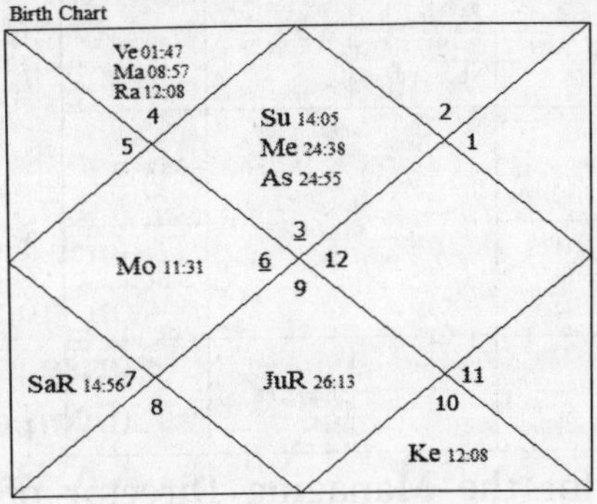

Birth Chart

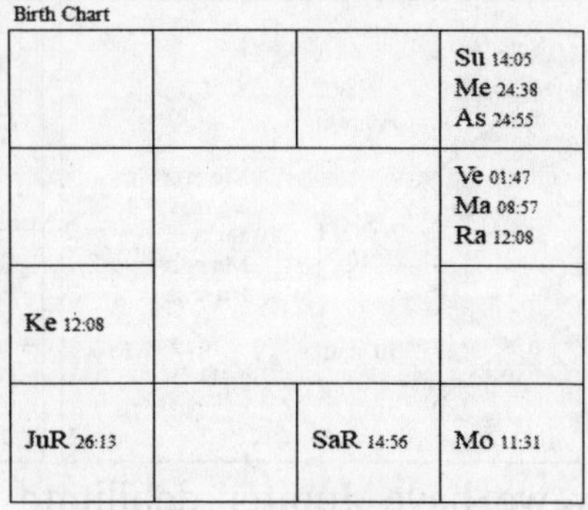

He was President of Italy for two terms and is the only one who has been President for two terms. He assumed the post of President in May 2006 in dasha of Mercury/ Jupiter. He resigned in 2015 due to old age of 89 years in the dasha of Ketu/ Jupiter. He was declared senator for life in 2005 in dasha of Mercury/ Rahu. He contested his first election in 1953 in Rahu/ Venus and never lost an election. He was married in 1959 and has two children.

CANCER

Sun

Saravali – He will be extremely intelligent, rich, strong and has conveyance. He will succeed in his undertakings, have sons, be valorous, unconquerable and great.

Saral – Sun is Digbali. He will have riches and hold a high position in society. His mother may not keep good health. He will acquire wealth through service, commerce, trade, government, performance of religious rites and agriculture.

Example Dominique Strauss Kahn – DOB 25 April 1949, TOB 11.10, POB Neuilly Sur Seine France

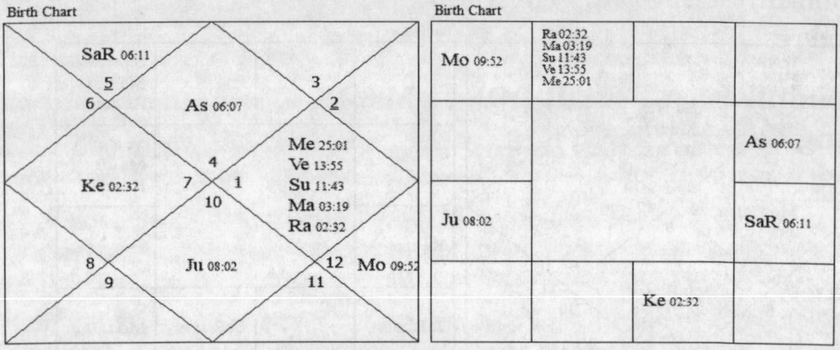

Now we have Jupiter debilitate for the Managing Director of International Monetary Fund. He was a professor of Economics and Minister of Finance in French Government. Debilitate Jupiter in seventh house involved him in financial and sexual scandals. Fourth house has Ketu in it and Fourth lord is with malefic. Aspect of Venus on fourth house and benefic relation with Venus make him escape the punishment. He was professor of Economics. He was minister of Economy and Finance of France from 1997 to 1999 and minister of industry from 1991 to 1993. He remained MD of IMF from 28 September 2007 to 18 May 2011. He married four times. He has five children. Conjunction of Sun, Venus and Mars causes Dhana and raj yoga.

Moon

Saravali – The person is wealthy, will have many sons, be long lived, will have attendants to serve him, be intelligent, sharp, valorous and spendthrift.

Saral – Moon is exalted and is lord of lagna. He will give long life, all gains and good progeny when it has benefic association. If there is only malefic relation with Moon, then the person is always agitated and cannot control his emotions. The person will enjoy good health. He is fortunate to have a beautiful wife. He will become famous. He will have gains in his all enterprises and get benefit from elder brother and friends who are highly placed in life. Moon in fourth or in eighth Navamsha may not give gains. For good results, Moon must have a benefic aspect or association.

Example Randy Kraft DOB 19 March 1945 TOB 14.18 POB Long Beach CA

Birth Chart

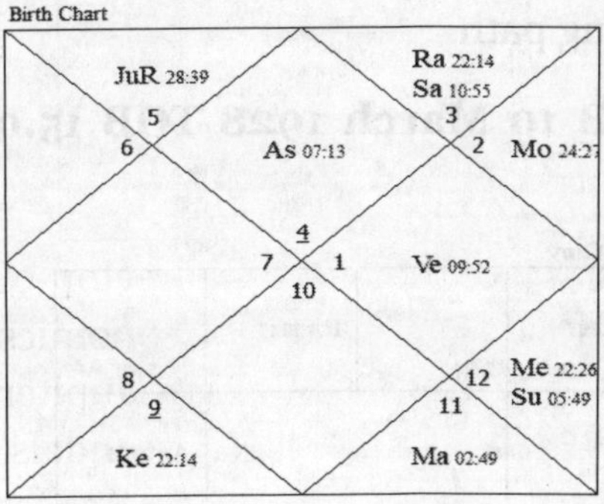

Birth Chart

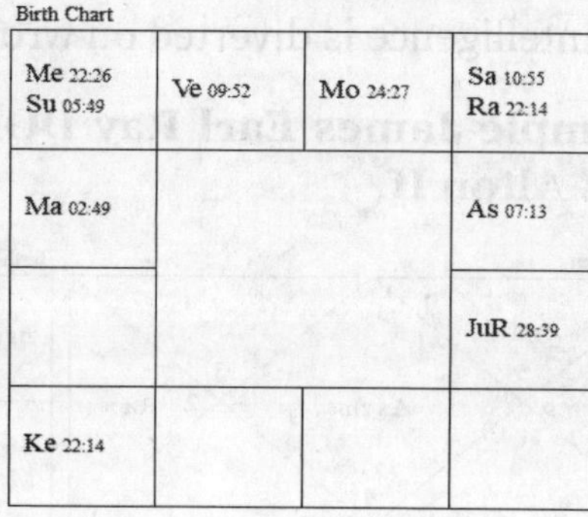

He is known as Freeway Killer. He killed 16 young men between 1972 to 1983 in California. It is believed that he committed 51 rape and murder. He was an intelligent student and joined US Air Force after graduation. He was discharged on 26 July 1969. He was arrested on 14 May 1983 and verdict of death was awarded on 11 August 1989 which was upheld by Supreme Court on 9 August 2000. He is in death row in prison. Sixth house has Ketu and have no benefic relation. Sixth lord Jupiter is aspected by Mars. The life of the person will be miserable. Moon is aspected by strong Mars only. Lagna lord is having only malefic relation.

Mars

Saravali – He will lose his wife, will suffer from disease, will take to bad ways, be miserable, sinful, devoid of wealth, distressed and emaciated.

Saral – Mars is yoga karaka and gives high position to the person. He is like a king with authority to punish and reward. This Mars gives separation from wife. The person will face challenges in life but will win over his enemy. Mars is forming Ruchaka yoga. Tenth lord placed in seventh house will give a wife from good family. She will be helpful in his earnings. Fifth lord Mars, he will get help from his son. When this Mars is under malefic influence then the karma and intelligence is diverted on wrong path.

Example James Earl Ray DOB 10 March 1928 TOB 15.0 POB Alton IL

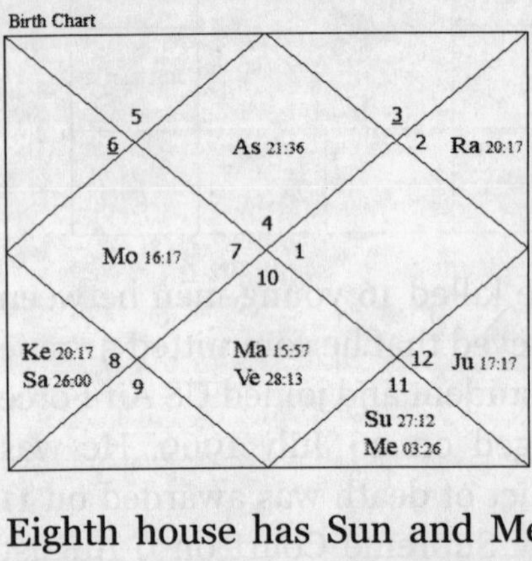

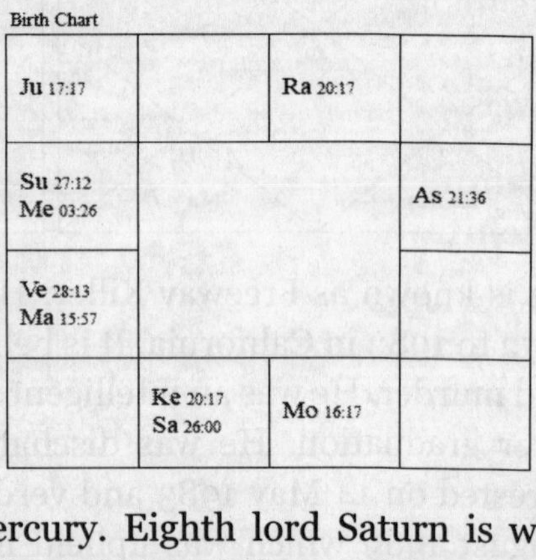

Eighth house has Sun and Mercury. Eighth lord Saturn is with Ketu. Life is miserable. Exaltation of Mars is boosted because of conjunction with Venus. He is the eldest of nine children of his parents. Rahu is in eleventh house. He dropped out of school after twelfth standard. He joined US Army at the close of WW2 and was discharged in 1949. He was involved in many crimes and was given two years for burglary in 1948, two years in 1952 for robbing a taxi driver, mail fraud in 1955 and got 4 years and given 20 years in

1959 for stealing 120 dollars. He escaped from jail hiding in a bakery truck in March 1968. He purchased a gun and shot Martin Luther King on 4 April 1968. He was given 99 years jail but died in jail on 23 April 1998. His ninth house is very strong. He murdered Martin because he was a strong racist.

Mercury

Saravali – The person will always toil hard, devoid of near and dear, skilful, has Coborn, very cunning and fickle minded.

Saral – He will use all tricks to have success and earn money. He will spend his money on charity also. He is worldly wise. This Mercury should not be associated with malefic. If it is so then the person is very courageous and ready to face dangers. Third lord is placed in third house and his younger brothers will prosper. Twelfth lord in exaltation and twelfth house has a benefic relation then the person gets salvation. As third lord Mercury will give short travels.

Example Bryce Poe DOB 10 October 1924 TOB 0.44 POB Wichita Kansas

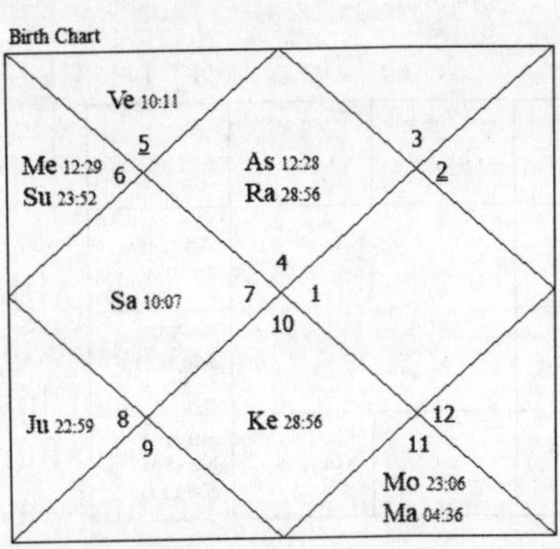

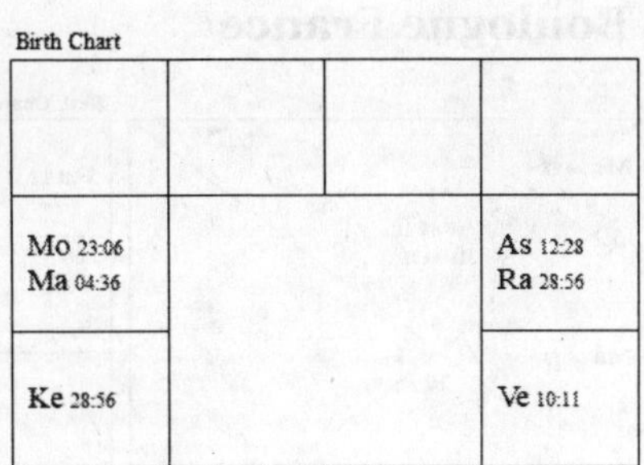

He was a four-star US Airforce General. He commanded the logistic command from 1978 to 1981. He retired on 31 July 1981. He died on 20 November 2000 at the age of 96 years. Lagna lord is in eighth house and eighth lord is exalted. There is no malefic influence on eighth lord. Mercury is with Sun and is aspected by Mars. Sixth house also has malefic relation only. Malefic in third and sixth will make a person to head an Army.

Jupiter

Saravali – He will be attractive in appearance, be energetic, long lived, will act after assessing consequences, be learned, courageous and great.

Saral – When Moon also joins this Jupiter this gives very long life. This creates disputes in married life. His father is an eminent person. He is respectful to his Guru and religion. He has no evils in life. Sixth lord in lagna will make him brave or a commander. He will be employed with Government and have much power and authority. Sixth lord can give disease during its dasha period. As ninth lord Jupiter makes his father very rich and he earns through his own efforts. Placement of Jupiter in Sagittarius Navamsha is not good. Jupiter is forming Hansa yoga.

Example Jacques Calvet DOB 19 September 1931 TOB 2.0 POB Boulogne France

Birth Chart

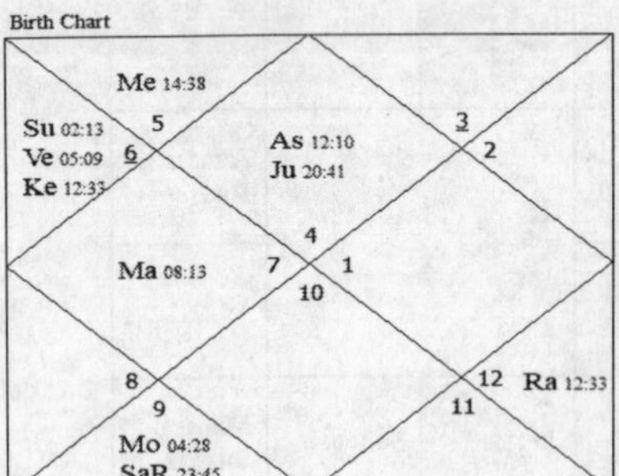

Birth Chart

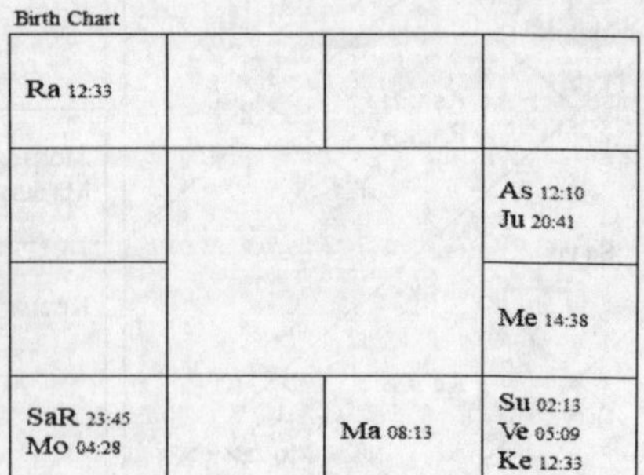

He was a finance management advisor. He became MD of Bank of Paris in 1976 but resigned in 1981. He became adviser to automobile industry. He joined PSA group of industry comprising of Peugeot and Citron car. He joined the group in 1984 when they were 30.5 billion Fracs in debt. He left them in 1997 when they were worth 17.6 billion in equity. He died on 9 April 2020 at an age of 89 years. The great help was from presence of Mukut yoga and conjunction of Saturn with Moon. Shakat yoga becomes Mukut yoga when Jupiter is exalted or in own sign. Here there is exchange of sign between Jupiter and Moon.

Venus

Saravali – When Venus is placed in ninth house, the person will possess a spotless and broad physique, wealthy, charitable, has wife, pleasures, friends, will honour Gods, Guru and elders.

Saral – He will have good character, house, happiness and luxury provided Venus is not afflicted. If it is afflicted then he is not able to enjoy these things. Venus as fourth lord placed in ninth house will give large amount of parental property. He earns through education but his mother may not keep good health. As eleventh lord, he earns through preceptor, father or charitable deeds. As eleventh lord Venus is a malefic. Venus in second or fourth Navamsha is not considered good. In third Navamsha, Venus will give some hobby as a living. Venus is a malefic for Cancer lagna. If it is associated with trishadaya house/ lord then the malefic nature is controlled to some extent.

Example Steven Seagal DOB 10 April 1952 TOB 13.54 POB Lansing MI

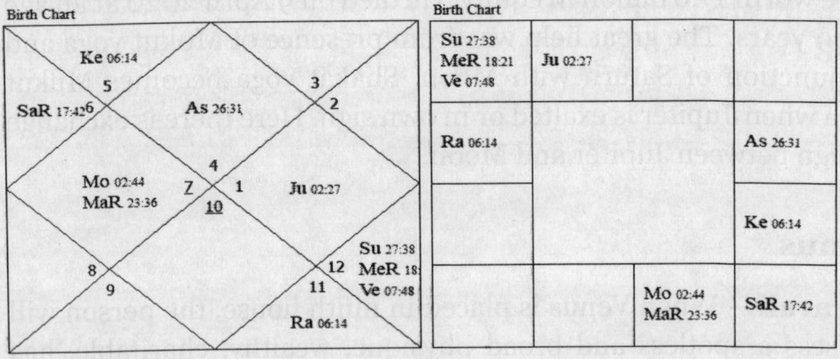

He began as a martial art instructor. In 1988, he moved to Los Angeles and started acting. He was a good player of Guitar and has many albums to his credit. He got Russian citizen ship and was appointed special envoy to US. He faced many cases of sexual assault from 1990 to 2018. The three lords of Kama trikona are mutually related. He faced 8 law suits and was fined. He married four times and have 7 children. The potency of exalted Venus is lowered by aspect of Saturn.

Saturn

Saravali – The person suffers heart disease or is a broken heart, devoid of relatives, conveyance, wealth, intelligence and happiness. He will suffer sickness in childhood and has prominent hair and nails.

Saral – He is a politician or a lawyer who deals with public at large. His wife has strong influence on him. This placement of Saturn as seventh lord is good but as eighth lord the benefits of fourth house are denied. Saturn is lord of a Kendra and becomes neutral. As eighth lord also he is neutral. Saturn will give results according to its association or aspect. Saturn is forming Sasha yoga.

Example Marilyn Monroe DOB 1 June 1926 TOB 9.28.30 POB Los Angeles CA

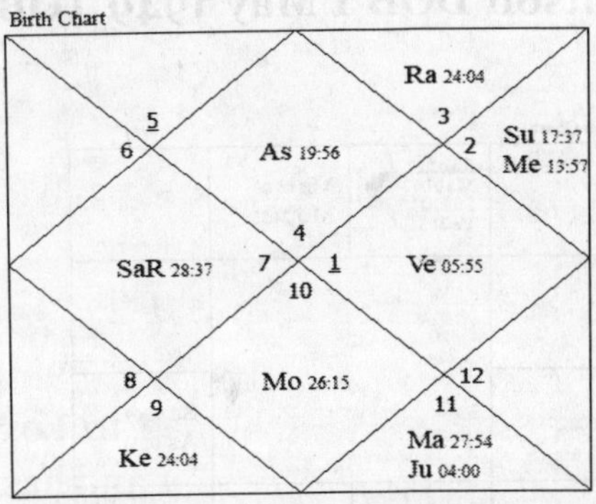

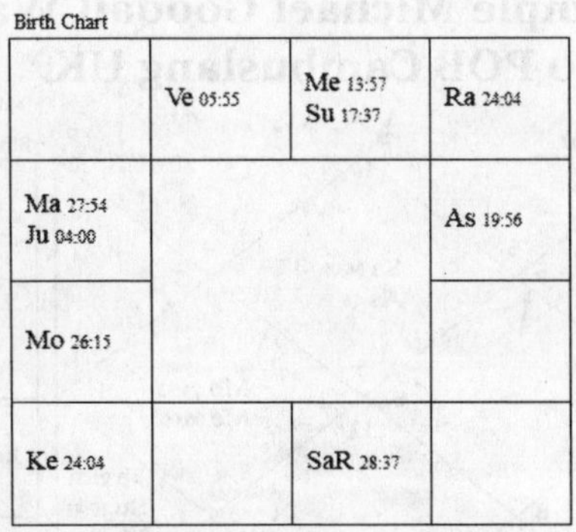

She comes from a poor family. She was with foster parents till the age of 7 years. She was sexually abused in her teens. She was the most marketable star in 1953. She formed her own company in 1954 and won Golden Globe award in 1959. She had three marriages. Her end came on 5 August 1962 due to over dose of drugs. Saturn is aspected by Jupiter. This has increased the value of exaltation of Saturn. Sixth lord is placed in eighth house with a malefic and strong Vipreet yoga is caused giving fame and wealth.

LEO

Sun

Saravali – The person will be wealthy, have children and friends, will be interested in worshipping Gods and brahmins, will not be well disposed towards his father and wife and will not be calm.

Saral – lagna lord is placed in ninth house and promotes the effects of ninth house. His father is highly placed and is a reputed person. He will do charitable deeds and devoted to preceptors and will be orthodox. He will acquire property from his father. If Sun is placed in sixth or eighth Navamsha then it is not so. When Sun is joined with ninth lord and is afflicted then he may not gain and goes astray in his conduct.

Example Michael Goodall Watson DOB 1 May 1949 TOB 14.40 POB Cambuslang UK

Birth Chart

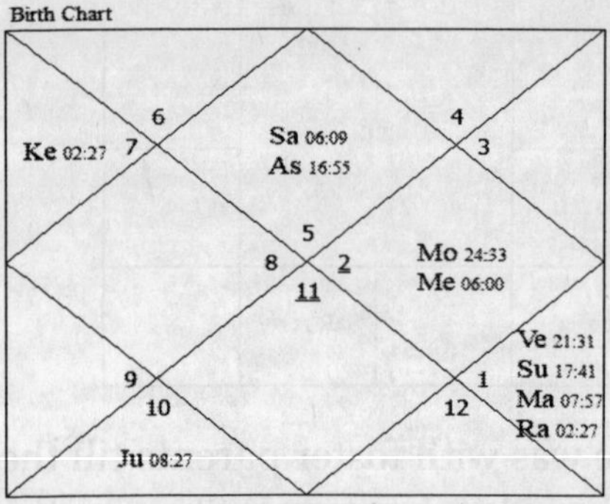

Birth Chart

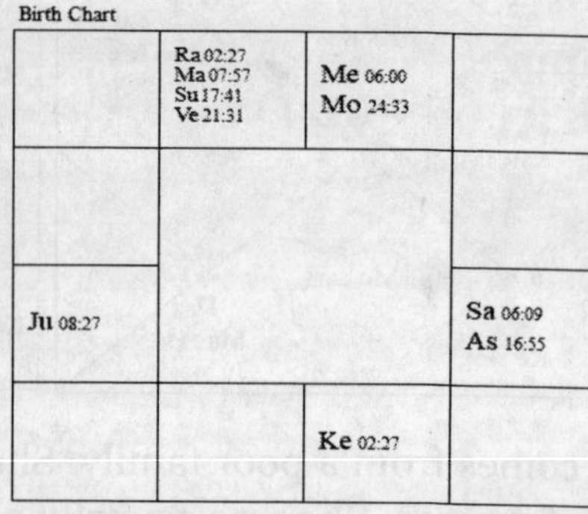

He is a politician and was elected twice as member of parliament. His first term was in 1989 and second term was in 1992. He was charged for setting fire in a hotel. He was charged on 15 November 2004. He admitted his guilt on 1 September 2005 and was sentenced for 16 months in jail. But he was released early on 23 May 2006. He was readmitted in the Labour party in July 2012 and now he is Education spokesman in the house of lords. He was knighted as lord. Conjunction of ninth and tenth lord is a raj yoga. Third house has Ketu. Third lord is with malefic and is the reason of disgrace. Sun and ninth lord are with Rahu. Sixth lord is in lagna in enemy sign and is in direct motion. There is no feeling of guilt for wrong doing.

Moon

Saravali – The person will not suffer grief, be dutiful, successful in his undertakings, pure, affluent, very strong, valorous and charitable.

Saral – When Moon is waning, the wealth will be fluctuating, his job is not permanent and keeps shifting his profession. When Moon is waxing then it gives good position. He will inherit wealth from his maternal grandfather (Nana). With malefic association he will waste his wealth. Benefic combination will cause expenditure for virtuous purpose. Moon in fifth Navamsha is best. All other Navamsha positions of this Moon are good.

Example Jean Claude Trichet DOB 20 December 1942 TOB 23.00 POB Lyon France

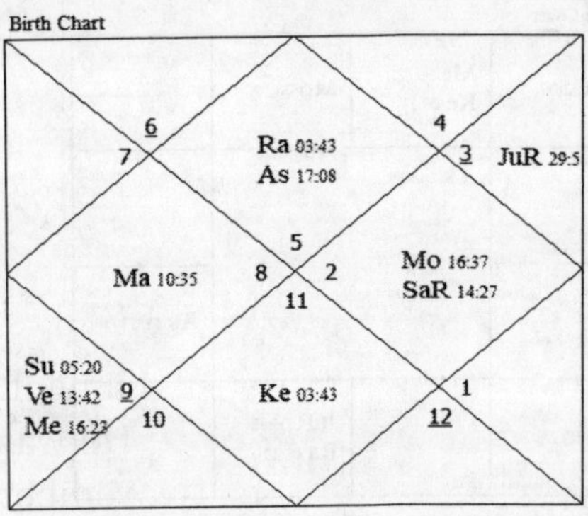

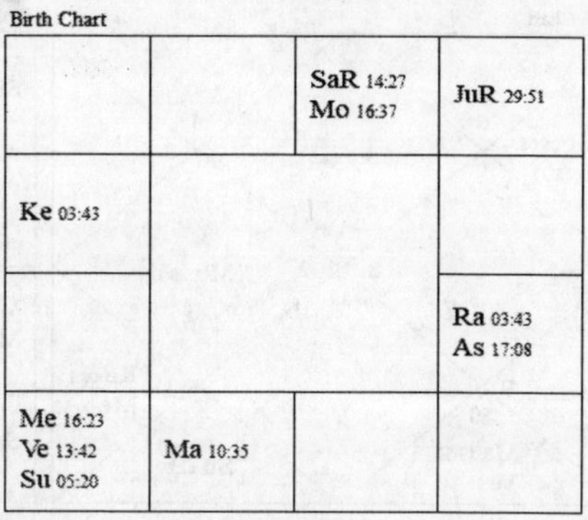

He was President of European Central Bank from 2003 to 2011. Before that, he was Governor of Bank of France from 1993 to 2003. He is ranked fifth most powerful economist of the world. He was married in 1970 and has two children. Conjunction of Moon with Saturn and aspect of Mars has given him sharp and logical mind. Mercury in Prishtodaya sign gives him shrewdness. Fifth house is aspected by its lord Jupiter. Placement of Mars in seventh from Moon could make a criminal but association of three benefic with lagna lord, Sun, has directed these qualities in right direction.

Mars

Saravali – He will have powerful digestive fire, be libidinous, be beautiful, tall, strong and great among his relatives.

Saral – His father will be highly placed in the Government and wield great authority. His mother is a religious lady. Mars as fourth lord placed in sixth will make his maternal uncle a prominent person. This can cause accidents due the significations of the planet associated with or aspecting Mars. Ninth lord in sixth can give sickness to father. Aspect of Mars on lagna will give strong body.

Example Elio De Angeles DOB 26 March 1958 TOB 15.45 POB Rome Italy

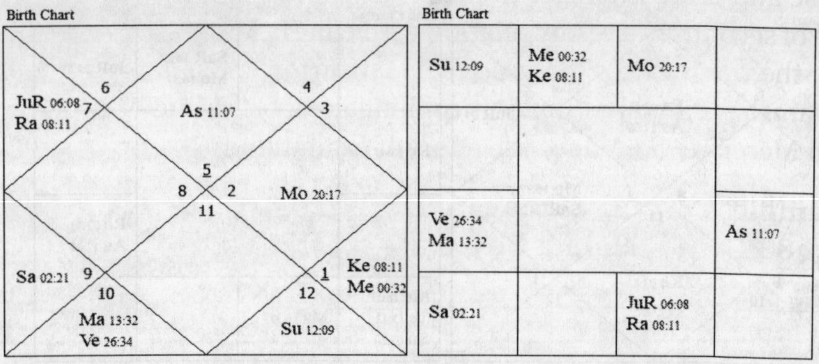

He was a car racer. He used to test run the cars. He participated in formula I race in 1979 and 1986. On 15 May 1986, he was testing Brabham car model BT55. The car caught fire and he died. His father was a boat racer. He was an excellent pianist.

Placement of eighth lord in third house is a Vipreet yoga. The yoga effects are felt fully if there is no benefic relation. Mercury is aspecting Jupiter and has spoiled the yoga. This placement supported by other divisional chart is the cause of short life.

Mercury

Saravali – He will earn wealth through his own intelligence, will enjoy food and drinks, be auspicious in speech and will have good conduct.

Saral – This Mercury gives abundance of wealth. He is learned and a strong orator who can captivate the listeners. He will earn a lot during the dasha of second lord if lagna lord is strong. Family and education will thrive. Second house is eighth from seventh house and there is danger to life of the spouse. Mercury is maraca lord of second house. Any relation with trine lord is good for wealth but the maraca factor also gets stronger. Mercury in last Navamsha will make him multi-millionaire. Any relation of Jupiter with Mercury will reduce the effect of exaltation.

Example Patrick Flanagan DOB 11 October 1944 TOB 03.48 POB Oklahoma City

Birth Chart

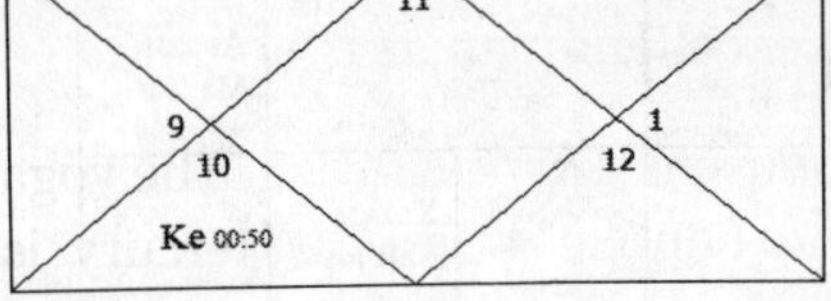

Birth Chart

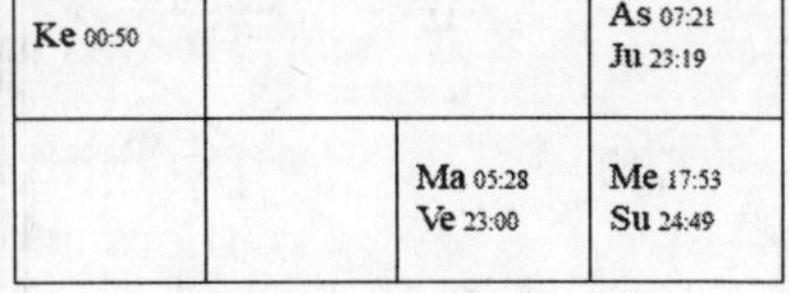

He was an author and an inventor. At the age of 13 years, he invented a neuro phone which can transmit sound waves via nervous system to brain. He wrote books on egophony geometry and pyramidology. Pyramidology is the power of pyramids. He was a new age writer. He died on 19 December 2019. Conjunction of Mars and Venus is raj yoga.

Jupiter

Saravali – The person will be indolent, odious, be devoid of speech and luck, and in all probability in servitude.

Saral – He is likely to have grief due to children or will not have any child. He can have a good house in a foreign country. He will be long lived but may suffer from chronic disease. He will face sudden events in life. Fifth lord in twelfth may give pleasures of bed. Fifth house indicates intellect and mind also. During dasha of Jupiter his mind may be disturbed and can have mental disorder. Placement of eighth lord in twelfth is a yoga. The potency of yoga is increased if Jupiter is conjoined or aspected by sixth or twelfth lord and have no other relation. In case Jupiter has other influence then the yoga is cancelled and only bad results will happen.

Example Alois Hitler DOB 7 June 1837 TOB 10.30 POB Dollersheim Austria

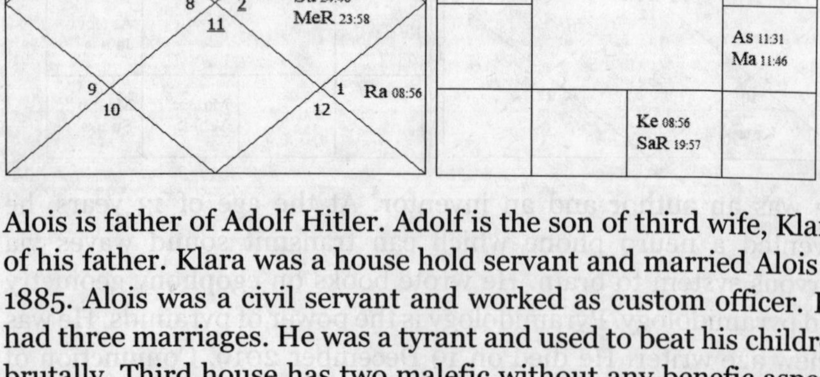

Alois is father of Adolf Hitler. Adolf is the son of third wife, Klara, of his father. Klara was a house hold servant and married Alois in 1885. Alois was a civil servant and worked as custom officer. He had three marriages. He was a tyrant and used to beat his children brutally. Third house has two malefic without any benefic aspect. He had 8 children. He purchased a 9-acre plot in Germany and moved there in 1895. Alois died on 3 January 1903. Jupiter is placed in eighth house from fifth house and has given bad treatment to children. If Moon was not conjunct with Jupiter, it would have denied him any child.

Venus

Saravali – He will be long lived, will enjoy incomparable happiness, be very rich, be equal to king and will always be delighted.

Saral – If Venus is having malefic association the he will be a famous person and will be very wealthy. Third lord in eighth in exaltation and with benefic will be bad for Coborn. Only malefic relation will not harm. When associated with sixth, eighth or twelfth lord then will have wealth. Tenth lord in eighth can give unstable but elevation in job with every change. This cause obstacles to education.

Example Maria Eagle DOB 17 February 1961 TOB 17.20 POB Bridlington UK

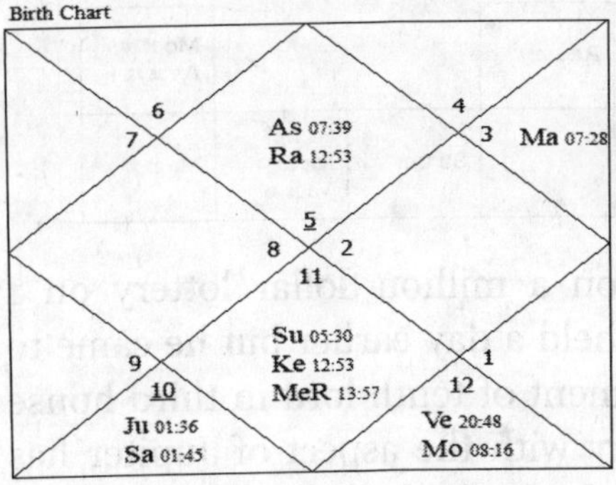

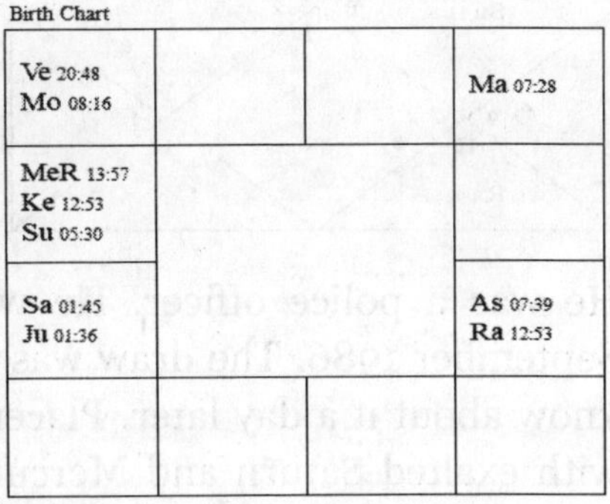

Maria has a twin sister. Both sisters are member of Parliament. She is an MP since 1997 and is the Minister of State for Justice. Venus is aspected by Saturn and has given good position to her and her sister. A good yoga is debilitation of Jupiter and aspect of Sun on lagna.

Saturn

Saravali – He will be of dark complexion, will maintain physical cleanliness, be base, will have indolent attendants, be courageous, charitable and will have great intelligence.

Saral – He may have delayed marriage and his wife will be very dominating. He will be famous after marriage. Lord of sixth in third gives bad relation with brother but his maternal uncle will support his brother. If Venus is afflicted, he may not have any brother. Seventh lord in third house will make the father – in – law fortunate. The person may marry twice. Seventh house is maraca also and can be bad for brother or the person will travel away from home.

Example Lottery Winner DOB 29 November 1953 TOB 0.30 POB Montreal Canada

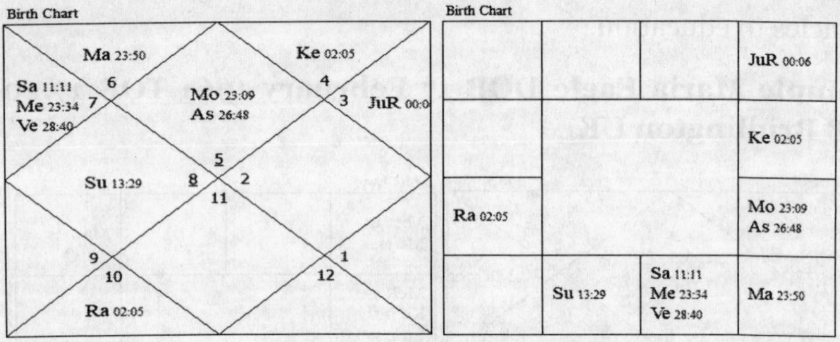

He was a police officer. He won a million-dollar lottery on 1 September 1986. The draw was held a day earlier but he came to know about it a day later. Placement of tenth lord in third house with exalted Saturn and Mercury with the aspect of Jupiter has given sudden gains. Mercury is the lord of eleventh and second house.

VIRGO

Sun

Saravali – He will have deformed eyes, devoid of wealth and happiness, be short lived and suffer separation from relatives.

Saral – Twelfth lord in eighth will give happiness and unhappiness in equal amount. Benefic relation gives more happiness. Malefic relation gives Vipreet yoga. Relation with sixth lord will also give good results. Twelfth house is outside world. Twelfth lord exalted in eighth house can give sudden gains from outside world.

Example Coretta Scott King DOB 27 April 1927 TOB 16.00 POB Marion Alabama

Birth Chart

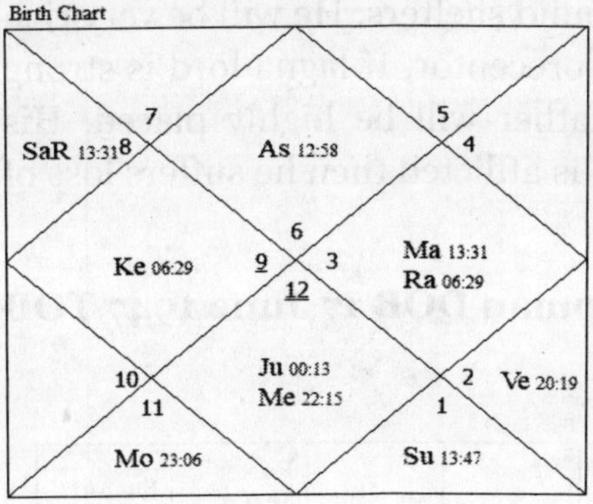

Birth Chart

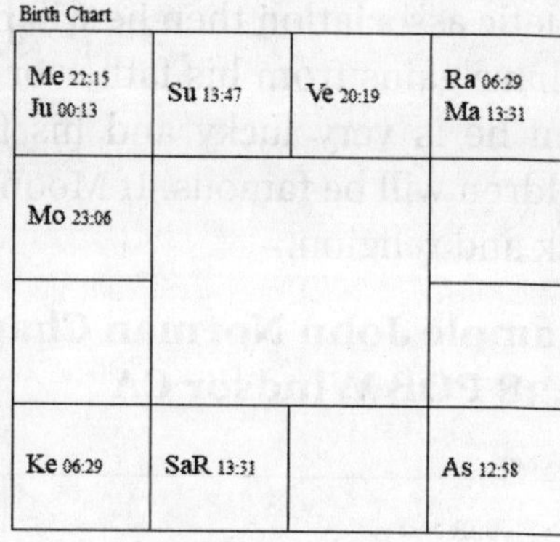

D9 Navamsha (spouse)

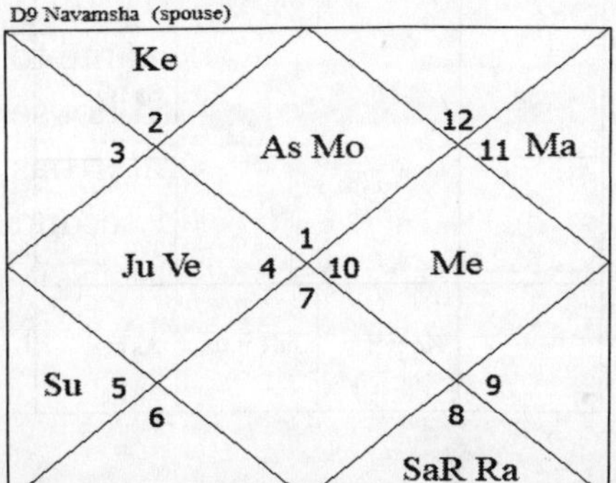

D9 Navamsha (spouse)

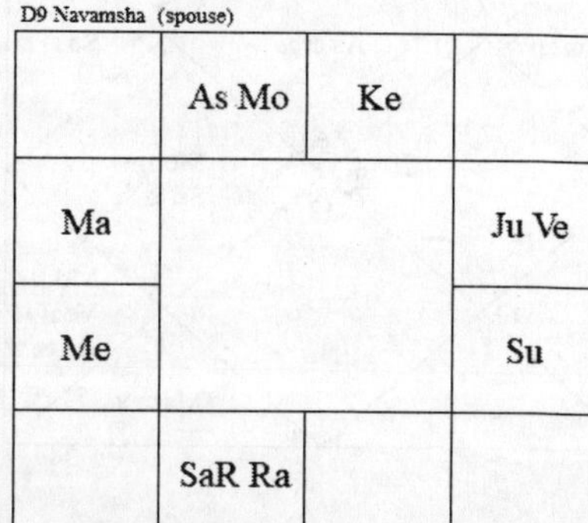

She was a singer holding BA and BM degrees in music. She married Martin Luther King. They had four children. Martin was assassinated in April 1968 in her dasha of Mercury/ Rahu. In Navamsha, eighth house is under malefic influence giving death to husband before her death. She was honoured with Gandhi Peace prize and finds place in the National Women Hall of Fame. She suffered paralytic stroke in August 2005 and died on 30 January 2006 in dasha of Sun/ Saturn/ Sun. A coincidence, she also died on the date Gandhi died.

Moon

Saravali – He will be devoted to divine and his parents, will be happy, wealthy, intelligent, sons and will attract fair sex.

Saral – He can be a spendthrift. When Moon is not having any malefic association then he will build shelters. He will be very rich or have gains from his father or preceptor. If lagna lord is strong then he is very lucky and his father will be highly placed. His children will be famous. If Moon is afflicted then he suffers loss of luck and religion.

Example John Norman Chapman DOB 17 June 1947 TOB 12.38 POB Windsor CA

Birth Chart

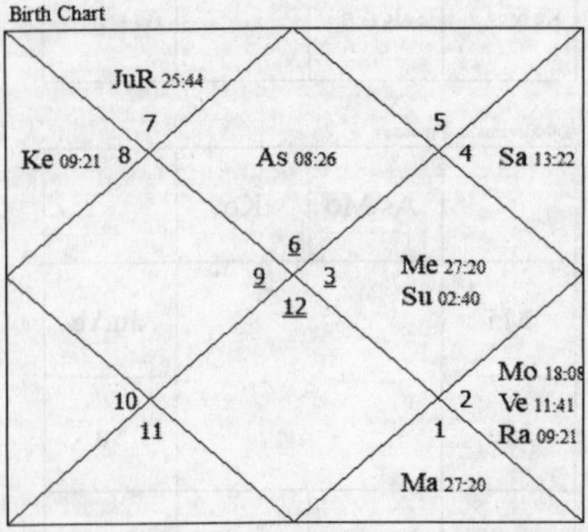

Birth Chart

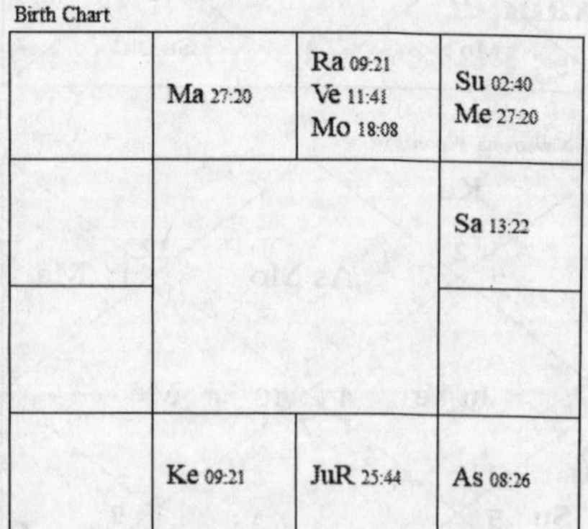

His lagna lord is having malefic conjunction. Fourth lord is afflicted by Mars. Mars is a malefic for Virgo lagna. He used to abduct young woman of 13 to 21 years of age. He will beat and rape them. After this he will murder them by stabbing or by strangulation. Maximum crimes were committed between July 1967 to July 1969. The dasha was Rahu/ Mercury. He was arrested on 30 July 1969 and was awarded life imprisonment on 19 August 1970. He is still in jail.

Mars

Saravali – The person will not be happy, no wealth and sons, be fickle minded, be a talebearer, will incur evils, be wicked, distressed and mean.

Saral – Third lord in fifth house will give many brothers. Each brother will earn his living by his association with a temple or a wealthy person. He himself may be adopted by a rich person. Eighth lord in fifth may give perversion to him or his children. If fifth lord is weak then he may suffer loss of a child. Mars in second or fourth Navamsha will prove bad. Mars is a strong malefic for Virgo lagna. Mutual relation of Mars with other trishadaya lord is a yoga.

Example Kurt Waldheim DOB 21 December 1918 TOB 0.25 POB Saint Andrae Austria

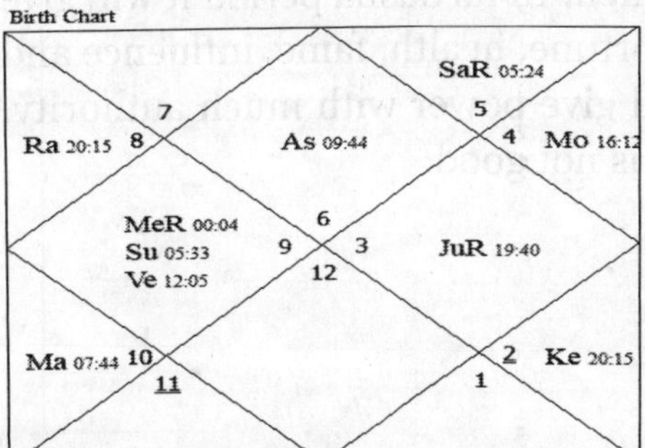

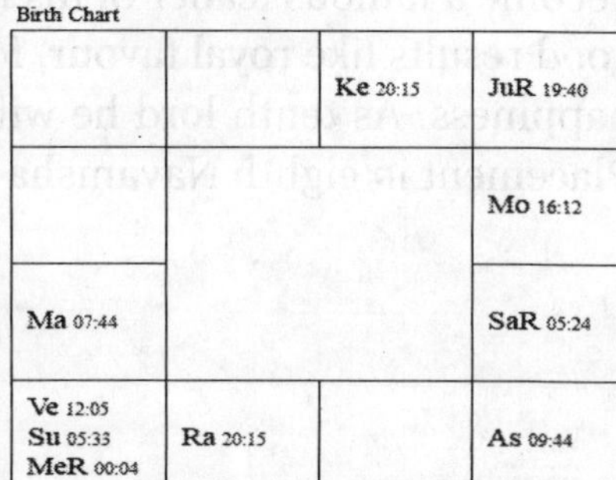

Mars is in mutual aspect with eleventh lord Moon. But placement of Mars in seventh house from Moon and placement of Mercury in Prishtodaya sign will make a person cunning. He can get his work done by any means. The saving factor is association of Venus with lagna lord Mercury.

He was fourth Secretary General of United nations from 1972 to 1981. The dasha was of Moon and Mars. He was President of Austria from 1986 to 1992 in dasha of Rahu. Earlier, he served as intelligence officer in WW2 in Nazi Government. He was a lawyer by qualification. Formation of raj yoga in fourth house is the reason of his rise. He was married and had three children. He married in Venus/ Venus in 1944. He died of heart attack on 14 June 2007 in Jupiter/ Saturn/ Mercury.

Mercury

Saravali – The person will have flawless physique, be intelligent, has knowledge of proper time and place, be versed with poetry and mathematics, skilful, sweet speaker and long lived.

Saral – Mercury is lagna lord and tenth lord. Mercury is exalted in lagna. This will give a charming and healthy body and good profession. This Mercury should be free from malefic aspect or association. Bhadra yoga is caused. Lagna lord in lagna will make the person very powerful, having qualities of lagna lord and will become a famous leader of his men. In its dasha period it will give good results like royal favour, fortune, health, fame, influence and happiness. As tenth lord he will give power with much authority. Placement in eighth Navamsha is not good.

Example Francois Mitterrand DOB 26 October 1916 TOB 4.00 POB Jarnac France

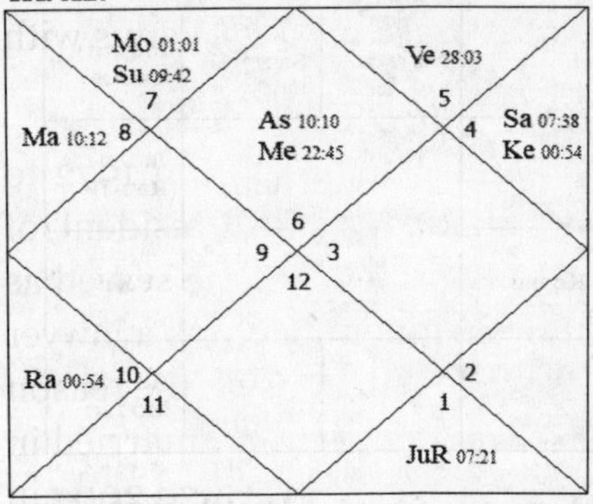

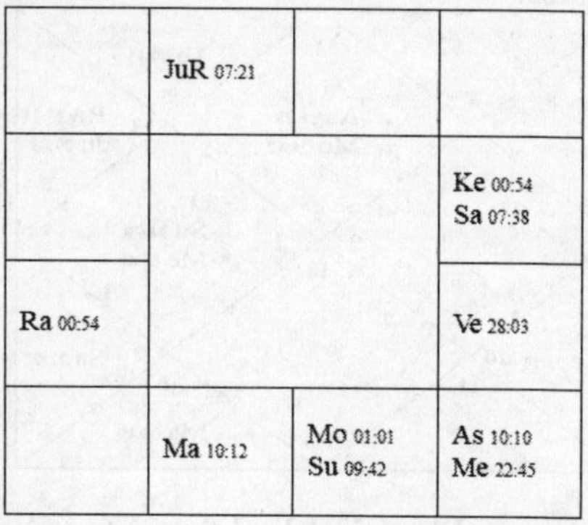

He was President of France from 1985 to 1995. He became President in Mercury/ Mars. Mercury is aspected by fifth lord Saturn. Tenth house is aspected by Mars. Mars is eighth lord placed in third house is a strong yoga. He served in Army for four years from 1937 to 1941. He got married in 1944 and has four children. He died on 8 January 1996 in Ketu/ Mercury/ Venus.

Jupiter

Saravali – He will enjoy many gains, conveyance, servants, be virtuous but will have limited education and sons.

Saral – Jupiter will aspect seventh house. He will have good partners and high position in life in the dasha of Jupiter. He will be very helpful to his partners. Jupiter is in eighth from fourth house and can deny comforts of fourth house. He will inherit the wealth of mother or can have a step mother. As seventh lord Jupiter can give many wives. If Jupiter is afflicted by malefic then his wives may die and he lives a life of struggle like carrying bundles of load on his back. He can earn from other countries. Placement of eleventh lord will decide the way of earnings. Jupiter in eighth Navamsha is bad and can deny the comforts.

Example Arthur Ashe DOB 10 July 1943 TOB 12.55 POB Richmond Virginia

Birth Chart

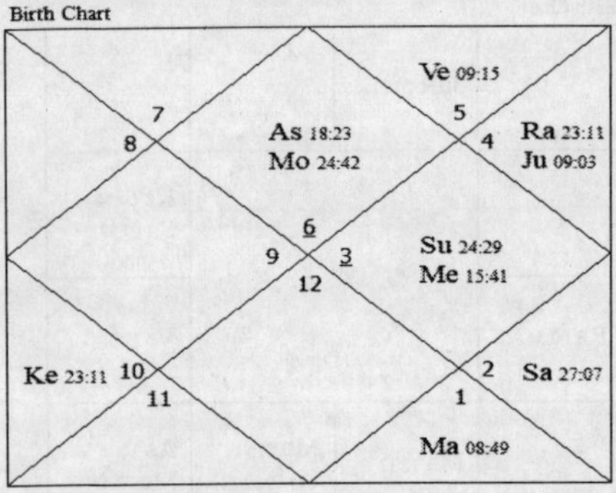

Birth Chart

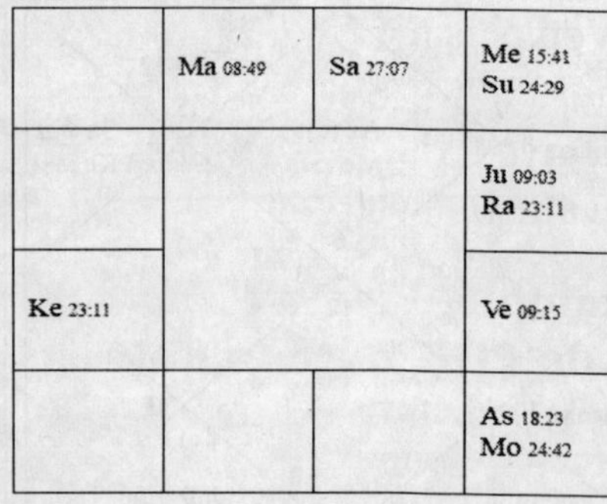

He was the only black men to win three tennis single titles. He won US open in 1970 in Jupiter/ Jupiter, Australian open in 1970 in Jupiter/ Saturn and Wimbledon in 1975 in Jupiter/ Venus. He was operated for heart bye pass surgery on 13 December 1979 in Jupiter/ Moon/ Saturn. Second surgery came in 1983 in Saturn/ Saturn. In the year 1988, he suffered paralysis of right arm and was tested positive for AIDS. He founded Arthur Ashe foundations for AIDS in April 1992 in the dasha of Saturn/ Venus. In September 1992 he suffered heart attack. He died on 6 February 1993 in the dasha of Saturn/ Venus/ Rahu. The health problems started in Jupiter Maha dasha. His Jupiter is with Rahu and is aspected by Mars and Saturn.

Venus

Saravali – He will have an excellent and chaste wife, he can have many marriages, be a leader and lucky.

Saral – Venus is lord of second and ninth house and is a benefic. It gives lot of wealth and a good and loving partner. His father is highly placed in life and will be very supportive to the person. Venus can prove a maraca. Venus is causing Malavya yoga. Second lord in seventh house will give earning from foreign country and from women. As ninth lord he will do meritorious deeds in foreign country. His preceptor or father may be living in foreign country. If Venus is afflicted then his father may be poor and pass away in other country. Second and seventh house are maraca places and can give trouble in its dasha period. Placement of Venus in fourth Navamsha will reduce the good effects with an element of surprise.

Example James Ronald Ryan DOB 29 April 1947 TOB 17.00 POB Wichita Kansas

Birth Chart

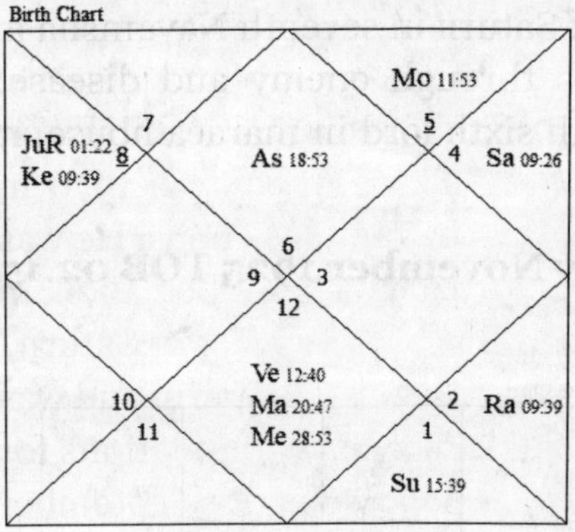

Birth Chart

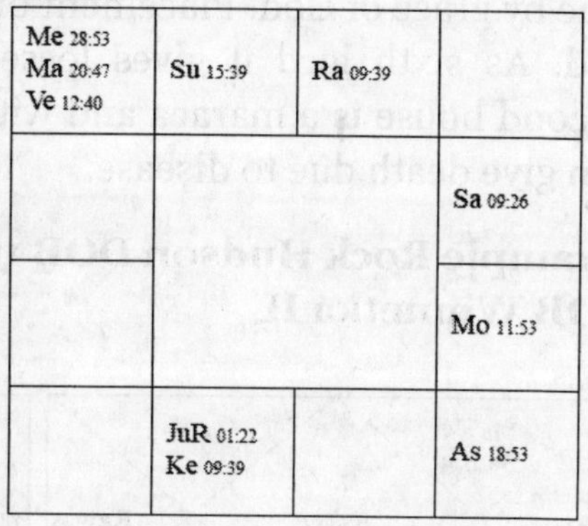

He is a politician and track and field athlete. He won silver medal in 1968 summer Olympics. He was member of US house of representatives from 27 November 1996 to 5 January 2007, when he was defeated. He remained member from Rahu/ Saturn to Rahu/ Moon. His Rahu is giving results of ninth house Venus. He married a girl who asked for his autograph after he won silver medal. They were married in 1969 in the dasha of Sun/ Rahu. They have four children. On 15 December 2000, he purchased a town house in the dasha of Rahu/ Mercury.

Saturn

Saravali – He will have an ugly face, will enjoy worldly prosperity, devoid of his own men, will render justice, in later life goes to other countries and will earn money and conveyance.

Saral – Saturn is fifth and sixth lord. Sixth lord in exaltation will give sense of competition, strong enemies and incurable disease if related to eighth lord. He will give lot of intelligence to the person. Fifth lord exalted in second house gives wealth. His family will live happily and his speech will be respected and his saying will come true by grace of God. Placement of Saturn in seventh Navamsha is bad. As sixth lord it gives losses through enemy and disease. Second house is a maraca and with sixth lord in maraca house, it can give death due to disease.

Example Rock Hudson DOB 17 November 1925 TOB 02.15 POB Winnetka IL

Birth Chart

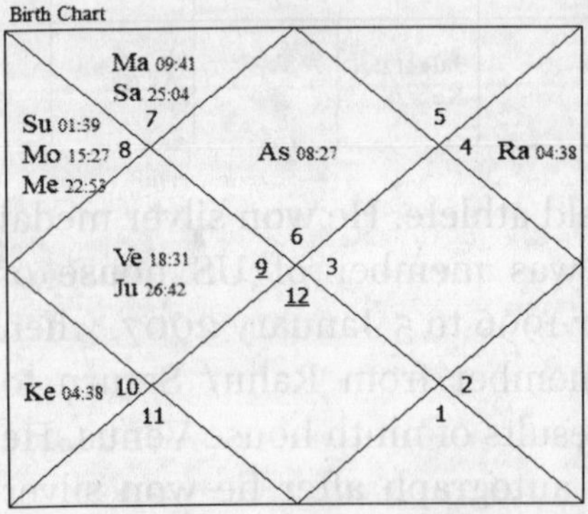

Birth Chart

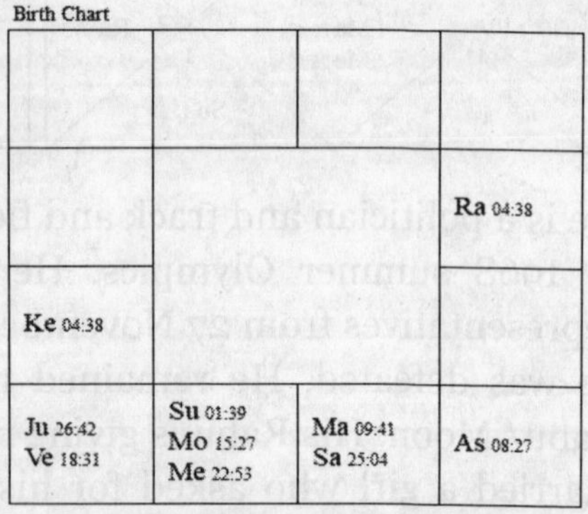

Rock Hudson is a famous film star of Hollywood. He acted in more than 70 films. He was nominated for academy award along with Elizabeth Taylor in 1956 for his movie 'Soarid Giant'. His best period was Moon dasha which saw the peak and the end of his career. He died on 2 October 1985. He was suffering from Aids. The dasha was Moon/ Venus.

LIBRA

Sun

Saravali – He will be poor, insulted, will suffer bodily disease, royal displeasure and imprisonment, will take to bad ways and will not be well disposed towards wife.

Saral – Eleventh house is the strongest of Trishadaya house. Exaltation of eleventh lord will spoil the house it is placed. He can have two marriages. The person will earn through partners/ wife or from foreign country. If Sun is placed in Virgo or Scorpio in Navamsha then he may be separated from his wife.

Example Jim Jeffords DOB 11 May 1934 TOB 18.05 POB Rutland Vermont

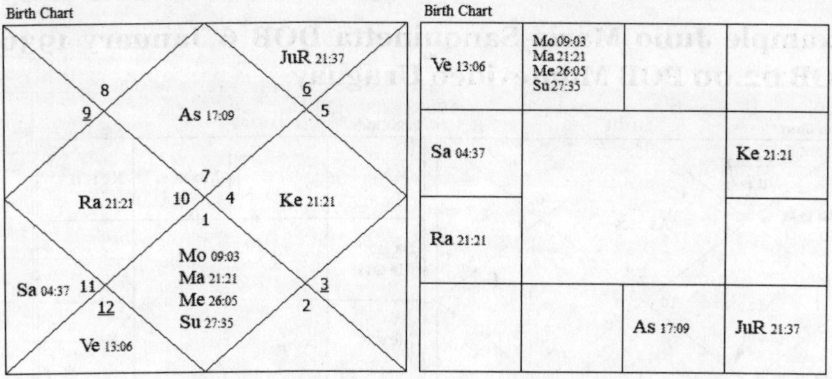

He was a Senator from Vermont and served from 1989 to 2001 as a republic party member. Dasha in 1989 was of Rahu/ Mercury. Rahu is in second house and Mercury is in tenth house in D 10. He also served as an independent senator till 2007. Dasha in 2007 was of Jupiter/ Venus. Jupiter is lagna lord and Venus is third lord of D 10. His father was Chief Justice of Vermont Supreme court. He was representative of Vermont from 1975 to 1989. Dasha in 1975 was Mars/ Saturn and was Rahu/ Mercury in 1989. He married twice but the same lady. He was married in 1961 in dasha of Sun/

Ketu and was divorced in June 1978 Mars/ Sun. He again married her on 26 August 1986 in Rahu/ Saturn. Eleventh lord in seventh house caused separation. She died of Ovarium cancer on 13 April 2007. He has two children. He was suffering from Alzheimer disease and expired on 18 August 2014 in dasha of Jupiter/ Venus.

Moon

Saravali – He will be very intelligent, very splendorous, will suffer from disease, if Moon is weak, he is short lived.

Saral – Tenth lord is placed in eleventh house from tenth. It gives sudden gains in profession. When Moon has benefic relations then the gains are more. If Moon is having only malefic relation, then he will lose his job frequently. There can be loss of land and vehicles if Moon has malefic relation.

Example Julio Maria Sanquinetta DOB 6 January 1936 TOB 02.00 POB Montevideo Uruguay

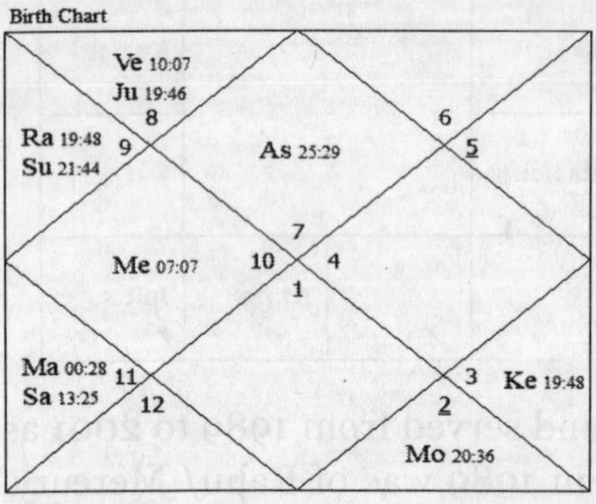

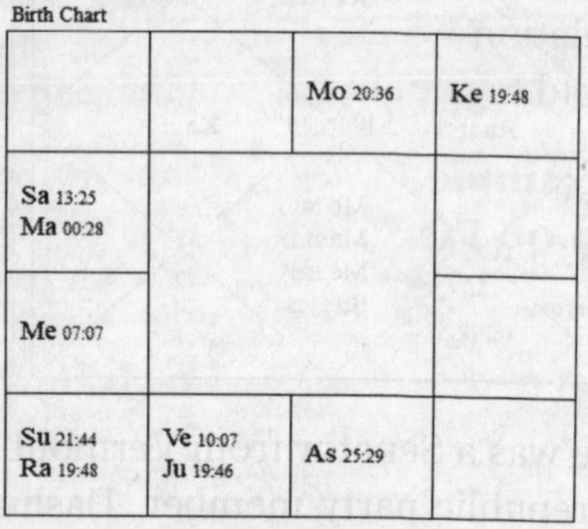

He was President of Uruguay for two terms. First term was from March 1985 to March 1990. Dasha at assuming charge was Saturn/ Ketu and at the end of term was Saturn/ Moon. His second term was from March 1995 to March 2000. This was from dasha of Saturn/ Rahu to Mercury/ Ketu. He was a lawyer by qualification having graduated in 1961 in Rahu/ Moon. He remained a minister of Industry and of Education between 1969 to 1972. His tenth lord is having two benefic aspects. Lagna lord Venus is aspected by yoga Karaka Saturn. The best combination is the mutual aspect of lagna and tenth lord and the ninth lord aspecting tenth house.

Mars

Saravali – The person is devoid of relatives, have no conveyance, be very miserable, will live in other's house and be distressed.

Saral – Mars is second and seventh lord. Second lord in fourth will ensure wealth, lands, education, friends and conveyance if Mars is having benefic relation. He may come across a hidden treasure. With malefic relation all these things will be lost. As seventh lord, Mars will take him to foreign lands and give a happy wife as Mars will aspect seventh house. He will have good relations with relatives of his wife. Seventh and second are maraca place and his mother may die in the dasha of Mars. Mars is aspecting tenth house and gives an adventurous life or works in Army. Mutual relation with Saturn will be a good Raj yoga and the person will hold high position. Ruchaka yoga is present.

Example Eugene Priest Forrester DOB 17 April 1926 TOB 19.00 POB Watertown Tennessee

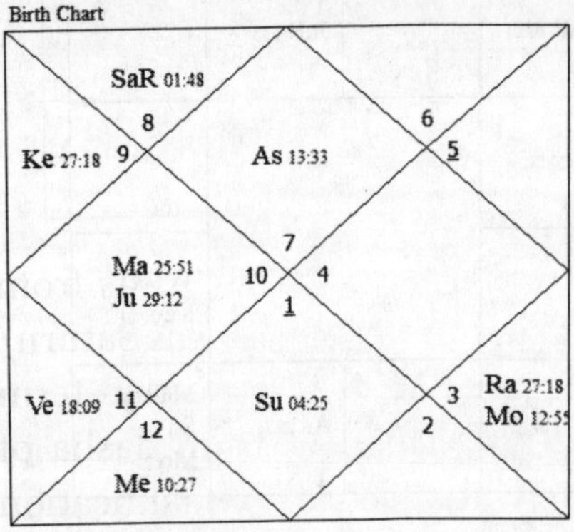

Birth Chart

Me 10:27	Su 04:25		Mo 12:55 Ra 27:18
Ve 18:09			
Ju 29:12 Ma 25:51			
Ke 27:18	SaR 01:48	As 13:33	

True to Mars aspect on tenth house, he was a senior General in the Army. He graduated from US military academy in 1948 in dasha of Jupiter/ Mars. He was commander of Western Command from 1981 to 1983. He always got accelerated promotions. He served in Korean and Vietnam wars and got gallantry and many more awards. He died on 25 July 2012 at the age of 86 years. Dasha at death was Venus/ Mercury.

Mercury

Saravali – He will keep up his promise, be indolent, be humiliated, be a good speaker, learned, pitiable and cruel.

Saral – If ninth lord is in twelfth house along with twelfth lord, then it is bad for ninth house. His father will have troubles of all kind. The person may travel abroad. He will spend money on charity or for his religion. He will be a staunch follower of his religion. If Mercury is placed in Aquarius, Aries or Leo Navamsha then the results will be bad. As twelfth lord in twelfth, the person will be engaged in philosophical pursuits.

Example Mohammed Merah DOB 11 October 1988 TOB 9.50 POB Toulouse France

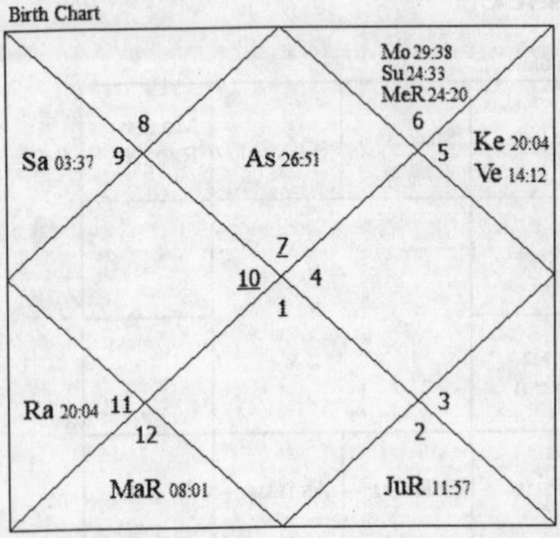

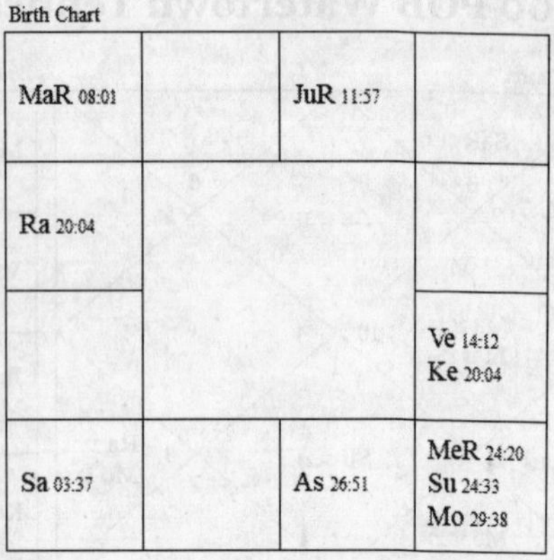

Three features in the horoscope are very prominent. Lagna lord Venus is with Ketu and have no benefic relation. Fourth house is in strong Papa Kartari. Mars is placed in seventh house from Sun and Moon. These factors give criminal tendency and no happiness in life. He was a serial killer and a Jihadi. He travelled to Pakistan and Afghanistan for training and was on the watch list of France intelligence. He admitted killing of seven people including three children. He used to film all his killing and send it to Al Jazeera. His first arrest came in 2005 in dasha of Rahu/ Venus and was in jail for 18 months. He tried to commit suicide by hanging on 25 December 2008. He was killed in Police siege and standoff on 22 March 2012 in the dasha of Jupiter/ Jupiter/ Mars. His funeral was attended by a big crowd including Imam who lamented that he has not killed more Jews.

Jupiter

Saravali – He will have successful beginning in his undertaking, be honourable, does efforts, gets happiness, wealth, relatives, conveyance and fame.

Saral – Third lord placed in tenth will make him thrive in profession. Jupiter with benefic will make his brother occupy high post in Government. If third lord is conjoined with tenth lord Moon, then he faces difficulty in his daily routine. If Jupiter is under malefic influence, then his Coborn will not be a good person. As sixth lord, Jupiter will do bad deeds if it is with benefic. With malefic, this Jupiter give low job. Jupiter will aspect sixth house and create enemies. It is best not to have any influence on this Jupiter. Jupiter is the lord of two trishadaya house and therefore a pure malefic for Taurus but its placement in Upchaya house is considered good. For better results Jupiter should be placed in sixth or eighth Navamsha. Exaltation of Jupiter in Kendra is Hansa yoga.

Example Patrick J Kennedy DOB 14 July 1967 TOB 14.33 POB Boston MA

Birth Chart

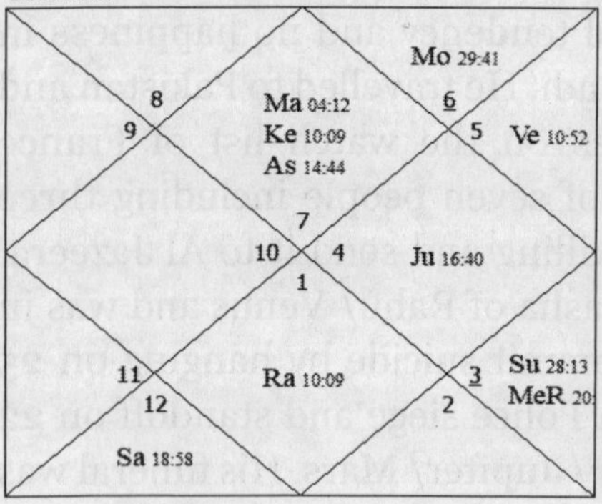

Birth Chart

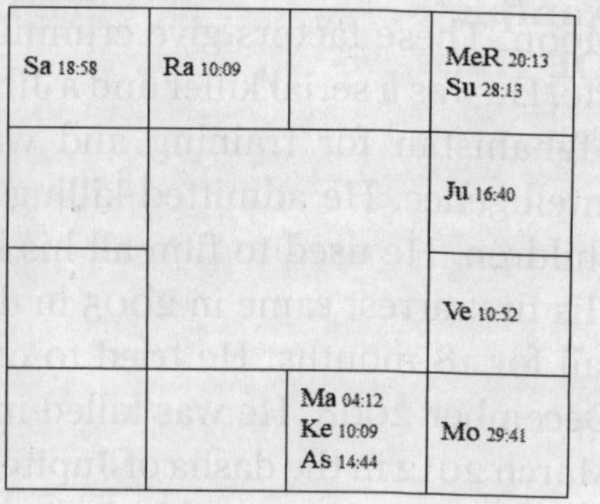

He is a politician and a mental health advocate. He is a nephew of J F Kennedy. He was a Democrat member of house of representatives from Rhode Island from 1995 to 2011. He joined in the dasha of Jupiter/ Mercury and left in Saturn/ Ketu. He met with a car accident on 4 May 2006 when he was under the influence of intoxicating drugs like Phenergan. He was awarded one year probation and 350 Dollar fine. He married late on 15 July 2011 in dasha of Saturn/ Ketu.

Venus

Saravali – He will greatly dislike his wife, will have many foes, be devoid of wealth, very much startled and be mean.

Saral – Venus is lord of eighth house. When Venus and Saturn are placed in Upchaya house then the person has long life. Lagna lord in sixth house can give high position in Army or in medical profession when it is with malefic or aspected by malefic. Eighth lord in sixth gives Vipreet yoga when it is influenced by malefic or other trik lords. There is still a possibility of disease in the dasha of sixth lord. There is danger of thieves and worries. As lagna lord in sixth house, Venus can give suffering from Government, litigation and suffer wounds.

Example Katherin Hepburn DOB 12 May 1907 TOB 17.47 POB Hartford Connecticut

Birth Chart

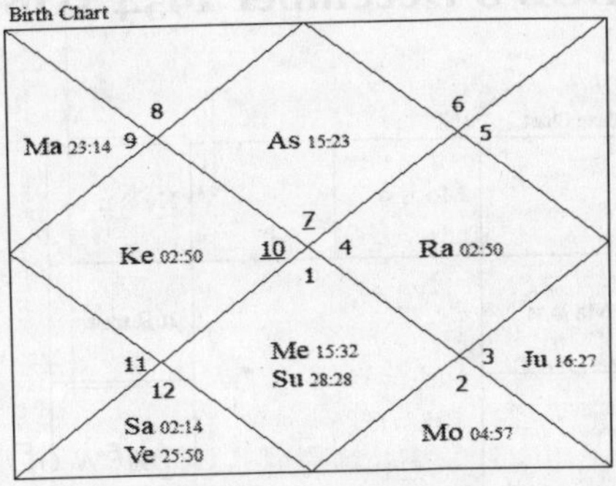

Birth Chart

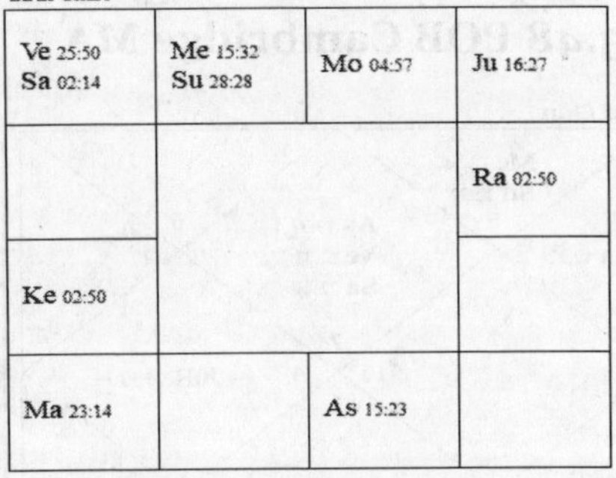

She was an American actress who served for more than 60 years in films. She got four academy awards for best actress. Her first award was in her third film in 1933 in dasha of Rahu/ Saturn. She was born in a wealthy family. She had many affairs but only one marriage. She was married on 12 December 1928 in Rahu/ Rahu/ Venus. She divorced in 1934 in Rahu/ Mercury. In May 2003, she was diagnosed with tumour in the neck died of cardiac arrest on 29 June 2003 in Ketu/ Mercury. Saturn and Venus in sixth house has given long life.

Saturn

Saravali – When Saturn is in exaltation or in own sign in lagna then the person is equal to a king, will head a country or a city. In other signs, he will give misery in childhood, dirty disposition and indolence.

Saral – Fourth lord placed in lagna will give high education in many subjects and all comforts of life. He will live in palatial house and will be brought up by his mother with care and affection. As fifth lord Saturn will give power to punish. He will be a friend of the king and liked by all. He will have limited progeny and will be kind to all. These are the effects when Saturn has benefic relation. When Saturn has malefic relation then he may be cruel by nature and have no progeny. Sasha yoga is formed. Saturn in sixth or eighth Navamsha is not welcome.

Example Harold Hongjukoh DOB 8 December 1954 TOB 03.48 POB Cambridge MA

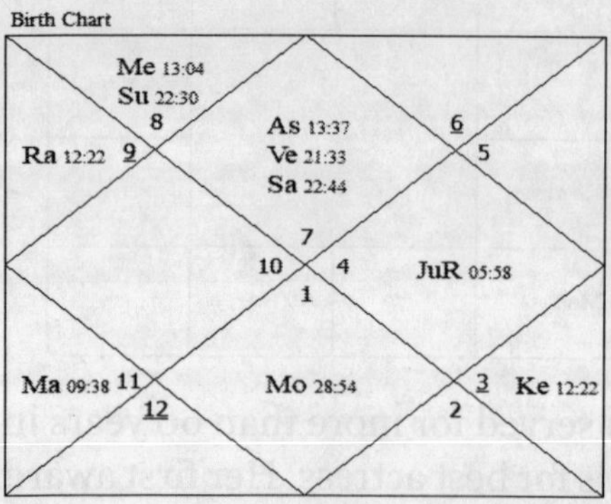

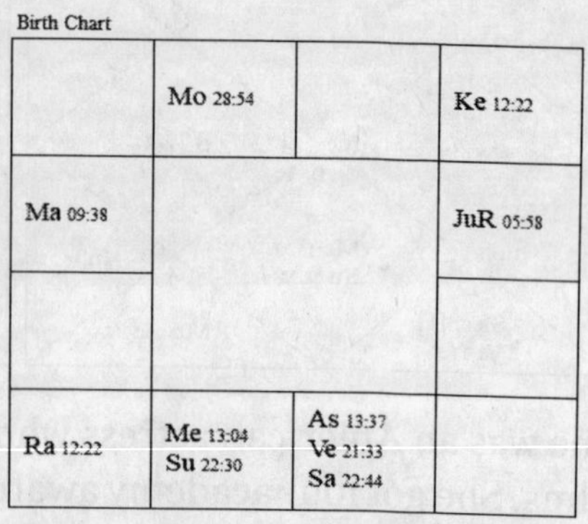

He was legal advisor in the department of state in Obama administration. His appointment was confirmed by Senate on 25 June 2009 in Jupiter/ Rahu. He resigned in January 2011 and joined Yale University as sterling professor of international law. He is a Korean and did his doctorate in Sociology. He had suffered Polio stroke at five years of age in Moon/ Moon.

SCORPIO

Sun

Saravali – The person is very libidinous, will have powerful digestive power, be strong, affluent, famous for virtues and be either a king or an army chief.

Saral – Tenth lord in sixth house will give employment in court, army or as a doctor. His maternal uncle is likely to be a powerful person. If Sun is under influence of malefic then the person will be cruel. He will perform last rites of people. Placement of Sun in third or seventh Navamsha is bad.

Example David Carpenter DOB 6 May 1930 TOB 21.16 POB Sanfrancisco CA

Birth Chart

Birth Chart

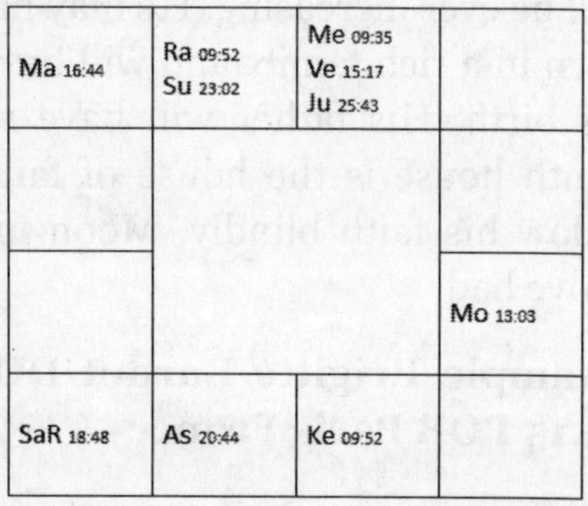

Let us first examine the basic horoscope. Lagna lord Mars is not having any benefic relation. Three benefic are in Kendra and a malefic is in second house. This gives poverty to the person and will not be able to have any wealth. Mercury is placed in Prishtodaya sign and the person can do cruel deeds. He had committed ten murders. His early life was not happy. His father was alcoholic and mother was very dominating. He married in 1955 in the dasha of Sun/ Ketu and had three children. His first murder attempt was in 1960 in dasha of Moon for which he got seven years in jail. In 1970 he was held for kidnapping and again got seven years imprisonment. He was arrested on 14 May 1981 in Rahu/ Saturn. He was convicted to die in gas chamber on 10 May 1988 in Rahu/ Sun. this judgement was overturned in 1995 in Jupiter/ Saturn. He is still in jail.

Moon

Saravali – He will be amiable, happy, will possess a good physique and be sensuously disposed. If Moon is weak then the person is pitiable and sick.

Saral – Ninth lord is in eleventh from it. The fortunes and wealth will be ever increasing. He may have wealth in foreign lands. He is born in a rich family and will have all comforts and luxuries from his birth. His father will have royal patronage and get wealth. Ninth house is the house of faith and religion. The person will follow his faith blindly. Moon in fourth or sixth Navamsha can prove bad.

Example Brigitte Bardot DOB 28 September 1934 TOB 13.15 POB Paris France

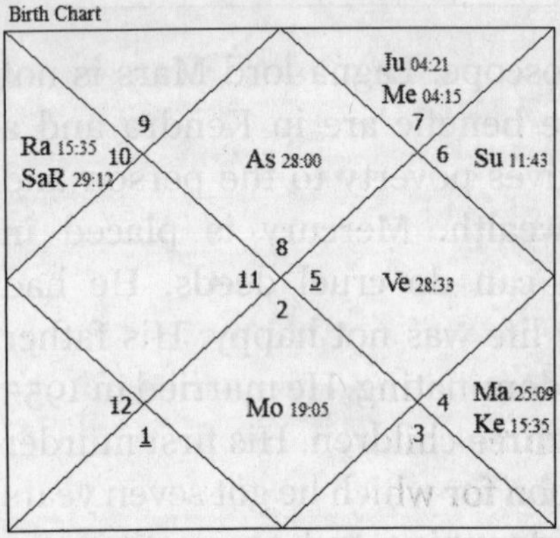

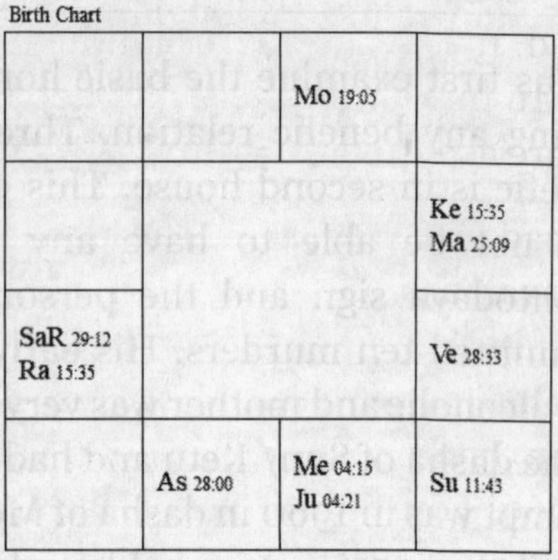

D10 Dashamsha (great successes)

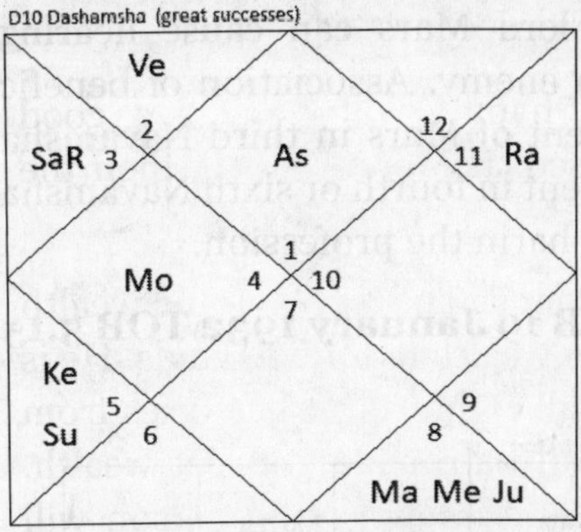

D10 Dashamsha (great successes)

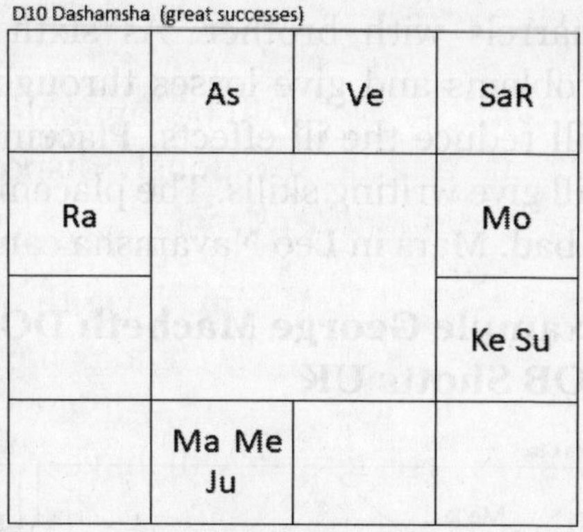

She was a famous actress and an animal rights activist. She remained a sex symbol during the fifties and sixties of 20th century. This spanned in her Rahu and Jupiter dasha. She left the entertainment world in 1973 in Jupiter/ Sun. her career started in 1952 in Rahu/ Saturn. She had been fined five times for racial hatred. In Navamsha Her ninth lord is in eighth house with eighth lord. In birth chart Ketu and debilitated Mars are in ninth house and are aspected by Saturn.

She had four marriages. The lagna lord of Navamsha is in own sign in Navamsha. Her first marriage was in 1952 in dasha of Rahu/ Mercury and ended in 1957 in Rahu/ Venus. Second marriage was in Rahu/ Sun ending in Jupiter/ Jupiter in 1962. Third marriage was in Jupiter/ Jupiter in 1966 which ended in Jupiter/ Mercury in 1969. Fourth marriage was in 1992 in Saturn/ Saturn and is going on.

Mars

Saravali – He will be courageous, unconquerable, have no Coborn, be delighted, will have all virtues and be famous.

Saral – When lagna lord is placed in third house, it will give lovable younger brother or sister. He will be courageous, study religious books and be interested in music. If afflicted he can have quarrels with brother. As sixth lord Mars can cause hearing problems and give losses through enemy. Association of benefic will reduce the ill effects. Placement of Mars in third Navamsha will give writing skills. The placement in fourth or sixth Navamsha is bad. Mars in Leo Navamsha can harm the profession.

Example George Macbeth DOB 19 January 1932 TOB 5.15 POB Shotts UK

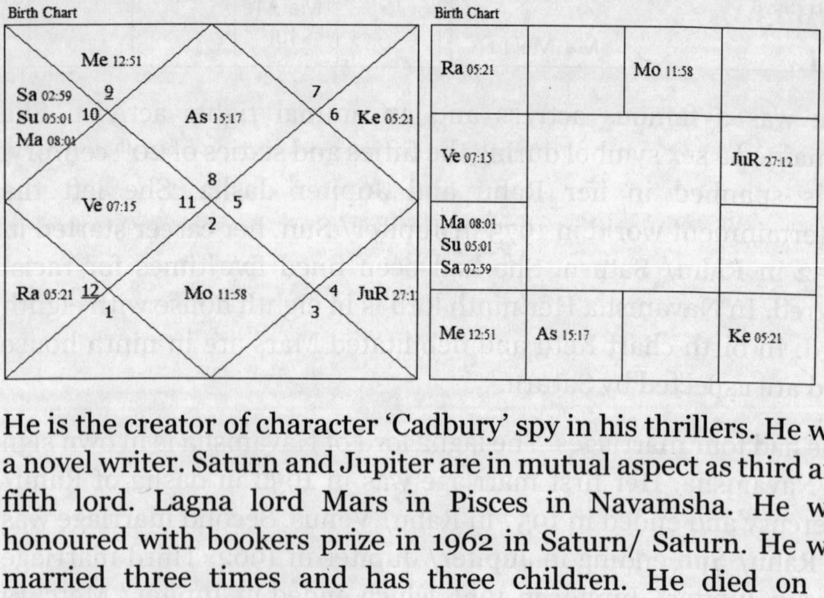

He is the creator of character 'Cadbury' spy in his thrillers. He was a novel writer. Saturn and Jupiter are in mutual aspect as third and fifth lord. Lagna lord Mars in Pisces in Navamsha. He was honoured with bookers prize in 1962 in Saturn/ Saturn. He was married three times and has three children. He died on 16 February 1992 in the dasha of Saturn/ Sun/ Saturn. He was suffering from neurone disease.

Mercury

Saravali – He will be rich, be an amicable worker, be learned, happy and endowed with wide enjoyment, be long lived and famous.

Saral – Placement of eighth lord in eleventh house will spoil the significations of eleventh house. There will be losses in business, trouble to elder brother and financial difficulty with debt. Association with maraca lords will shorten the life but association with trine lord will give long life.

Note- if a planet owns two signs and is placed in one of its signs, then he will give the results of its other sign. As such the results of eleventh house will not be experienced.

Example Abdulrahman al Awlaki DOB 13 September 1995 TOB 13.16 POB Denver Colorado

Birth Chart

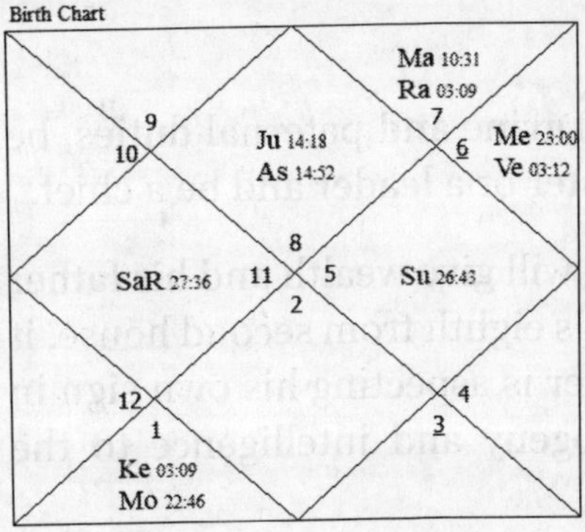

Birth Chart

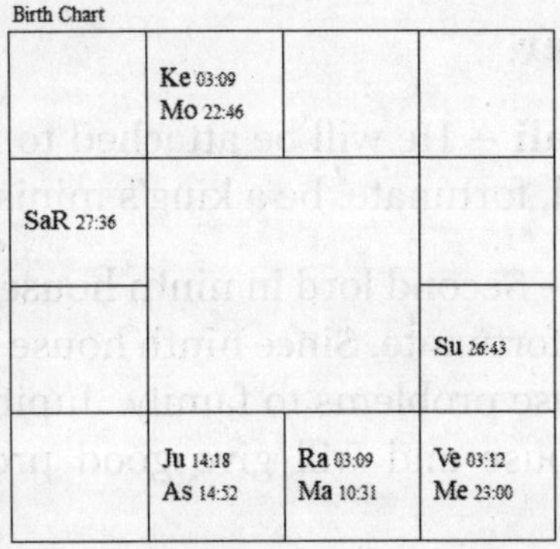

D8 Ashtamsha 1/8 Accidents

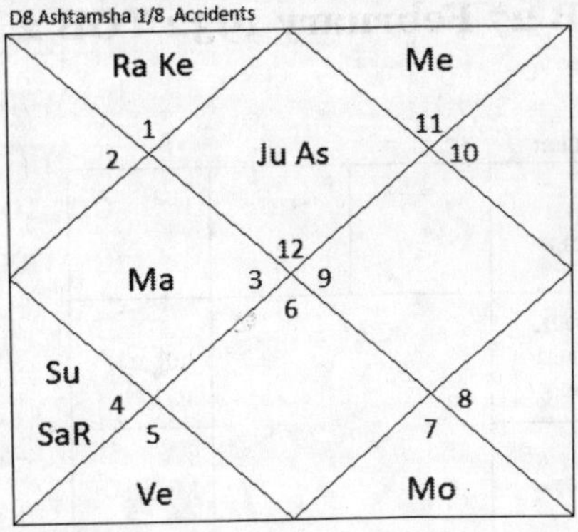

D8 Ashtamsha 1/8 Accidents

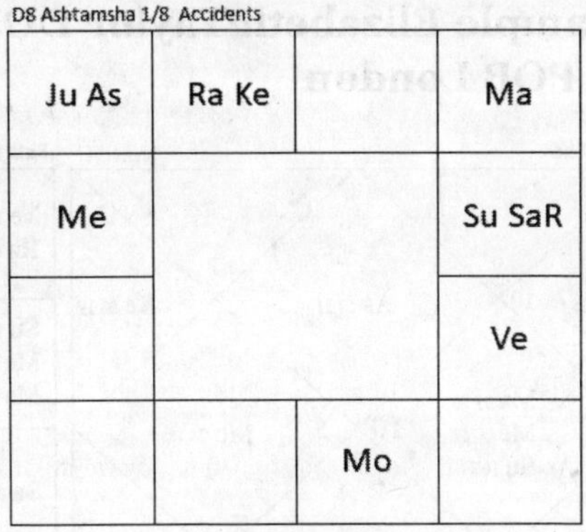

In this chart also, we examine the first basic rule. Lagna lord is with Rahu and have no benefic relation. Mars is placed in seventh from Moon. This gives criminal tendency to the person.

He was killed in US drone strike ordered by President Obama on 14 October 2011. He was 16 years old. His father was operational leader of Al Qaeda in Arabian Peninsula. His sister was also killed in commando attack on 21 January 2017 at the age of 8 years.

His Mercury gives effects of eighth house. Mercury is with Venus who is lord of twelfth and seventh house in birth chart. In D 8 Jupiter is in lagna showing sudden events in life. Tenth house of D 8 is aspected by Mars giving sudden bad event.

Jupiter

Saravali – He will be attached to Divine and paternal duties, be learned, fortunate, be a king's minister or a leader and be a chief.

Saral – Second lord in ninth house will give wealth and his father will be fortunate. Since ninth house is eighth from second house, it can cause problems to family. Jupiter is aspecting his own sign in fifth house and will give good progeny and intelligence to the person.

Example Elizabeth Taylor DOB 27 February 1932 TOB 2. 30 POB London

Birth Chart

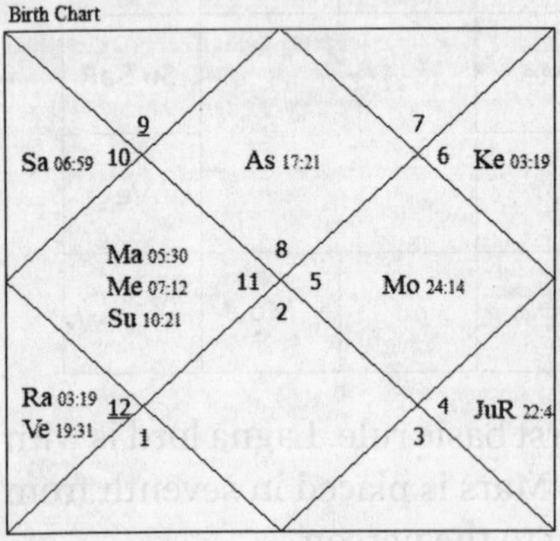

Birth Chart

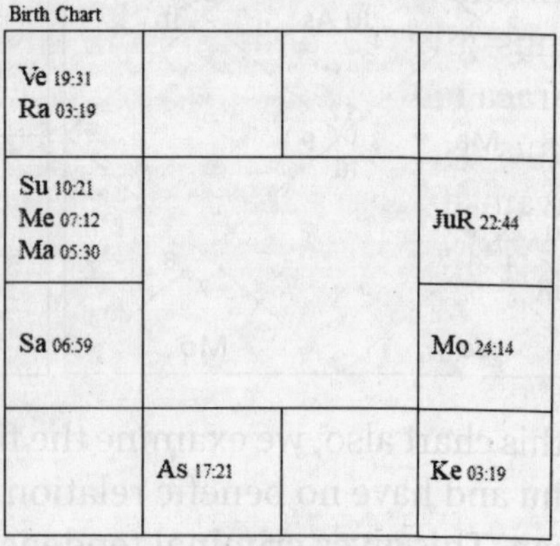

She was a well-known actress. She started her film career in in 1940 as a child artist in the dasha of Sun. She has won many awards in her long spell of acting. She is most talked about her eight marriages. Her lagna lord of Navamsha is Jupiter. Jupiter is debilitated in second house in Navamsha and aspects eighth house. Death of spouse was not the cause of remarriage in any of her marriage. lagna lord of Navamsha in debilitation gives many affairs or marriages. Her first marriage was in Mars MD and this continued till dasha of Jupiter. Her Venus is also exalted and she had the most expensive jewellery. She had four children. Her end came on 23 March 2011. She died of heart failure in dasha of Saturn/ Jupiter/ Moon.

Venus

Saravali – He will have happiness, sons and friends, be fond of sexual union, be very affluent, full of everything and be a minister or a justice.

Saral – Venus is seventh lord placed in fifth house. It is good for children but can give two marriages. Twelfth lord placed in fifth will give earning and knowledge from other countries. Any relation with Moon will be a very good yoga. Mutual relation of Jupiter and Venus gives wealth in their dasha. But Jupiter and Venus are maraca for Scorpio and can give problems. Relation of Saturn with Venus is not considered good. Placement of Venus in third Navamsha is not good.

Example Shirley Temple Black DOB 23 April 1928 TOB 21.00 POB Santa Monica CA

Birth Chart

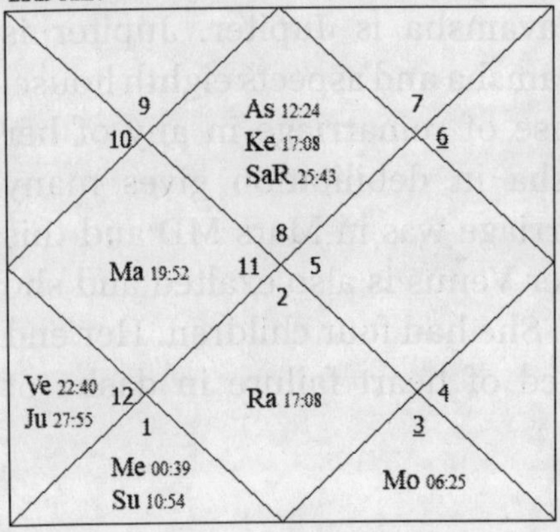

Birth Chart

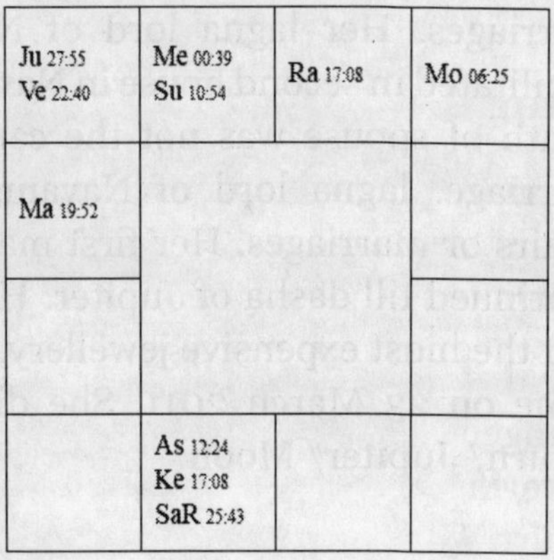

Another famous actress was also a singer, dancer, business women and diplomate. She started as child artist in 1934 in dasha of Rahu/ Saturn and worked as child artist till 1938. Her weekly salary was 150 dollars in 1934. It was raised to 1000 dollars/ week plus 15000 in bonus for a completed film. It was big money at that time. She retired from films on 16 December 1950 in dasha of Jupiter/ Saturn as other big things were waiting for her. She was chief of protocol of US. She was US ambassador to Ghana from 6 December 1974 to 13 July 1976. The dasha at appointment was Saturn/ Mars and was Saturn/ Rahu at the end if this job. She was again made Ambassador of Czechoslovakia from 23 August 1989 to 12 July 1992. The dasha at start was Mercury/ Moon and Mercury/ Rahu at the end.

Her first marriage was on 19 September 1945 in Rahu/ Mars/ Jupiter. This marriage was attended by more than 500 guests. This marriage ended in divorce on 5 December 1949 in Jupiter/ Saturn/ Sun. She got married again on 16 December 1950 in dasha of Jupiter/ Saturn/ Jupiter. Her husband died on 4 August 2005 in dasha of Venus. She was diagnosed with breast cancer in 1972 in

Saturn/ Sun. Her death was on 10 February 2014 in Venus/ Rahu/ Mercury due to pulmonary disease. Venus is seventh lord and Rahu is in seventh house.

Saturn

Saravali – He will be poor, deformed of some limb, tormented by expenses, addicted to courtesans and will not have permanent livelihood. A female will not have lasting family ties.

Saral – Saturn as third lord placed in twelfth house will harm his younger Coborn who may live in a distant country. His mind is wavering and he is not able to take firm decision. As fourth lord Saturn will provide good education and comfortable living. He gets mother like affection from people.

Example Mark Pottenger DOB 9 February 1955 TOB 03.23 POB Tucson Arizona

Birth Chart

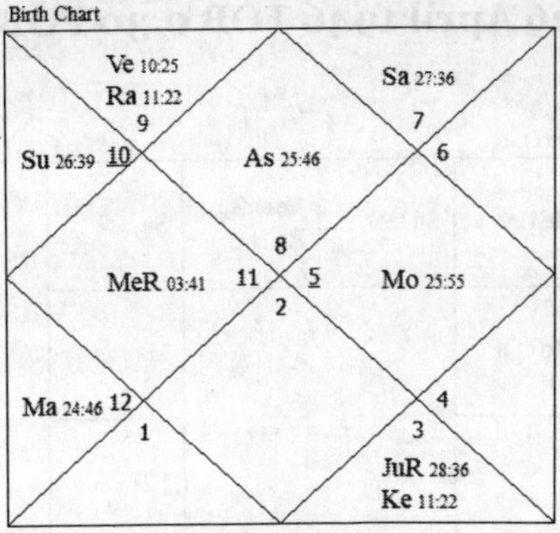

Birth Chart

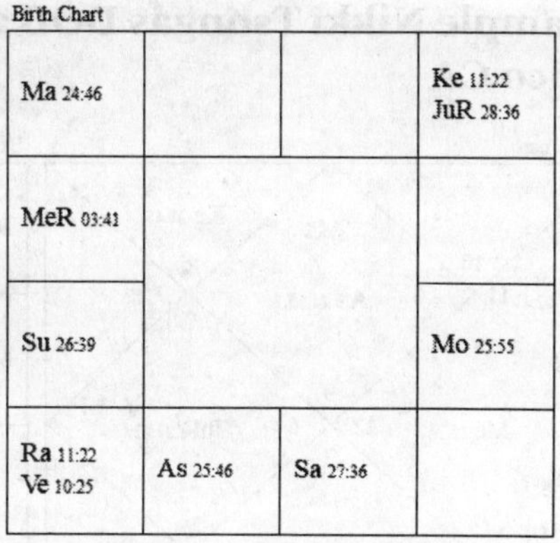

Mark is an astrologer and his researches led to the creation of Astro data bank. He started his work in 1981 in the dasha of Rahu with International Society for Astrological Research. With a data of 7465 he completed his research on 13 February 1988 in Rahu/ Mercury. Mercury is eighth lord and Rahu is in second house. By the year 1992 he had 29837 entries. At present it has a data bank of 94625 entries. Jupiter is aspecting Saturn and has improved the quality of Saturn.

SAGITTARIUS

Sun

Saravali – He will not have happiness, sons and wealth, will live by husbandry, will move in hills and fortresses, be fickle minded, scholarly, devoid of strength and be short loved.

Saral – Ninth lord exalted in fifth house will bring fortunes to his father, grandfather and children provided Sun is not afflicted. He will get help from father or a rich preceptor. The lagna lord should be strong to enjoy all good results. The dasha of trine lords will be important to the person. For this lagna Saturn is a malefic and is lord of second house.

Example Nikki Tsongas DOB 26 April 1946 TOB 0.30 POB Chico CA

Birth Chart

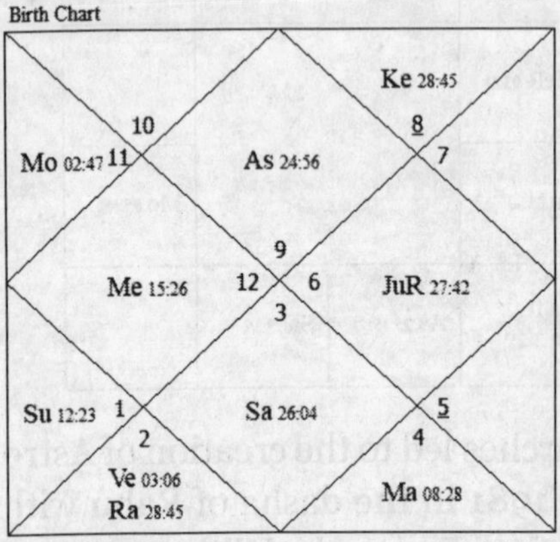

Birth Chart

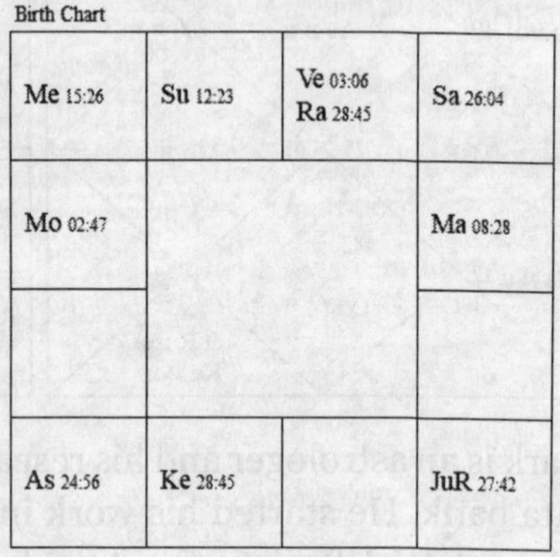

She is the eldest of four daughters. Eleventh lord Venus is with Rahu in sixth house which is eighth from eleventh house. Eleventh house is aspected by Mars. Her political career started in 1975 in

Jupiter dasha. She was representative from Massachusetts from 2007 to 2019. She won the election on 16 October 2007 in Mercury/ Sun. Mercury is tenth lord. This ended in 2019 in Ketu/ Venus. She is the head of the foundation to provide education to the children of 9/ 11 attack. She retired from politics in August 2017 in dasha of Mercury/ Saturn. She was married in 1969 in Jupiter/ Saturn. She died of liver failure on 18 January 1997 in dasha of Saturn/ Rahu/ Saturn. Saturn is a malefic and a lord of second house. Saturn is placed in another maraca seventh house.

Moon

Saravali – The person will suffer from stomach disease. If Moon is weak then he is short lived.

Saral – Eighth lord is exalted in sixth house. It is Vipreet yoga provided it is influenced by malefic only. Eighth lord will give research, occult science and deep knowledge. The person will not suffer chronic disease when Moon is under malefic influence. Moon is harmful to maternal uncle and give fear of thief to the person. He will be long lived.

Example Slemmons David DOB 31 December 1922 TOB 7.45 POB Alameda CA

Birth Chart

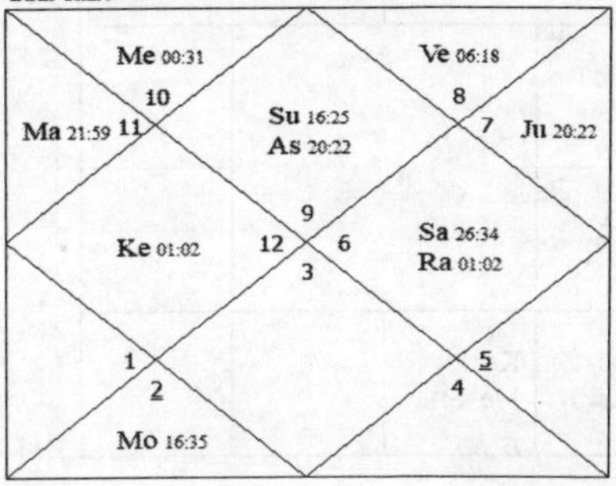

Birth Chart

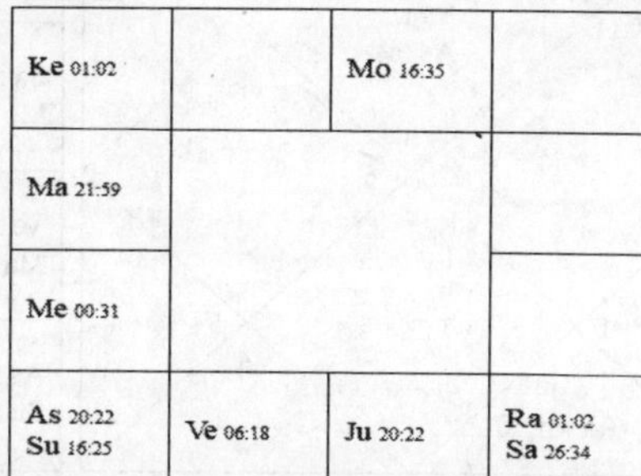

He was a scientist in Geology field. He obtained his doctorate in 1953 in dasha of Jupiter/ Jupiter. He was appointed consultant to the Government in 1962 in dasha of Jupiter/ Venus. He taught in the University of Nevada. His researches were in the field of faults and earthquake magnitude. He was married on 7 September 1946 and have two children. His Moon is aspected by Mars and Venus. Venus is a functional malefic.

Mars

Saravali – He will not derive fruits of family and wealth. He will be without learning.

Saral – Mars is lord of fifth and twelfth house. To get good results of Mars, it should not be related to trishadaya lord. In such situation the trishadaya lord gains strength to bring harm to the person. If this Mars is mutually related to a Kendra lord, then only it will give good results. Twelfth lord placed in second with malefic will give quarrels in family. He will not get food in time. Fifth lord in second with benefic will give happy family.

Example Jean Thierry Mathurin DOB 27 December 1965 TOB 6.15 POB Arrondssement of Saint Laurent du marone French Guiana

Birth Chart

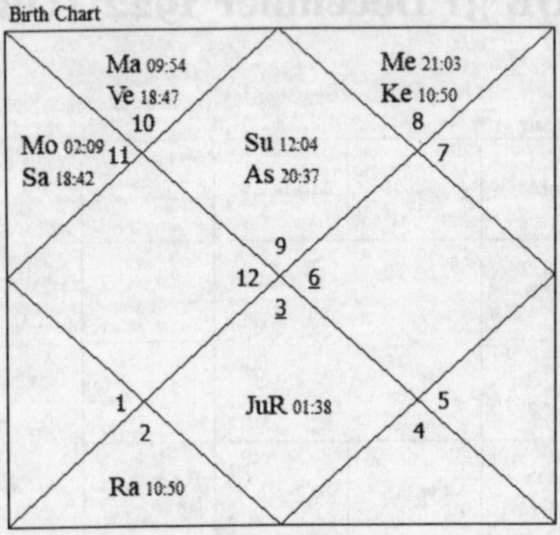

Birth Chart

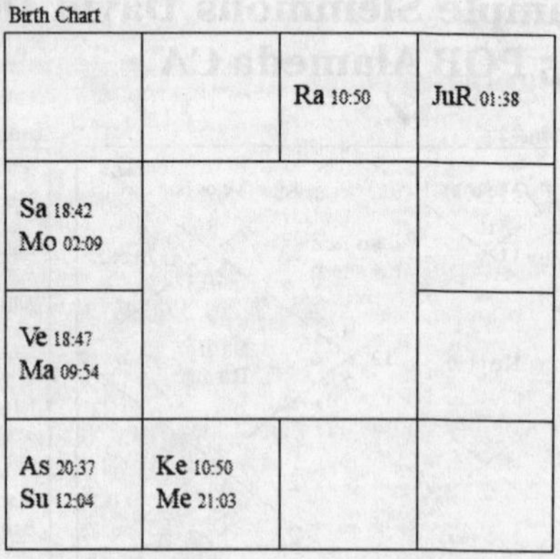

He was a drug addict and a drug peddler. His crime graph started on 14 November 1982 when he robbed an old woman and was arrested. On 5 October 1984 he robbed 50 dollars from two women and one of them died. From October 1984 to November 1984, he murdered eight elderly women. Between 20 December 85 to 14 June 86, he committed eight more murders. His last crime was on 25 November 1987, when he murdered a 79-year-old woman and attacked an 87-year-old. He was arrested on 1 December 1987 in Jupiter/ Jupiter/ Sun. He has committed 16 to 21 murders. He died of AIDS on 16 April 1989. The dasha was Jupiter/ Saturn/ Rahu. Ninth lord Sun is in Navamsha of Cancer which is eighth house. Eighth lord is in third house causing Vipreet yoga but this is spoiled by aspect of Jupiter. This Jupiter brought the end of Vipreet yoga and he was arrested.

Mercury

Saravali – He will possess distinguished intelligence, will perform distinguished acts, will attain success in undertakings, be very learned, courageous, strong will be endowed with various kinds of ornaments.

Saral – Mercury is lord of two Kendra house. It is neutral for Sagittarius lagna. Mercury placed in his sign in Kendra will prove maraca in his dasha. Seventh lord and tenth lord in exaltation will give good profession and marriage. It will give name and fame to the person. Any mutual relation with trine lord is a Raj yoga and the person will hold high position in society.

Example Sophia Loren DOB 20 September 1934 TOB 14.10 POB Rome Italy

Birth Chart

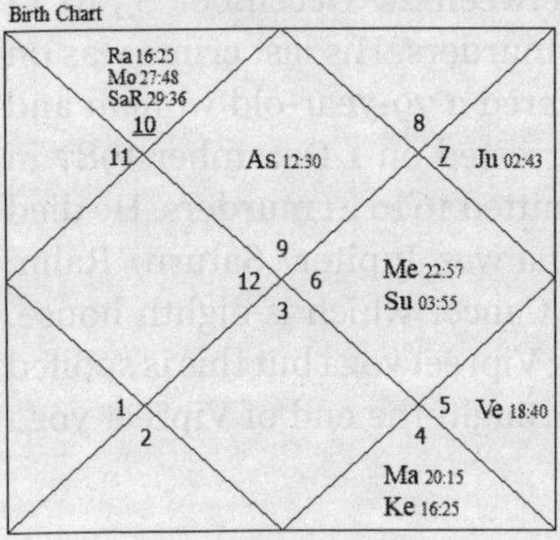

Birth Chart

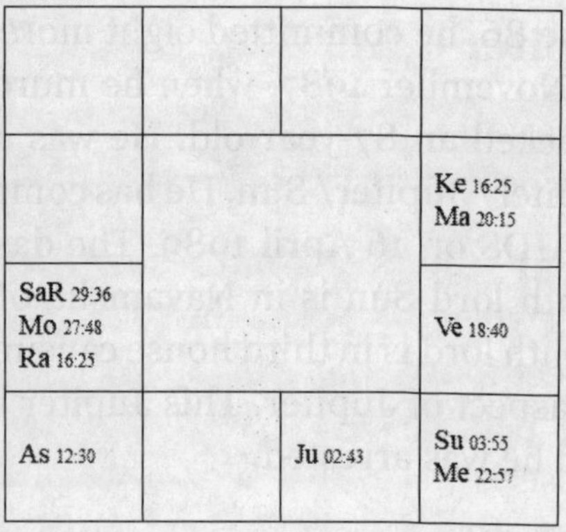

She is named the greatest female star of twenty first century. She started her career in minor roles after her selection as miss Italia. Her father abandoned her mother after her birth and she met him only thrice in life. Once when she was 5 years, then at her 17 years and last time on his burial in 1976. In D 12, ninth lord Saturn is placed in eighth house and ninth house has Ketu in it. The dasha was of Saturn. She married Ponti on 17 September 1957 and was attended by Ponti through proxy by two lawyers. The marriage was annulled in 1962 to save her husband from bigamy charges. He was 37 years old and she was 16 years at the time of marriage. In Navamsha, her eighth lord Saturn is in third house with lagna lord Moon. The dasha at marriage was Jupiter/ Jupiter. The final divorce was granted on 9 April 1966 in Jupiter/ Venus. After this she married again in 1966. Her husband died on 10 January 2007 due to pulmonary disease in dasha of Mercury/ Saturn. She has two children. First son was born on 29 December 1968 in Jupiter/ Moon and second son on 6 January 1973 in Jupiter/ Rahu. She started her film career in 1950 in Rahu/ Venus. Both Rahu and Venus are in eleventh house in D 10. She got best actress award in

1991. Her birth in day time with five planets including Jupiter placed in visible half is the reason of her success.

Jupiter

Saravali – He is insulted, long lived, be a servant, will serve his own people, be pitiable and will have union with dirty women.

Saral – Jupiter is lord of lagna and gets exalted in eighth house. This will ensure long life to the person. As fourth lord Jupiter will aspect fourth house and will promote the effects of fourth house. The person will have property and happiness of home. Eighth house is the house of research and occult. The person will have innovative ideas. As fourth lord, Jupiter has Kendradhipati Dosha, but being lagna lord it becomes a benefic. Jupiter will aspect second house and gives wealth. When Jupiter has a relation with Saturn then he will save good amount of money.

Example Michel Bon DOB 5 July 1943 TOB 20.45 POB Grenoble France

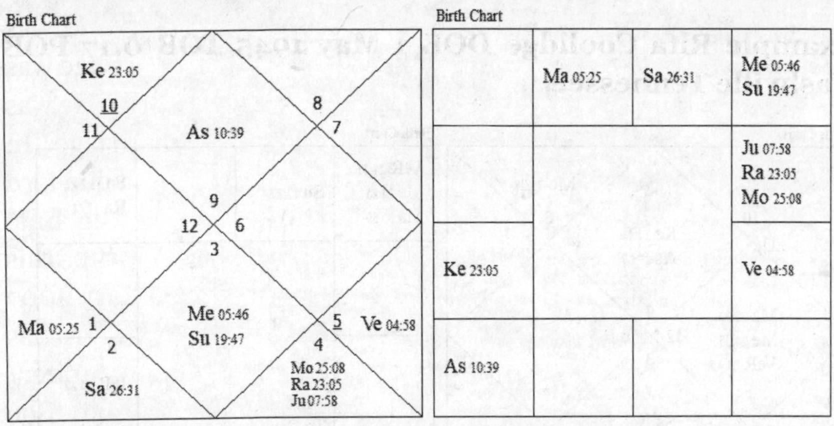

He has held high positions in business houses. He was chairman/ CEO of Carrefour chain of super market from 1993 to 1995. Dasha was of Mars. Mars is placed in third house with tenth lord in D 10. He was chairman of France Telecom from 1995 to 2002. The dasha was of Mars in 1995 and in 2002 it was Rahu/ Rahu. He holds a degree in Political Science from Stanford Graduate school of business. He was the first leader of young leaders of French American foundation in 1981. The dasha was Sun/ Ketu. Sun is ninth lord and is placed in seventh with tenth lord. In D 10 Ketu is in tenth house.

Venus

Saravali – He will be blessed with relatives, friends and happiness, be splendorous, will have conveyance, be beautiful, rich and fortunate.

Saral – Malavya yoga is caused. Venus is lord of two trishadaya houses and If Venus is having only benefic relation, then his mother and property will suffer. His mother may be short lived and his brothers will take away his property. His education will not be completed. But if Venus has more or only malefic relation then these bad results are not experienced. With this malefic relation with Venus and lagna is strong then good results are more.

Example Rita Coolidge DOB 1 May 1945 TOB 0.17 POB Nashville Tennessee

Birth Chart

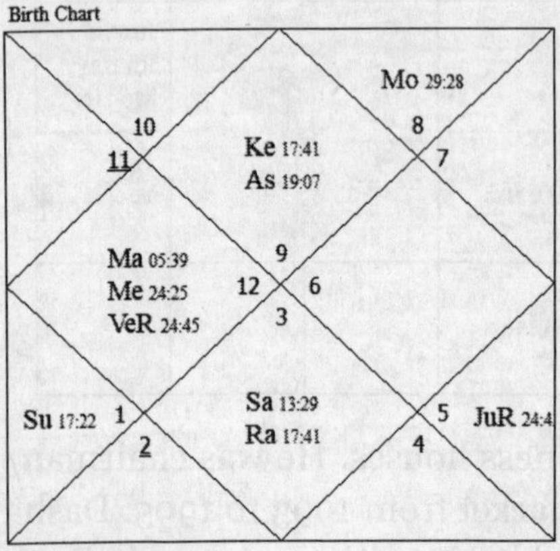

Birth Chart

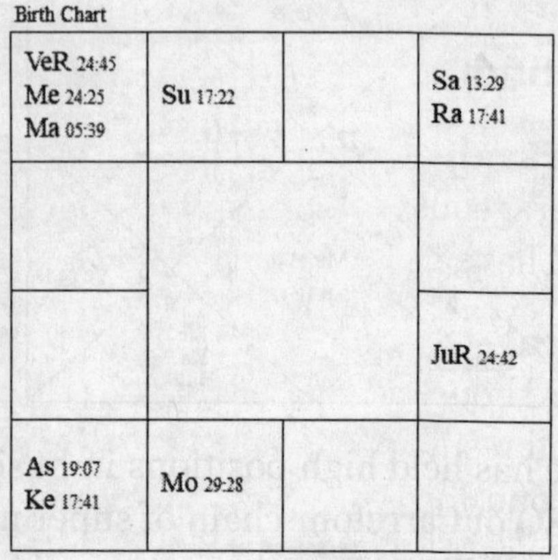

D9 Navamsha (spouse)

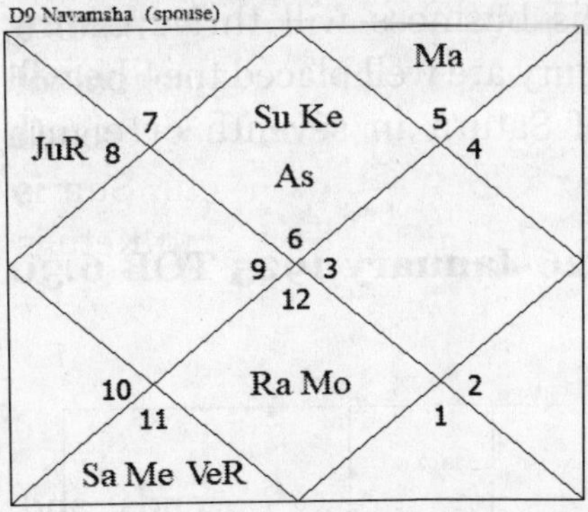

D9 Navamsha (spouse)

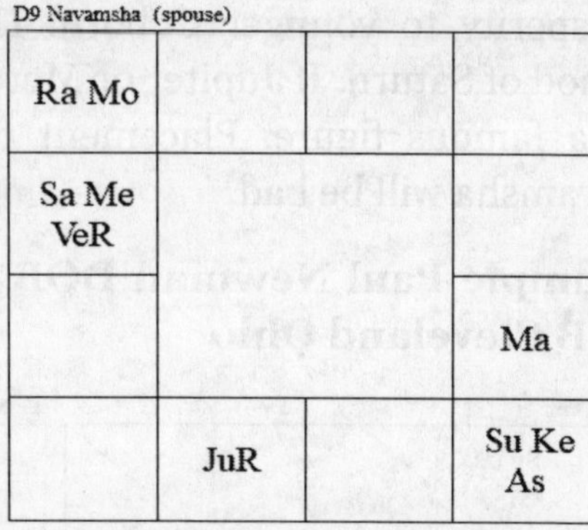

She is an actress and recording artist. She is the winner of two Grammy awards. She had sung the theme song of James Bond thriller "Octopussy". She started working in 1970 in Venus dasha. Her first marriage lasted from 1973 to 1980. She has a daughter from this marriage. The dasha at the time of birth of her daughter was Sun/ Mars. The marriage came in Sun/ Moon. Her marriage was volatile because of alcoholism and infidelity of husband. She had a miscarriage in 1977 and the marriage deteriorated. The dasha was Sun/ Mercury. Her second marriage was on 19 June 2004 with a Japanese professor. The dasha was Rahu/ Mercury. Generally, Sun Moon conjunction, opposition or exchange in Navamsha does not give happy marriage.

Saturn

Saravali – The person is long lived, have lasting riches, be courageous, will have knowledge of arts, be devoid of sickness and will have money, people and wealth.

Saral – Saturn is lord of neutral second house and lord of malefic third house. Saturn should be influenced by a strong malefic to give good result. Any benefic relation with Saturn will give bad results. Second lord in eleventh house will give gains. The gains will be from sources indicated by the planet associated with Saturn or by the lord of Navamsha sign of Saturn. As third lord Saturn will give prosperity to younger Coborn. His business will thrive during period of Saturn. If Jupiter or Mercury are well placed then he will be a famous figure. Placement of Saturn in seventh or eighth Navamsha will be bad.

Example Paul Newman DOB 26 January 1925 TOB 6.30 POB Cleveland Ohio

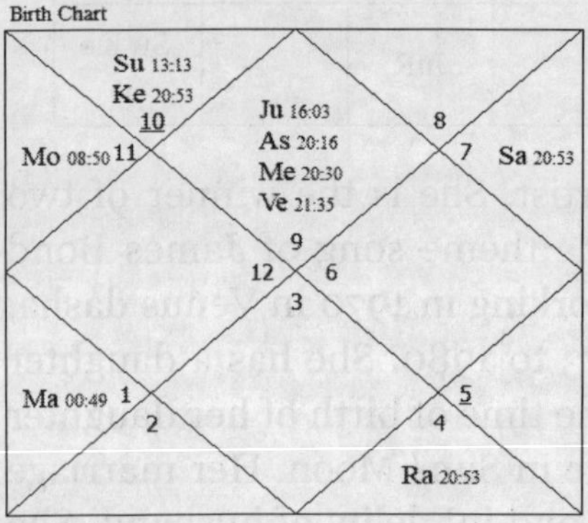

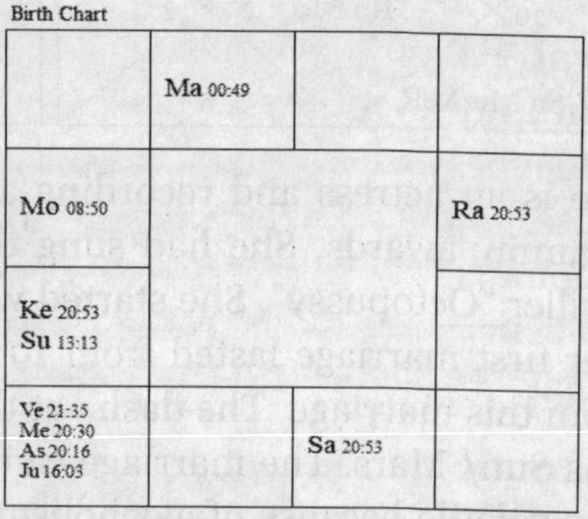

He was a highly paid actor. He charged more than one million dollars per film. He has done more than 60 films with this much fees. He started his career 1953 in the dasha of Jupiter/ Mars. He was nominated seven times for Oscar award but could not make it. He was offered honorary award in 1985 but he declined. Finally, he won an Oscar on 30 March 1987 in Venus/ Jupiter/ Jupiter. He married in 1949. His wife and he had a daughter before the formal marriage. He has six children. He is a great philanthropist. On 1 June 2007, he donated 10 million dollars to a school and made many more donations. His biggest contribution is 21 million dollars to Newman Foundation. He was nominated "Most Generous Celebrity" in 2008. He owns 22 houses in California. He retired in May 2007 when diagnosed for lung cancer. He died on 26 September 2008 in dasha of Venus/ Rahu/ Sun.

His eighth lord Moon is in third house and has no benefic relation. This is the reason of his fame, wealth and long life.

CAPRICORN

Sun

Saravali – The person will not have conveyance and relatives, will suffer heart disease, will destroy parental house and wealth and will serve a bad king.

Saral – Eighth lord is considered a neutral and a trik lord. But eighth lord is giver of concentration, new researches and suddenness. As a malefic, he will destroy the effects of fourth house. Malefic relation with Sun will give no comforts or happiness. Any influence of trishadaya lords will aggravate the problems. Influence of benefic can save the problems to a great extent.

Example Susan Atkins DOB 7 May 1948 TOB 01.03 POB San Gabriel CA

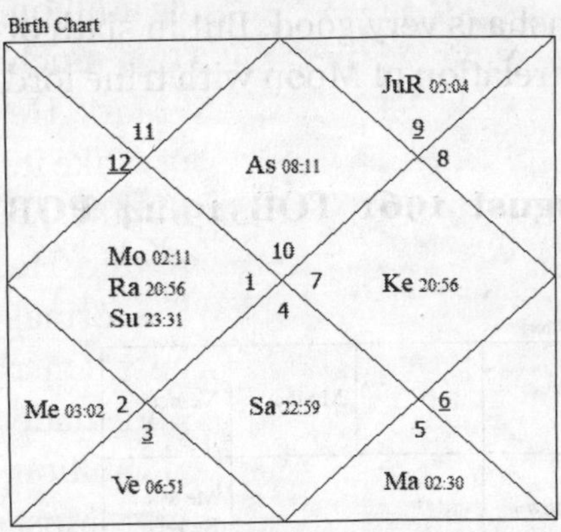

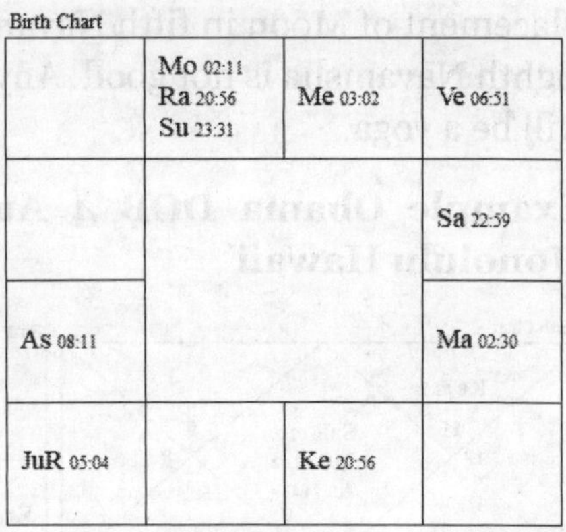

She was an active member of Charles Manson's family. She had a traumatic childhood. Her parents were alcoholic. After the death of her mother in 1963, her father abandoned her. Her mother died of cancer in her Venus/ Rahu dasha. She met Manson in 1967 and became his follower. She treated Manson as Jesus. She was known as sexy Sadie in the group. She gave birth to a boy on 7 October

1968 in Venus/ Saturn/ Sun. The boy was adopted by someone and she had no further contact with him. Between 25 July and 10 August 1969, the group murdered nine people. Her dasha was of Venus/ Saturn/ Rahu. She was convicted to death but the sentence was converted to life imprisonment by Supreme Court. She is the longest serving female prisoner in jail. Sun is with Rahu and is aspected by third lord Jupiter. Jupiter is not a functional benefic. Eighth lord and fourth lord are in exchange of sign. Aspect of Saturn can be good as Saturn is lagna lord.

Moon

Saravali – He will be of timid disposition, will earn learning, clothes, food, will have many sons and friends, be a scholar and be passionate.

Saral – Seventh lord placed in fifth house will promote both houses. He will get help from distant place and from partners. Placement of Moon in fifth Navamsha is very good. But in sixth or eighth Navamsha is not good. Any relation of Moon with trine lord will be a yoga.

Example Obama DOB 4 August 1961 TOB 19.24 POB Honolulu Hawaii

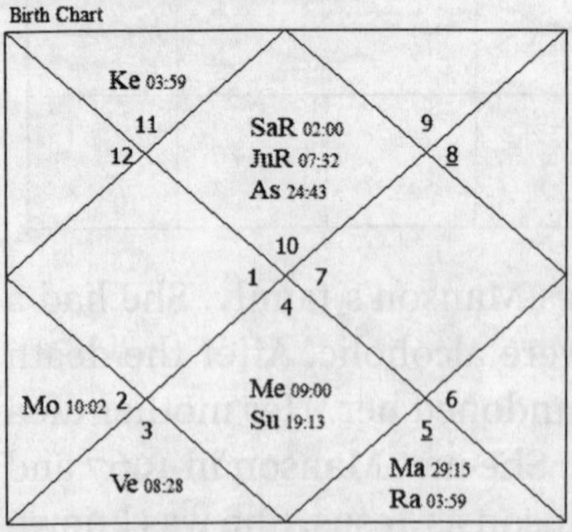

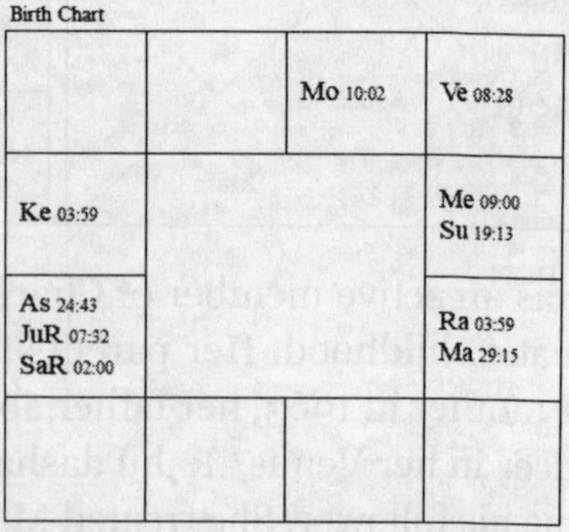

His childhood was not stable. His parents separated by divorce in 1964 in Moon/ Jupiter. His father died in a vehicle accident in 1982 in Rahu/ Jupiter. At the age of six years, he moved to Indonesia to join his step - father. His early schooling was done in Indonesia. He speaks Indonesian language with the ease of a child. In 1971 in Mars dasha, he returned to Honolulu to stay with his maternal grandparents. He completed his high school in 1979 on scholarship. He met Michelle in 1989 and they married on 3 October 1992 in dasha of Rahu/ Venus/ Ketu. She had a miscarriage and did invitro fertilization. They have two daughters. His mother got her doctorate degree in 1992 but she died in 1995.

He was 44th President of USA from 20 January 2009 to 2017. He became President in Jupiter/ Moon/ Venus and left in Saturn/ Mercury/ Mars. Prior to this, he was Senator from Illinois from 2005 to 2008.

Mars

Saravali – He will be cruel, adventurous, dull witted, short lived, honourable, courageous, will have an injured physique, be attractive in appearance and fickle minded.

Saral – Fourth lord in lagna will give a strong character to the person. He will be dignified in his actions. As eleventh lord, it will expand the deeds of lagna. Any malefic relation is not good. Exchange or conjunction of Mars and Saturn will make him a dare devil. Relation with trishadaya lords is not welcome. An exalted trishadaya lord will spoil the other planets aspected by it or are in conjunction with it.

Example Camilo Gorriaran DOB 6 February 1932 TOB 7.00 POB Havana Cuba

Birth Chart

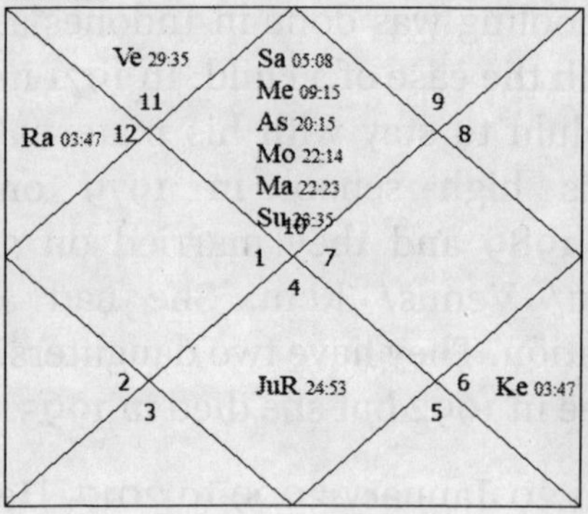

Birth Chart

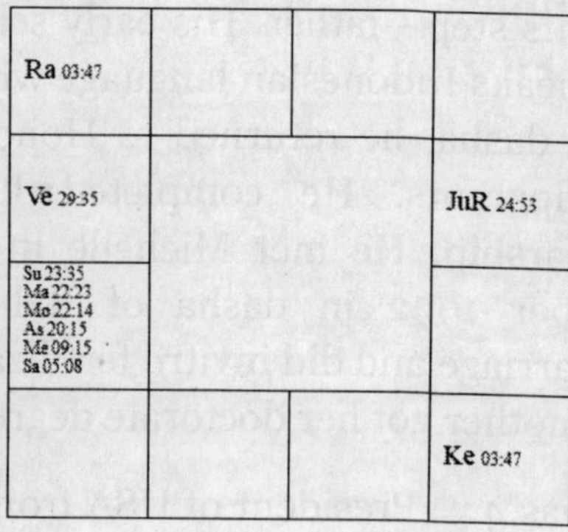

He played a very prominent role in liberation of Cuba from the dictator Balista. He was a member of 1956 Granma expedition launched by Fidel Castro. He was the top guerrilla commander. After winning the key battle of Cuban revolution, he was known as 'Hero of Yaguajay'. This was in 1959 in dasha of Jupiter/ Jupiter. He was appointed head of Cuban armed forces at the age of 27 years. His airplane went missing on 28 October 1959 and he was presumed dead. The dasha was Jupiter/ Jupiter/ Rahu. His father was a tailor and mother a domestic servant.

Mercury

Saravali – The person will be very affluent, scholarly, of good conduct and habits, eloquent in speech, skilful of great order and be virtuous.

Saral – Ninth lord placed in ninth house and under benefic influence will promote the effects of ninth house. His father will be highly placed in life and the person is upright and a follower of his Dharma. He will do charities. If it is under malefic influence then these will not happen. His father may not keep good health or longevity. As sixth lord in ninth house, Mercury will give army, police or judiciary related job. A relation with eighth lord can give deviation from religious path.

Example Carlo Dalla Chiesa DOB 27 September 1920 TOB 16.00 POB Saluzzo Italy

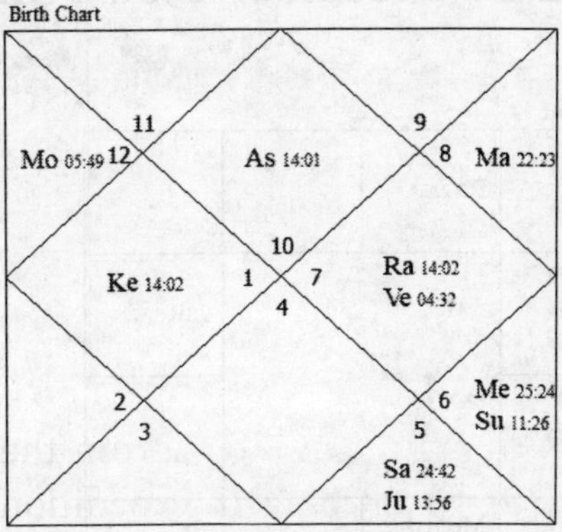

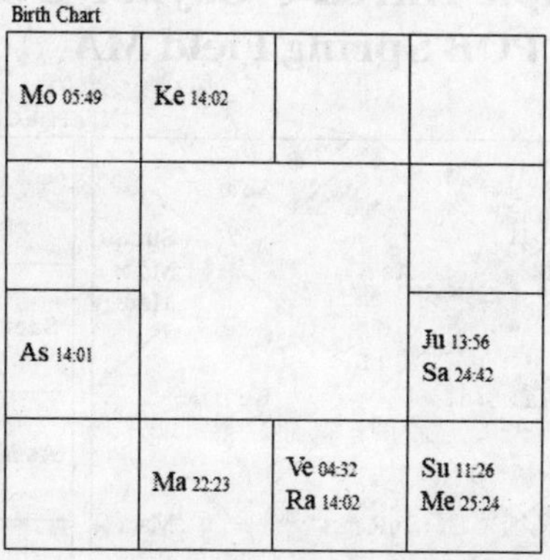

He was a general of police department. He joined police in World War 2. Soon he became a captain. He is known for his fight against Red Brigade mafia. He started his investigations of mafia attacks in 1949 in dasha of Mercury/ Jupiter. He commanded the Carabinieri region for 7 years. He revealed that banks were laundering money. He was given a warning by mafia and he was killed in terrorism. He was assassinated by Sicilian mafia on 3 September 1982 in dasha of Sun/ Rahu.

His third lord Jupiter is in eighth house with Saturn and is a strong Vipreet yoga.

Jupiter

Saravali – He will acquire a beautiful wife, be greater than his father, be an eloquent speaker, a poet, a superior person and be learned and famous.

Saral – Twelfth lord in seventh house brings evil to wife. Benefic association will bring money and she may stay abroad for some time. Malefic association will cause misery and troubles and the person will wander aimlessly. As third lord, Jupiter will promote third house and his brothers will be happy. Jupiter is trishadaya lord and will spoil the lagna.

Example Alfred J Gaynor DOB 10 December 1966 TOB 10.41 POB Spring Field MA

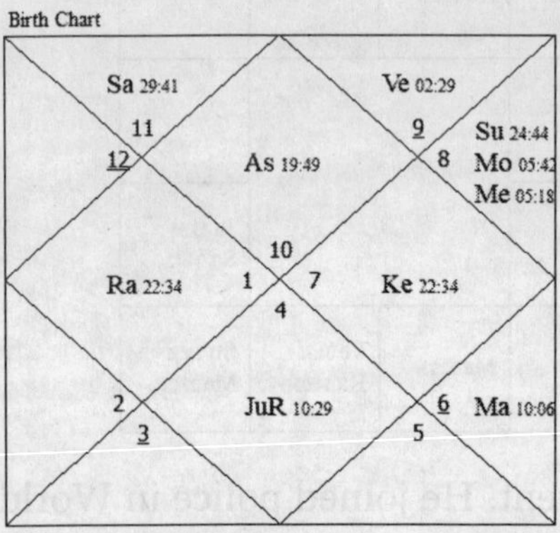

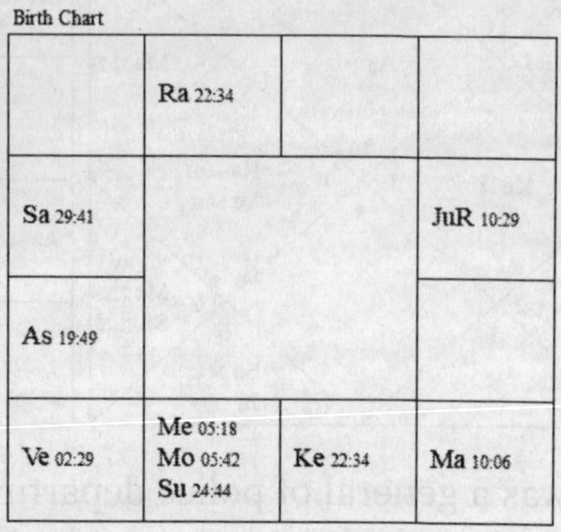

We examine few important points in this horoscope. Lagna lord is not having any benefic relation. Mercury is in Prishtodaya sign. Fourth house has Rahu and fourth lord is not having any benefic relations. These makes a criminal. He was a serial killer and committed nine murders between 1995 to 1998. He was arrested on 10 April 1998 in the dasha of Mercury/ Saturn/ Sun. he was found guilty in May 2000 and was given four life sentences. He is still in prison and makes paintings and sells them.

Venus

Saravali – Will be rich, happy, conquered by women, be vile, little enthusiastic and bereft of luck and paraphernalia.

Saral – Venus is yoga Karaka and its exaltation is excellent. Tenth lord when in third house it will give all round success in every field of his work. Person is courageous in his work and keeps his words.

Fifth lord in third will promote fifth house and the person is very intelligent and is an author. If Venus is associated with malefic then love life is a failure.

Example Andrea Ypsilanti DOB 8 April 1957 TOB 03.45 POB Russelsheim Germany

Birth Chart

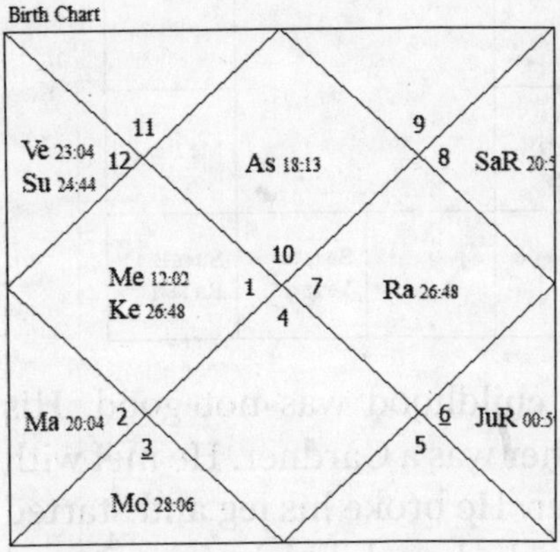

Birth Chart

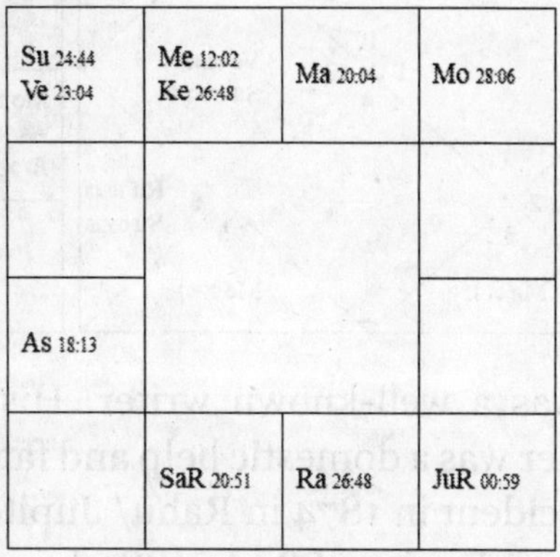

This is a rag to riches story. She is a daughter of a factory worker. After her school, she worked as secretary and a flight attendant for Lufthansa airline. She was married but divorced in 1992.

Due to hard work and Grace of God, she became Chairperson of Social Democratic party from 2003 to 2009. She contested for the post of Prime Minister and lost the election by 0.1 percent votes on 27 January 2008. The dasha was Venus/ Venus/ Rahu.

Saturn

Saravali – He will be wealthy, learned, valorous and be a minister or a justice or be a leader of a group, city or village.

Saral – Lagna lord placed in tenth house will give name and fame to the person. He will have good status and rank in life. He will be hard working. He will get promotions in service and hold influential post. Second lord on tenth house will make him rich.

Example H G Wells DOB 21 September 1866 TOB 16.30 POB Bromley UK

Birth Chart

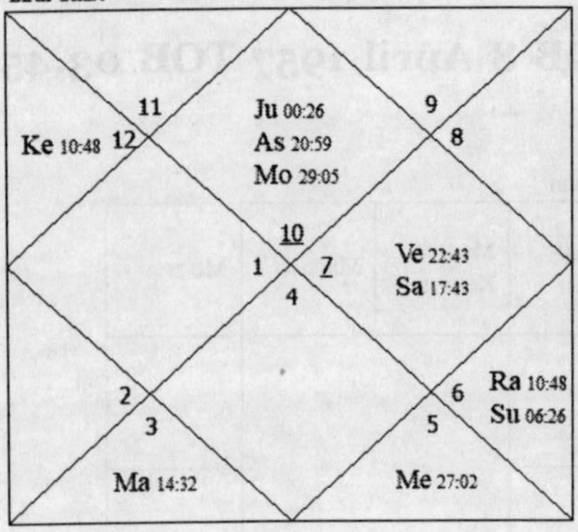

Birth Chart

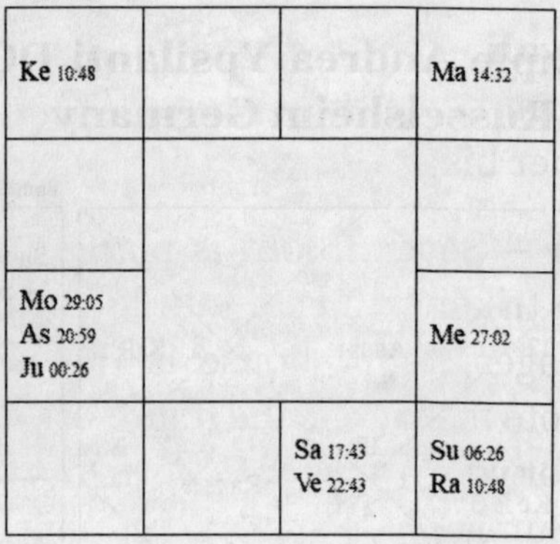

He was a well-known writer. His childhood was not good. His mother was a domestic help and father was a Gardner. He met with an accident in 1874 in Rahu/ Jupiter. He broke his leg and started reading. During 1880 to 1883 he worked as child labour and used to sleep in a dormitory with other labour. He was earning 21 Shillings a week. His father had a thigh fracture in 1887 and he had to leave the school. His good time started from Jupiter dasha when he wrote many novels. He had two marriages. The first marriage was in 1891 which ended in 1894. He again married one of his students in 1895 and it continued till her death in 1927. They had four children. He had many affairs but only two marriages.

The reason for his rise is the placement of sixth lord in eighth house without any other association. It would have been better if Mercury was under malefic influence.

AQUARIUS

Sun

Saravali – The person will be valorous, strong, will suffer loss of co born, be dear to people, good looking, very learned and will conquer his enemies.

Saral – Seventh lord is placed in third house. Third house is a Kama trikona and seventh lord will promote lust. It can give two marriages. Third house is the house of father-in-law and will promote it. Third is the house of younger Coborn. Your spouse will care for your younger Coborn and will be attached to her father. In case Sun is under malefic influence then your marriage is spoiled. The relations of your wife with her father and your Coborn will not be good. Benefic association will promote them. Seventh house is the house of professional progress and the person has to put in efforts to get good position.

Example Marco Pannelo DOB 2 May 1930 TOB 2.34 POB Teramo Italy

Birth Chart

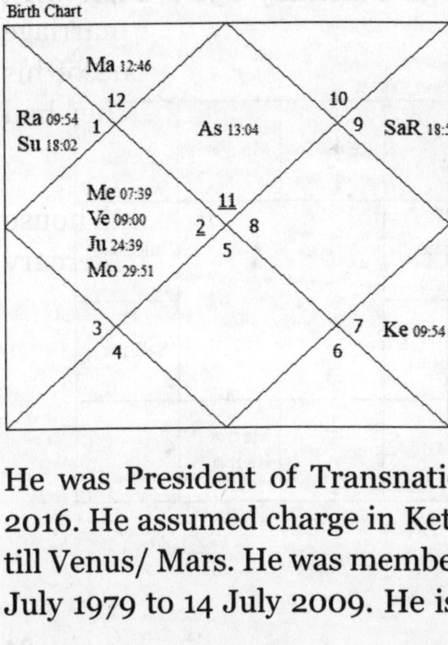

Birth Chart

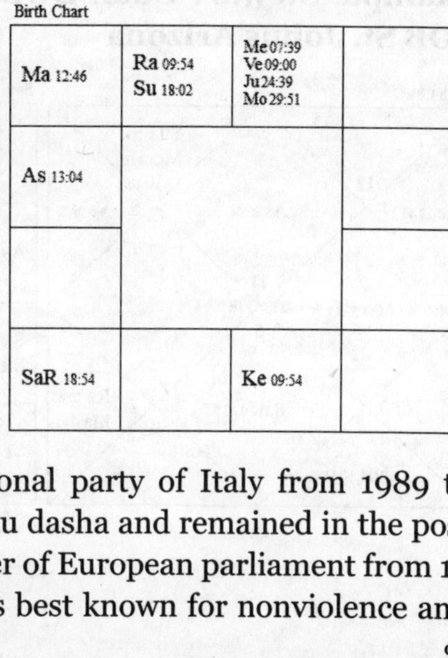

He was President of Transnational party of Italy from 1989 to 2016. He assumed charge in Ketu dasha and remained in the post till Venus/ Mars. He was member of European parliament from 14 July 1979 to 14 July 2009. He is best known for nonviolence and civil rights campaign. He never married but lived with his girlfriend from 1974 till his death. He had no child. His girlfriend was bi sexual and had 3 or 4 other relations. His seventh lord is with Rahu and have no benefic relation. He was suffering from cancer and it was not curable. He agreed for death after sedation. He died on 19 May 2016 in dasha of Venus/ Moon/ Mercury. His Moon is very strong and shows his mental strength.

Moon

Saravali – He will have relatives, conveyance, be charitable, fond of travelling by water and will neither be very happy nor be miserable.

Saral – Sixth lord is exalted in fourth house. Moon is aspecting tenth house. The profession will relate to the significations of sixth house like medical, law, money lending or brokerage. His maternal uncle and enemies are very powerful. He will live disease free life. If Moon is associated with Venus, it may give accidents. Moon in last Navamsha can give sudden changes in profession.

Example Stewart Udall DOB 31 January 1920 TOB 9.15 POB St. Johns Arizona

Birth Chart

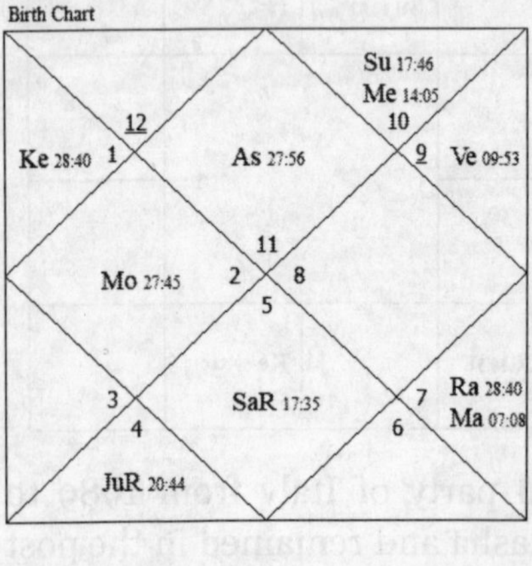

Birth Chart

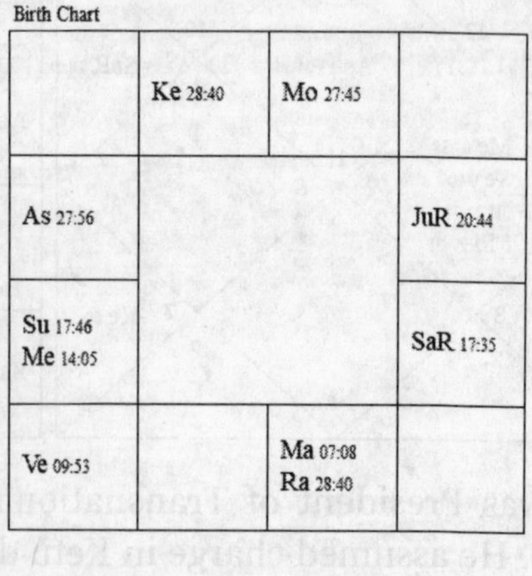

He was a law graduate. He was in politics, air force and also a professor. He served four years in Air force as a gunner from 1942 to 1946 in dasha of Jupiter. He completed his law degree in 1948 in Jupiter/ Mercury. He was a congressman from Arizona. He remained Secretary of Interior from 1961 to 1969 with President Kennedy and President Johnson. After this assignment he returned to University of Yales as visiting Professor. He was married and had two daughters and four sons. His wife died in 2001 in Venus/ Venus. He died on 20 March 2010. Saturn is lagna lord aspecting lagna from seventh house. Saturn in seventh can give respect from outside world.

Mars

Saravali – He will have diseased eyes, will fall in moral sense, will kill his wife, be a talebearer, be fierce and will contact humility and prison.

Saral – Mars is third lord and tenth lord. For success in foreign countries, Mars should have relation with a trine lord. Any association of other trishadaya lord will give failure in ventures if have malefic relation also. Benefic relation will give success. As third lord, Mars will take Coborn to other country. Mars will aspect third house and the person will be courageous and hard working. Tenth lord if joined with malefic planets can bring disgrace in profession.

Example Joe Malone DOB 18 November 1954 TOB 13.27 POB Newton MA

Birth Chart

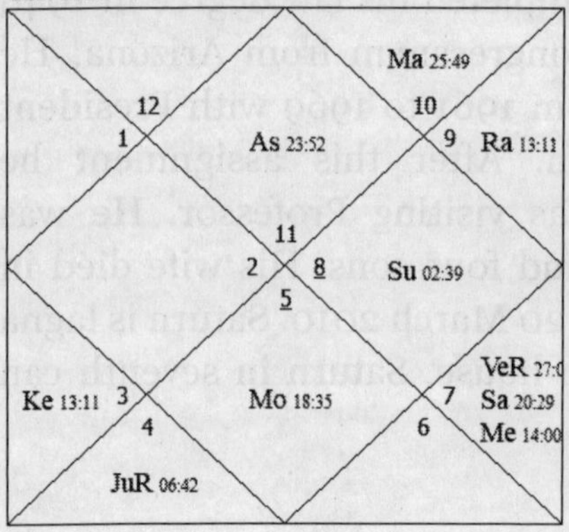

Birth Chart

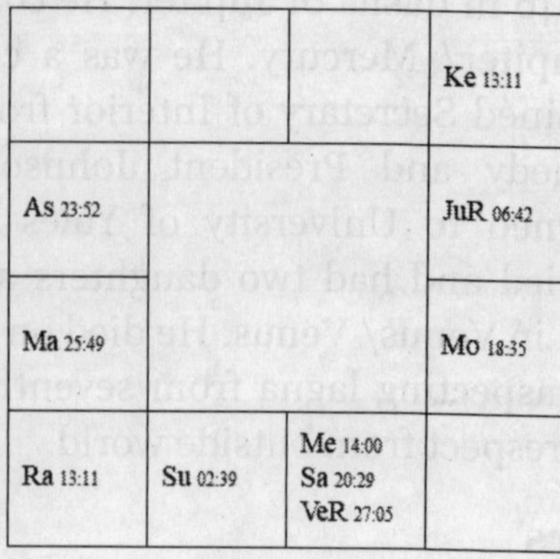

Mars is aspected by Jupiter. Jupiter is a natural benefic. In this horoscope Jupiter is lord of eleventh house and can prove bad. Jupiter is lord of two Dhana houses and is influencing tenth lord. She was a business woman. She was the treasurer and receiver general of Massachusetts state from 1991 to 1999. She was successful in reducing the operating budget of the state by 62 percent. But she was unsuccessful in the race for US senate against Ted Kennedy in 1988. Jupiter gave both effects. She is the co-founder of MD group which is a business development group.

Mercury

Saravali – He wins titles, be strong, long lived, will support his family and be equal to king or will become a justice.

Saral – Mercury in eighth house is praised by classics as giver of good results. Here Mercury is fifth lord and is placed in eighth house. With malefic influence, Mercury will deny progeny or give them short life. If Mercury is with benefic influence, then it will give enmity with father and his worship will go in vain. As eighth lord in eighth house it will give wealth and happiness. If lagna is strong then he will have long life.

Example Gwyneth Paltrow DOB 27 September 1972 TOB 17.25 POB Los Angeles CA

Birth Chart

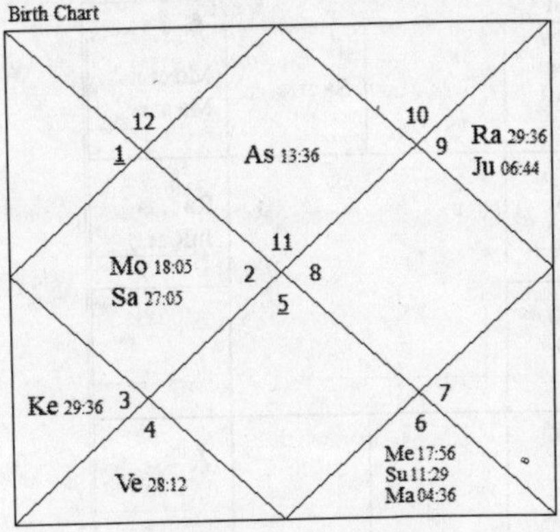

Birth Chart

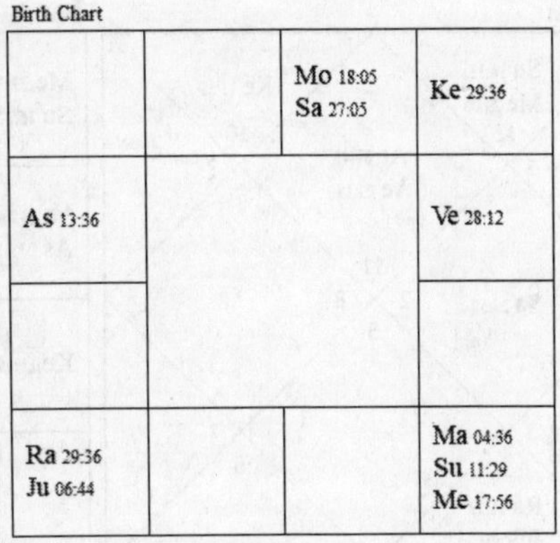

She is an actress, director, scriptwriter and a business woman. This is given by placement of third lord Mars in eighth house in enemy sign. She made her debut in 1989 in her father's TV film. She speaks French and Spanish besides her mother tongue English. She had affair from 1994 to 1997 but no marriage from this affair. She married in 2003 which ended in divorce in 2016. She has two children. She has written many books and won many awards. She was awarded best actress award in 1995, 96 and 99. These include Academy, Golden Globe and Emmy awards.

Jupiter

Saravali – He will lack digestive power and masculine virility, be humiliated, weal, indolent, will become famous on account of females, will destroy his enemy and be widely famous.

Saral – Jupiter is eleventh lord and is placed in sixth house. It will increase the effects of sixth house. If Jupiter has malefic relation, then he is adventurous and does not tolerate enemy. Benefic influence will reduce the bad effects. Jupiter is second lord. Its placement in sixth house will make him lose wealth to enemy. A relation of Jupiter with trine lord will give wealth.

Example Carl Buntion DOB 30 March 1944 TOB 5.28 POB Houston Texas

Birth Chart

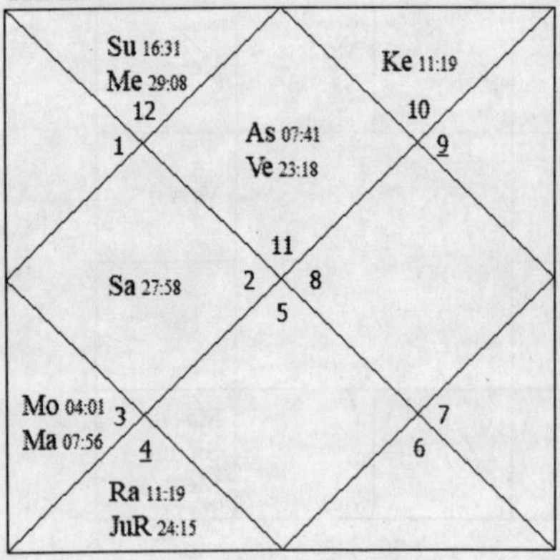

Birth Chart

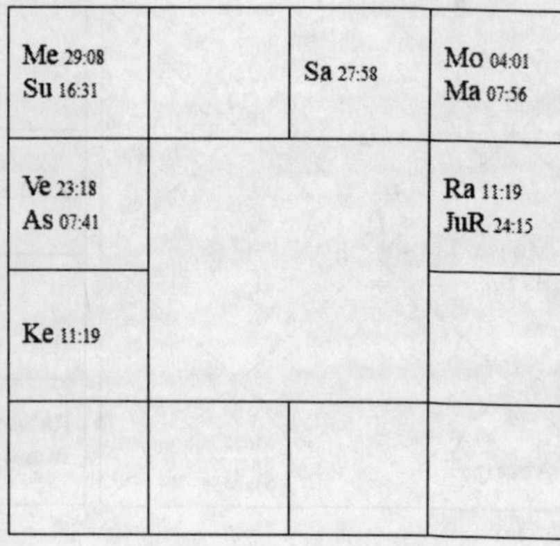

On 10 April 1990, he was going in a car with a friend. They were stopped by motor cycle policeman for making an illegal turn. He got out of the car and shot the policeman in head. Then he walked around the car and fired more rounds on his body and fired all around injuring another car driver. He was released from prison in May 1989 after serving 17 years in jail for a crime he committed at the age of 18 years.

Jupiter exalted and afflicted is very dangerous.

Venus

Saravali – He will enjoy abundant food, drinks and wealth, will derive excellent pleasures, will have good speech and wealth.

Saral – Venus is yoga Karaka and its exaltation is very good. Venus is fourth lord and is placed in second house. It will bring happiness to family. Venus as ninth lord in second house will give immense riches and the person is fortunate. He will enjoy good food and speech is sweet. If Venus is afflicted by malefic then good results are reduced.

Example Alexander Graham Bell DOB 3 March 1847 TOB 7.0 POB Edinburgh UK

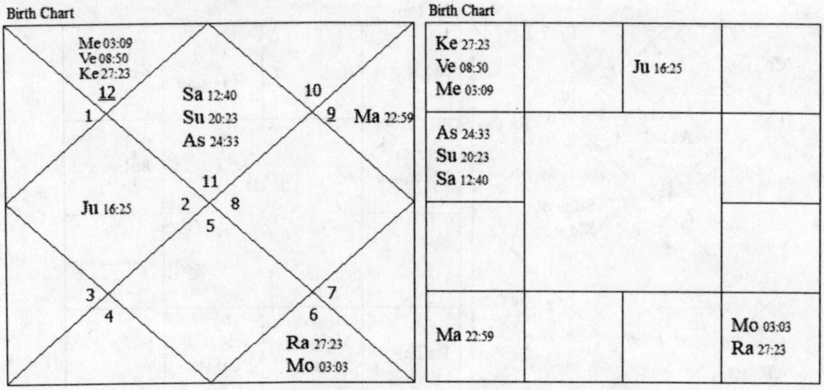

An important feature of the chart is the exchange of second and fourth lord. His work will be around his family and comfort. He is the inventor of microphone and first telephone. He got the patent of phone on 7 March 1876 in dasha of Rahu/ Mercury. He faced lot of opposition in getting his phone patented. Rahu is in eighth house and Mercury is eighth lord. He is the founder of American Telephone and Telegraph Company (AT&T). He was not good in school and left school at the age of 15 years. He got married in 1877 and have 4 children. He died on 2 August 1922 of diabetes in dasha of Mercury/ Mercury/ Saturn.

Saturn

Saravali – He will be devoid of religious merit, will not have much wealth, no co born, sons and happiness and will cause sorrow to others.

Saral – Lagna lord placed in ninth house will promote charity and riches. But as twelfth lord, Saturn is not considered good. If Saturn is associated with benefic then it will give good results and the person is lucky. With malefic influence, results are not good.

Example Bruce John Hegarly DOB 5 December 1954 TOB 12.19 POB Brighton MA

Birth Chart

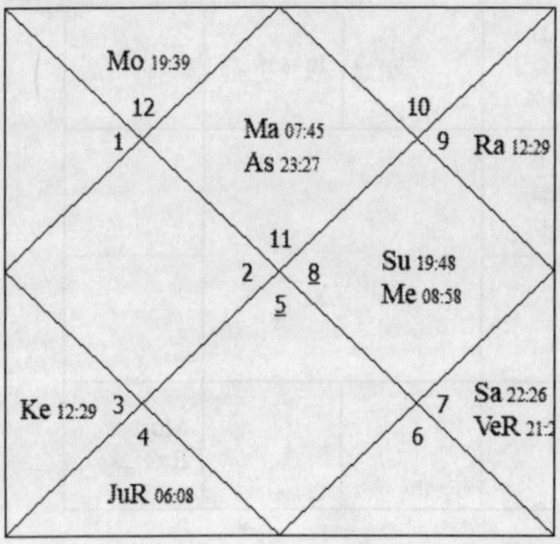

Birth Chart

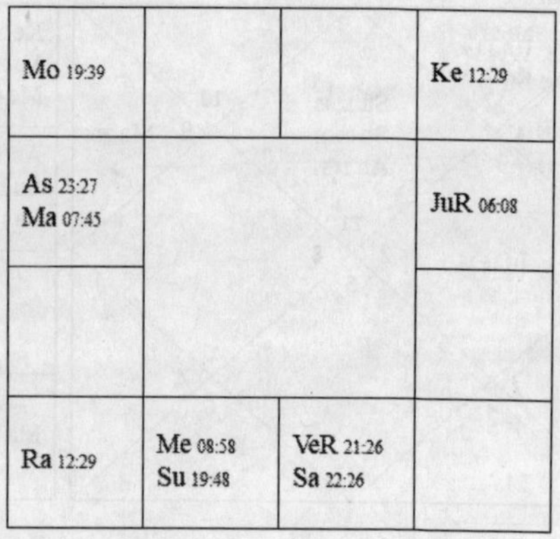

Saturn is with yoga Karaka Venus and have no malefic influence. He was an out of job plumber and wife was working as cashier. They were living hand to month type of life. They had three children. On 22 February 1993, he won the third largest lottery of Massachusetts. The amount was 26.7 million dollars. Dasha was of Venus. Second lord Jupiter is aspecting second house.

PISCES

Sun

Saravali – The person will have servants, and quadrupeds, will suffer facial disease, will not have happiness and wealth and will lose money through royal displeasure or through thieves.

Saral – Sixth lord is in the house of wealth and family. It will give gains from the enemy but there are disputes in the family. Sixth is a Vipreet house and malefic influence on Sun is welcome. He will have many servants. There will be gains of material things but the living things of second house will be damaged.

Example Miucca Prada DOB 10 May 1948 TOB 4.30 POB Milan Italy

Birth Chart

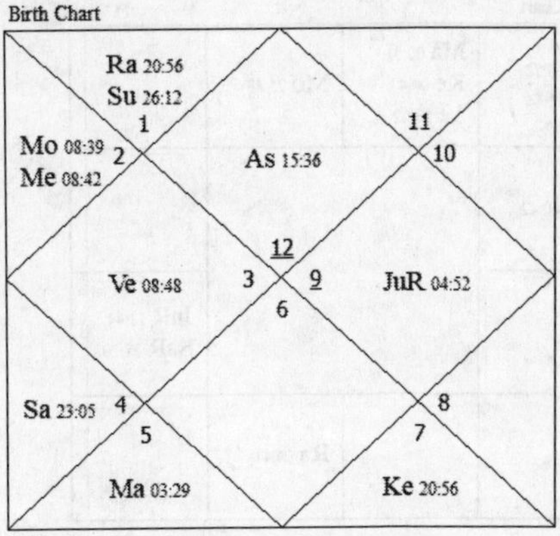

Birth Chart

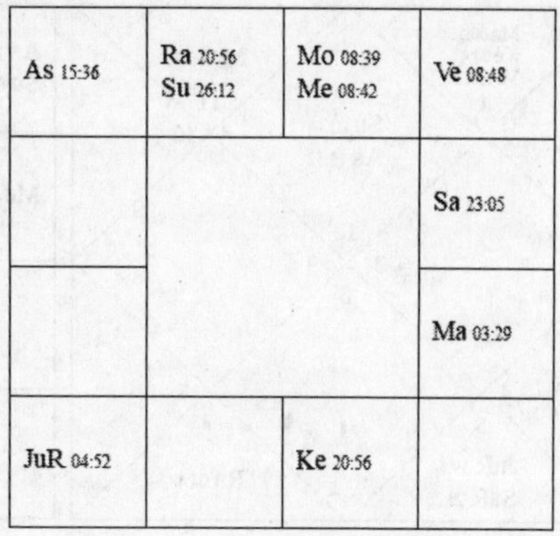

She is a billionaire fashion designer and business woman. She became head of family business in 1975 at the age of 27 years. She was adopted by her aunt in Prada family. Her worth was 11.1 billion in 2014. She is the CEO of Prada and Miu Miu. She is married and has two sons. Her rise started in Rahu/ Venus in 1975.

Moon

Saravali – He will enjoy incomparable happiness and friends and be wealthy. If the Moon is full, he will be very affluent and will speak less.

Saral – Moon is fifth lord and is exalted in third house which is eleventh from fifth. All significations of fifth house will thrive. He will be intelligent, have famous children and have blessings of his grandfather and father. To experience good results, Moon should have planets in Kendra from it.

Example Donald Mcintosh Kentall DOB 16 March 1921 TOB 7.00 POB Sequim Washington

Birth Chart

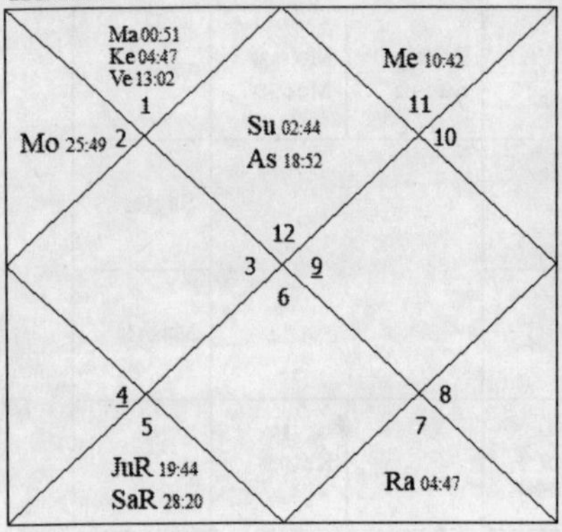

Birth Chart

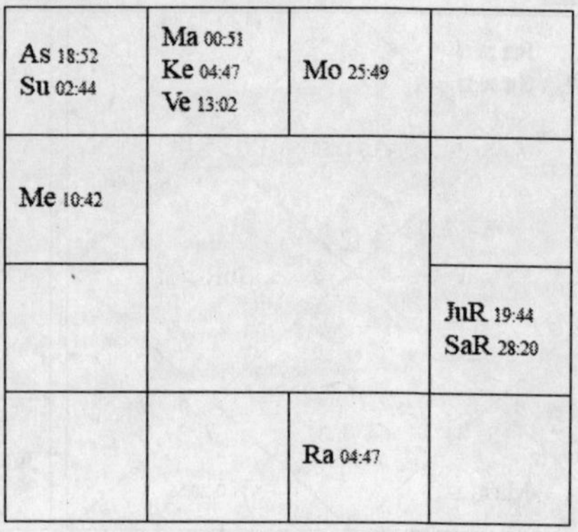

He was CEO of PepsiCo from 1971 to 1986. He served Navy in 1942 as a bomber. He earned three medals and distinguished flying cross in Air Force. He completed his law degree and joined Pepsi Cola in 1947 at the bottling plant. He rose to the position of VP in 1956, head of international operations in 1957 and to CEO in 1963. Position of Moon and Jupiter are the reason of his rise. He joined Pepsi in Jupiter/ Saturn.

Mars

Saravali – He will be virtuous, happy, courageous, wealthy, has grains and sons and will not have sorrow.

Saral – Mars is second and ninth lord and will give wealth, good family and gains from father. The wealth is according to the signification of Mars. Mars rules logic. Mars is aspecting second house and gives a sharp tongue to the person. His religious thoughts are also governed by logic. Mars is lord of trine and relation with Mercury or Jupiter is a Raj yoga.

Example Walter Benjamin DOB 15 July 1892 TOB 22.30 POB Berlin Germany

Birth Chart

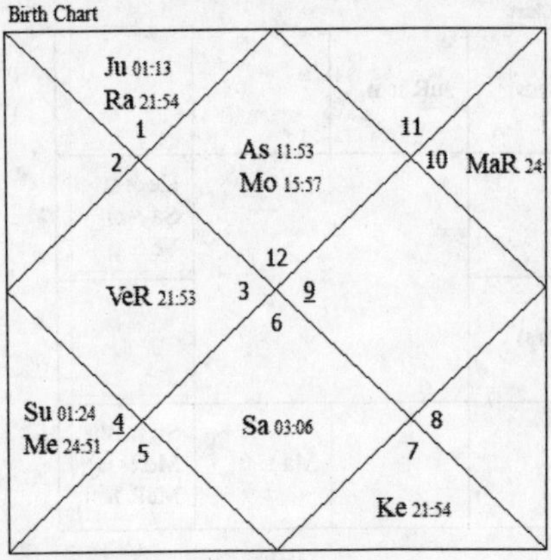

Birth Chart

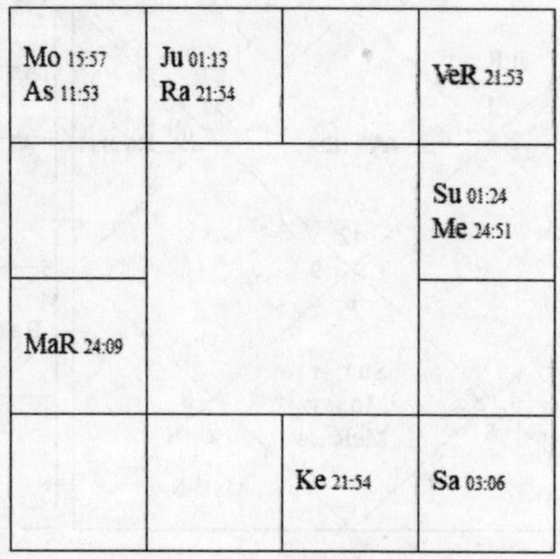

He was a German Jewish philosopher. His lagna lord is with Rahu and is aspected by Mars. Mercury is in Prishtodaya sign. Mars is placed in seventh house from Sun. this gives criminal tendency to the person. This is reflected in his works. Moon is in fifth Navamsha and saved him from turning into a criminal.

Mercury

Saravali – His wife will be very learned, beautiful in appearance, will not be of good descent, will promote quarrels and be very affluent. The person himself will be very great.

Saral – Mercury will form Bhadra yoga. Mercury is maraca also. It can give death if Mercury is influenced by trishadaya or trine lord. As fourth lord placed in seventh house, he will provide all happiness of fourth house when it is not afflicted. If Mercury is under malefic influence, then the happiness, comfort and marriage suffers. He will travel abroad and get honours. The good effects will increase if Mercury is with trine lord.

Example Vittorio Mussolini DOB 27 September 1916 TOB 19.30 POB Milan Italy

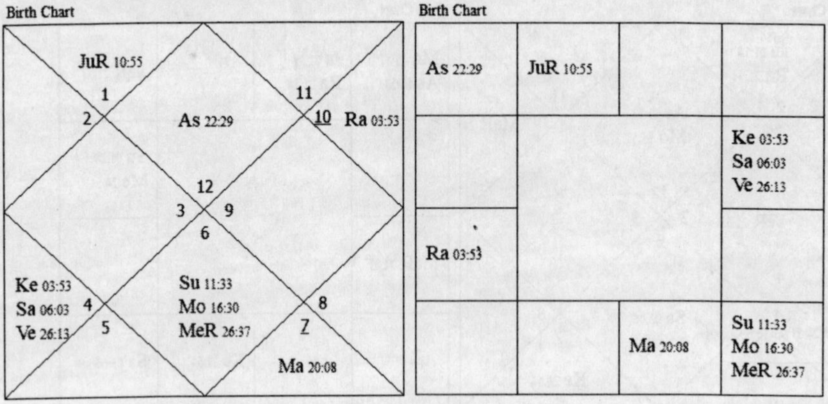

He was the second son of Benito Mussolini, dictator of Italy. He served as Lieutenant in Italian Royal Airforce and participated in WW2. He used to enjoy the killings as he called the bombs as budding rose. After WW2, he went to Argentina but returned back to Italy. He was a film critic and producer. He married Orsola, two-year senior to him, in 1934. His son was born in 1938. His death was on 12 June 1997 in Mercury dasha. Mercury is with trine lord Moon and aspected by eleventh lord Saturn.

Jupiter

Saravali – He will have abundant happiness, many sons and friends, be learned, courageous, wealthy and will always be happy.

Saral – Jupiter is lord of lagna and aspects lagna. The person will enjoy good health and physique. He will be honourable and will do good deeds. Jupiter is tenth lord and its placement in trine is a yoga. The fifth house is the house of prime minister. The person can be a minister or will hold high position in Government. But placement of tenth lord in eighth house from tenth will give suddenness and unexpected events in profession.

Example John Paul Stevens DOB 20 April 1920 TOB 4.12 POB Chicago IL

Birth Chart

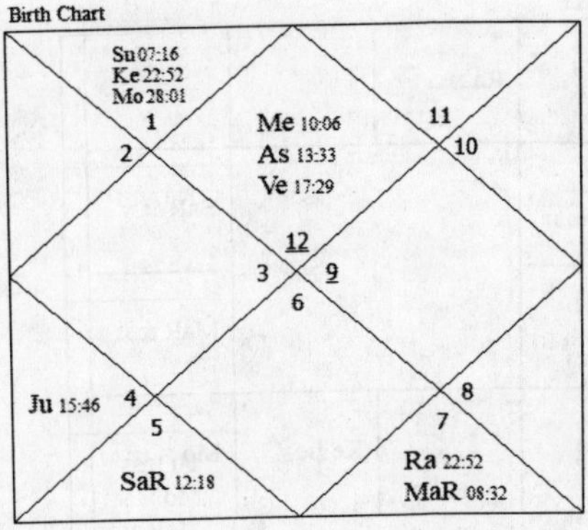

Birth Chart

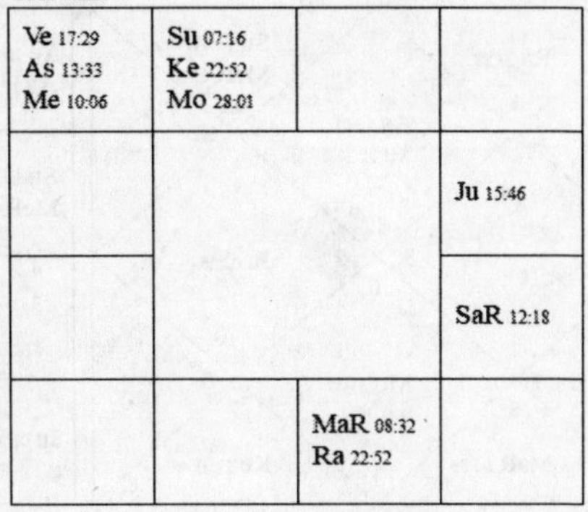

He was a lawyer and a justice of Supreme Court. He served as Lt. Commander in US Navy in WW2 from 1942 to 1945. He completed his law degree and joined a law firm. He was appointed in the Court of appeals in 1970. He remained Associate justice of US Supreme court from 1975 till 2010. He died on 16 July 2019 at the age of 99 years.

Venus

Saravali – The person will possess beautiful eyes face and physique, be happy, long lived, timid and attractive to females.

Saral – Venus is the lord of third and eighth house and is a serious malefic for Pisces lagna. Its exaltation will create more mischief. The bad results will increase if Venus is under malefic influence. When eighth lord is placed in lagna and lagna lord is afflicted then the person is very poor. As third lord this Venus will make him courageous. His courage will be more if Venus has benefic relation. Malefic relation will take the courage in wrong direction. Eighth lord exalted in lagna will give long life.

Example Ferguson John Enol DOB 27 February 1948 TOB 8.05 POB Miami Florida

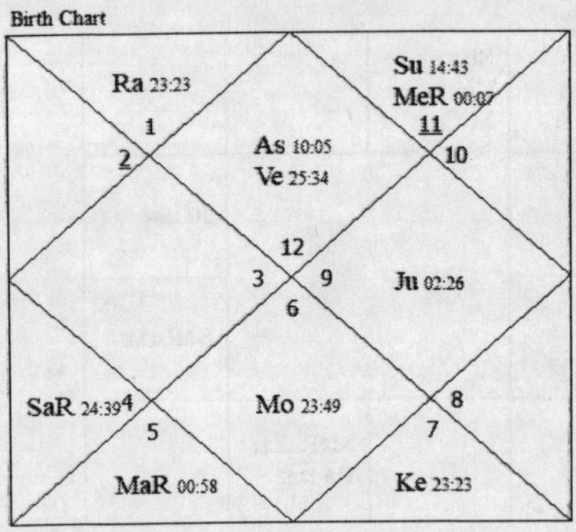

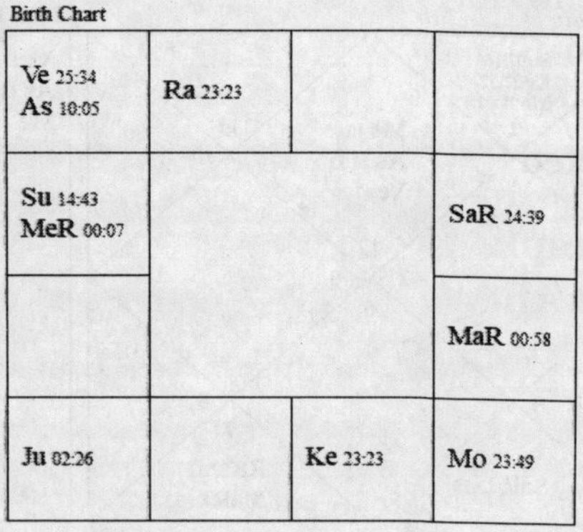

His lagna lord Jupiter is not having any aspect or conjunction. Mars is placed in seventh house from Sun. his Moon is severely afflicted. Moon and lagna are in papa kartari. Moon is aspected by Saturn and Venus. Venus and Saturn are most malefic planets for Pisces. In the year 1975, he was acquitted of six robberies and two assaults on a plea of insanity and was given a sentence of 18 months only. He was released in May 1977. He robbed and shot an elderly couple. On 27 July 1977 he shot eight people and out of them six died. He then faced rape charge. On 8 January 1978 he shot two children in a parked car. He was arrested on 5 April 1978. He was found guilty on 25 May 1978 and was awarded death by execution. He is still in jail and has filed many appeals to delay death sentence. All crimes were committed in Jupiter dasha. In the previous chart Venus is exalted but did not give bad results. The reason is the strength of lagna and lagna lord.

Saturn

Saravali – He will suffer from leprosy and fistula, will have short life and will fail in his undertakings.

Saral – Saturn is eleventh and twelfth lord. As twelfth lord, the placement in eighth house is yoga and gives good effects. But as eleventh lord it will give long life to the person but will harm elder Coborn. Saturn is aspecting tenth house and dasha of Saturn will be good for profession but with frequent changes in profession if afflicted.

Example Lee Lacocca DOB 15 October 1924 TOB 17.00 POB Allentown Pennsylvania

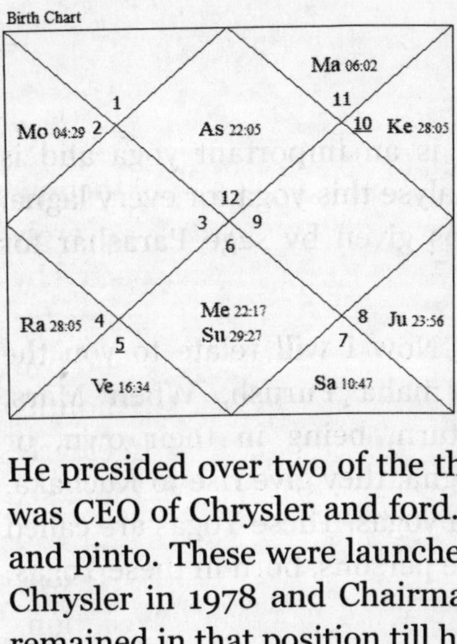

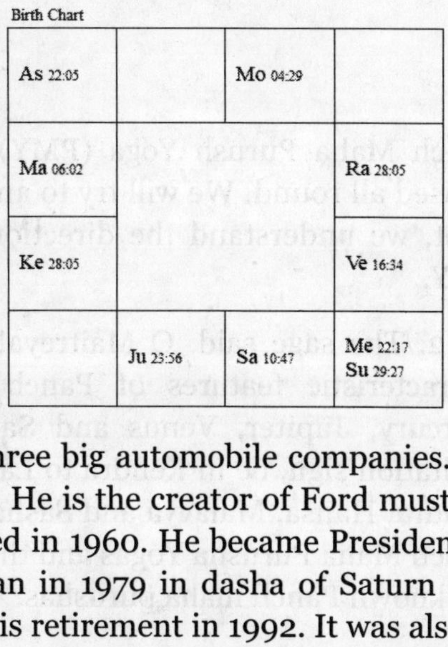

He presided over two of the three big automobile companies. He was CEO of Chrysler and ford. He is the creator of Ford mustang and pinto. These were launched in 1960. He became President of Chrysler in 1978 and Chairman in 1979 in dasha of Saturn and remained in that position till his retirement in 1992. It was also in Saturn dasha. He had three marriages and two children. He lived till the age of 94 years and died on 2 July 2019 in Ketu/ Saturn.

Chapter 02

Panch Maha Purush Yoga

Panch Maha Purush Yoga (PMY) is an important yoga and is praised all round. We will try to analyse this yoga for every lagna. First, we understand the directions given by sage Parashar for PMY.

1 - 2. The sage said. O Maitreya! Now I will relate to you the characteristic features of Panch maha Purush. When Mars, Mercury, Jupiter, Venus and Saturn, being in their own, or exaltation sign, be in Kendra to Lagna, they give rise to Ruchaka, Bhadra, Hansa, Malavya and Sasha yogas. These Yogas are called Panch Maha Purusha Yogas and the persons, born in these Yogas, are known Panch maha purushas.

3-7. The Ruchaka person possesses a long face, he is very enthusiastic, has spotless lustre, is powerful, has attractive eye brows, black hair and is fond of all things. He loves to fight wars, is of dark-red complexion, is victorious over enemies, is discriminating, is protector of thieves and has cruel temperament and slender thighs. He is a devotee of Brahmins, has marks of Veena, Vajra, Dhanush, Pasha and Taurus sign in his hands along with Chakra Rekha. He is well versed in occult sciences. He is 100 Anguls in height, his waist has the circumference equal to the length of his face and is 1000 Tulas in weight. He, as ruler of

Sahyashya and Vindhya Pradesh, will attain swarga the age of 70, by fire or weapons.

Note: Tula is ancient measure of weight.

8-12. The Bhadra native is splendorous, like a lion, has very developed chest (or chest with well-developed muscles), has the gait of an elephant, has long and thick arms, is learned in all respects. He is well versed in Yoga performance, is of Sattva-Guna and has beautiful feet, moustaches and head. He is fond of luxuries and comforts and has marks of Sankha (conch), Chakra, Gada, arrow, elephant, Dhwaja (flag) and Hala (plough) in his hands and feet. He is well versed in Shastras, has black and curly hair, possesses independent nature and is protector of his family. His friends share in the enjoyment of his wealth. He lives a happy and comfortable life with his wife and children as ruler of Madhya Pradesh, lives for one hundred years.

13-16. The Hansa native has voice, like a Hansa, has a handsome appearance and well-developed nose. He is a king with phlegmatic temperament, honey-like tawny -coloured eyes, red-coloured nails, sharp intelligence, sturdy cheeks, round forehead and beautiful feet. He has marks of Matsya (fish), Ankush (the iron hook, with which elephants are driven), Dhanus (bow), Sankha, Kamal (lotus) in his hands and feet. He is very passionate and his lust remains unfulfilled. He is 96 Anguls in height. He is fond of swimming and playing games in watery places. He enjoys life fully and, as ruler of a land, situated between the Ganges and Yamuna, he after enjoying all comforts leaves the world at the attaining the age of 100 years.

17-19. The Malavya native has beautiful lips and a slender waist. He is lustrous, like Moon, and has fragrance in his body. He is of normal reddish complexion, has a medium stature and clean and beautiful teeth. His voice is like that of an elephant and his arms are long enough to reach up to his knees. His face is thirteen Anguls in length and ten Anguls in breadth. He lives happily for seventy years, as ruler of Sindhu and Malwa, and then leaves for his heavenly abode.

20-22. The Sasha native has small sized teeth and face, but his body is not small. He is valorous. He has a slender waist and beautiful thighs. He is wise and enjoys wandering in forests and mountains. He is well versed in the loopholes of the enemy. He is lively, virile and fond of women. He usurps other people's wealth. He has marks of Mala (garland), Veena, Mridang (musical instruments) and weapons in his hands and feet. He rules happily over several parts of the earth and then leaves for his heavenly abode at the age of 70.

Phaldeepika (Translation by S. S. Sareen)

1. When Mars, Mercury, Jupiter, Venus or Saturn occupies an angle in his own or exaltation sign, the five yogas formed by these planets respectively are Ruchaka, Bhadra, Hansa, Malavya and Sasha.
2. The person born in the Ruchaka yoga will have a long face, have wealth acquired through daring acts, brave, conqueror of his enemies, powerful and arrogant, will be known for his merits, be a commander of an army and gain victory over all.
3. The person born in Bhadra yoga will enjoy longevity, will be of sharp intelligence, honest, praised by the learned, be a leader of men, rich and impressive when addressing in the assembly.
4. The person born in Hansa yoga will be a king who will be praised by the wise. Marks of Sankha, Padma, Matyas (fish) and Ankush may be seen in his feet and hands. He will possess a well-formed body, will enjoy sumptuous food and be of righteous disposition.

5. The person born in Malavya yoga will possess a stout body, be resolute, wealthy, endowed with wife, children and of good fortune. He will be prosperous, enjoy a hearty meal and all sorts of pleasures, possess vehicles, be famous and learned and of balanced mind.
6. The person born in Sasha yoga will be praised by one and all, will have faithful attendants and be strong. He will be the headman of the village or be a king. By disposition he will be a crocked man, having an eye on others' wives. He will rob others of their wealth to keep himself happy.
7. These five yogas can be operative even when counted from Moon lagna. In such case they will bestow on the person an empire and supremacy. The person having one, some or all these yogas in their birth chart will respectively be 1. A fortunate man, 2. Like a king, 3. A king, 4. An emperor and 5. Even greater than Emperor.

Notes

1. Five planets, except Sun and Moon, can form PMY when any one of them occupy a Kendra from Ascendant and is in its own sign or in exaltation sign.
2. Some authors include Trine position also. It is not in line with classic.
3. Phaldeepika has included the formation of these yoga from Moon also. This will enlarge the scope to a large number of horoscopes. Do we find mortals having the quality of PMY? If we consider the formation from lagna the large number of horoscopes are found. By including Moon, this number will increase.
4. For a movable Ascendant, six PMY are possible, for a Dual Ascendant, five PMY are possible and for a fixed Ascendant we can have three PMY for each Ascendant respectively.
5. Each of these five planets signify a character and a vice. With presence of this yoga the particular characteristics are

highlighted. Five Tatva are Ether, Water, Air, Fire and Earth. These are ruled by Jupiter, Venus, Saturn, Mars and Mercury respectively. Jupiter governs voice, Venus governs splendour or friends, Saturn governs complexion, Mars governs prowess and Mercury governs greatness.

6. We have functional benefic and malefic for each lagna. Each planet has good and bad significations. Formation of PMY will promote the results guided by the functional role of the planet.
7. **A very important rule applies to planets placed in Kendra in own sign. It says that such a planet can cause death in his dasha. This is more applicable if the house of placement is seventh house.**
8. The results attributed in classics are very general and are not specific.
9. We will analyse the results of these yogas for each Ascendant. The formation of these yoga by placement in own sign in Kendra is discussed here since exaltation is already covered in the chapter of exaltation.

General discussion for yoga in own sign

Ruchaka yoga

This Ruchaka yoga is formed by placement of Mars in Aries or in Scorpio and in Kendra from Ascendant. Placement in Aries needs a movable Ascendant. Placement in Scorpio needs a fixed Ascendant. Aries is the mooltrikona sign of Mars and gives stronger results. In Aries lagna, Mars is lord of eighth house also and its placement in lagna can give long life. For Cancer lagna, Mars is yoga Karaka and is Digbali. Mars can give success and adventure in life. For Libra, Mars is a maraca and gives wealth and death in its dasha. For Capricorn, Mars is lord of trishadaya house and Mars can spoil family happiness by creating disputes.

For Leo lagna, Mars is yoga Karaka and gives good results. In Scorpio lagna Mars gives good protection from disease. For Aquarius lagna, Mars is tenth and third lord and can give rise in profession through hard work. In Taurus lagna, Mars becomes a maraca but gives immunity from disease. Family life is disturbed. The cancellation by conjunction with Ketu will not promote the physical significations of the house.

Malavya yoga

Malavya yoga also need a movable or a fixed Ascendant. Libra is the mooltrikona sign of Venus. In Aries Ascendant, Venus is lord of second and seventh house placed in seventh house. Venus is strong maraca in his dasha. For Cancer Ascendant Venus is eleventh lord also and create problems of fourth house when related to benefic only. Venus placed in Ascendant in Libra is good for luxuries of life and gives strong enemies. For Capricorn Ascendant, Venus is yoga Karaka.

For Taurus lagna, Venus is in lagna. The effects will be centred on self. In Leo lagna, Venus is in tenth house and gives effects on profession and the person can hold high position is Venus is well related. In Scorpio lagna, Venus is in seventh house. The matters related to partners and position will be prominent. For Aquarius lagna, Venus is a yoga karaka and is placed in fourth house providing all comforts of life.

Bhadra yoga

Bhadra yoga is possible for dual signs only. Mercury is in lagna for Gemini lagna. The person is intelligent and can be selfish. In Virgo lagna, Mercury is in tenth house and promoted professional achievements. For Sagittarius lagna, Mercury is in seventh house and gives high position. In Pisces lagna Mercury gives comforts of fourth house. For Sagittarius and Pisces lagna, Jupiter considers Mercury as enemy.

Hansa yoga

This yoga is found in lagna of dual signs. In Gemini lagna Jupiter is in mooltrikona sign in seventh house. It will give importance to partnership and business. In tenth house Jupiter makes things easy for profession when it is having benefic association. In Virgo lagna charts, Jupiter is in fourth or seventh house. The results depend upon relation of Jupiter. Mercury considers Jupiter as neutral. Hansa yoga formed in Sagittarius or Pisces lagna are better since Jupiter is the lagna lord. The sign other than the placement of Jupiter will get strong.

Sasha yoga

Sasha yoga is also formed in movable or fixed sign lagna. For Aries lagna, Saturn is not a good planet but when placed in tenth house it gives very good results and gives great position to the person. It is not the case for Cancer lagna. For Libra lagna, Saturn is yoga karaka and promotes tenth house. It can subdue enemy. In Capricorn lagna, Saturn will be in lagna and will again aspect tenth house and gives frequent change, for better, in profession.

In the fixed sign of Taurus, Saturn will be in tenth house. For Leo lagna Saturn is in seventh house and is sixth lord also. Person gets respect from partners. In Scorpio lagna, Saturn is in fourth house and gives problem to fourth house affairs if it is under malefic influence. In Aquarius lagna, Saturn is in lagna and gives earning from the sources of fourth house.

ARIES

Ruchaka

Saral - Mars is in Aries. For Aries lagna Mars is the lord of lagna and eighth house. Parashar has taken Mars as a benefic if he is not afflicted. Affliction is caused by relation of Mercury, Saturn or malefic with Mars. Saturn is a malefic since it is the lord of eleventh house and a Kendra. Aspect or association of trine lord is yoga and gives good position to the person. Mars will aspect eighth house and will give long life to person. Mars will aspect fourth house and gives property in its dasha when fourth house is not afflicted. The person is respected in family. Aspect of Mars on seventh house can give separation from partners. The person will be truthful, valorous, king, is fond of war, adventurous and charitable. Mars alone without any relation can give effects of eighth house.

Example Gerald Ford DOB 14 July 1913 TOB 0.43 POB Omaha Nebraska

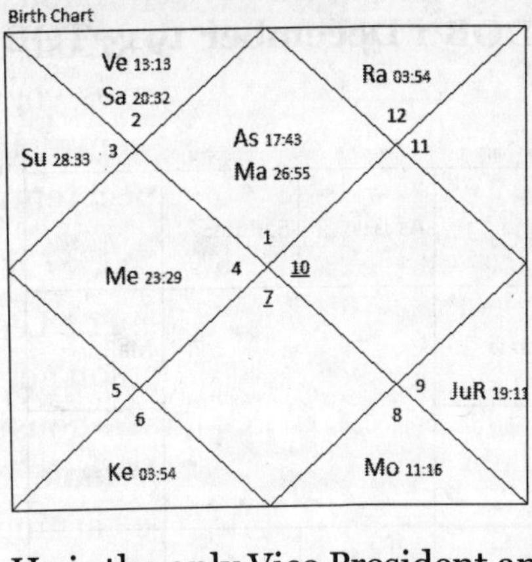

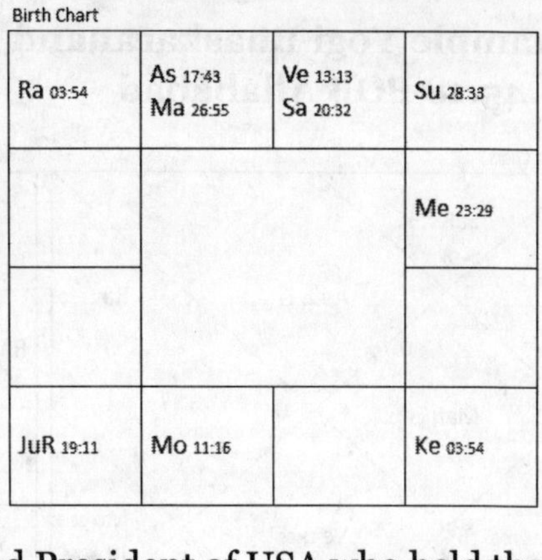

He is the only Vice President and President of USA who held these positions without being elected to these posts. He assumed post of VP after the elected VP resigned and President Nixon appointed him as VP on 6 December 1973 since he was leader of opposition. President Nixon had to resign due to water gate controversy on 9 August 1974 and he was made the President.

Mars is aspected by Jupiter. His Saturn is well placed in second house with second lord. The influence of ninth lord on lagna lord made him religious. He was a free mason which he joined on 30 September 1949. He was Grand master of masonry. He held a special ceremony in the oval hall on 11 January 1977. He died at an age of 93 years on 26 December 2006.

Malavya

Saral - Venus is placed in own sign, Libra, and cause this yoga. Venus is lord of Kendra and becomes neutral. As second lord, he is again neutral. The results will depend on the other association and aspect with Venus. Malefic aspect will spoil the marriage and the person desires company of low-class women. He will earn money by hard work and is interested in living in foreign country. Relation of trine lord will give yoga. He will protect his own people, be skilful, famous, honours Gods and brahmins and is a scholar. Venus is a maraca and can give death in its dasha.

Example Yogi Bhaskaranand DOB 1 December 1913 TOB 15.45.18 POB Allahabad

Birth Chart

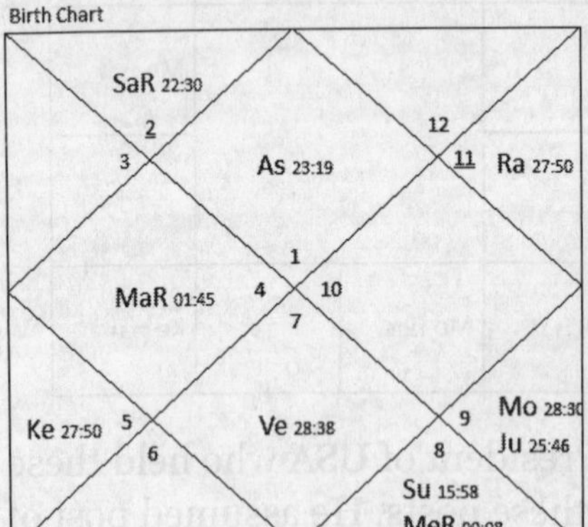

Birth Chart

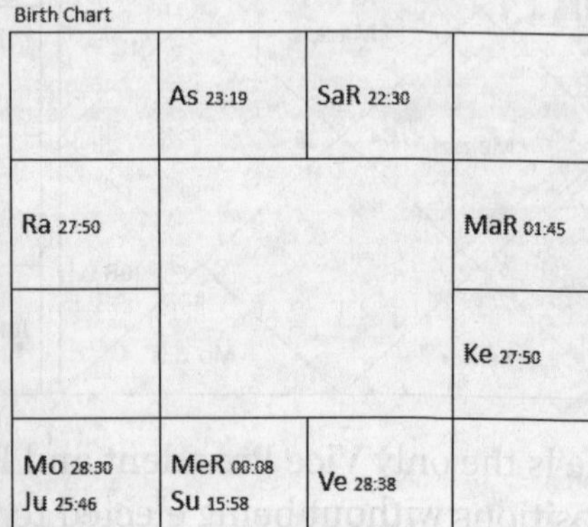

This birth data is taken from the records of Sh. K. N. Rao.

He was a great yogi and a great astrologer. Ketu is in fifth house and is aspected by ninth lord Jupiter. Saturn in second house as tenth lord has given high status. But Venus in seventh house and aspected by Mars has denied marriage. Mars is aspected by Saturn and Mars gives effect of eighth house and made him a yogi.

Sasha yoga

Saral - For Aries lagna, Saturn is considered a malefic. Now Saturn is placed in own sign in tenth house to give this yoga. Tenth lord placed in tenth house will give a good status to the person. Any relation of trine lord will increase the status but a relation of trik lord is harmful, Jupiter is trine lord. Saturn is the significator of masses and democracy. The person will be a public figure and well known in society. Saturn will aspect seventh house and can give delay or disturbance in marriage. This should not be predicted if Venus is well placed or well associated. He will lord over other's land. He will stay at his place of birth and his primary education and childhood is happy.

Example Alessandra Mussolini DOB 30 December 1962 TOB 13.00 POB Rome

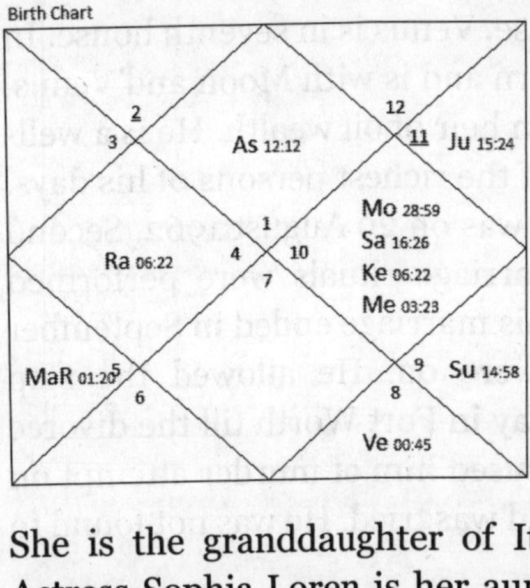

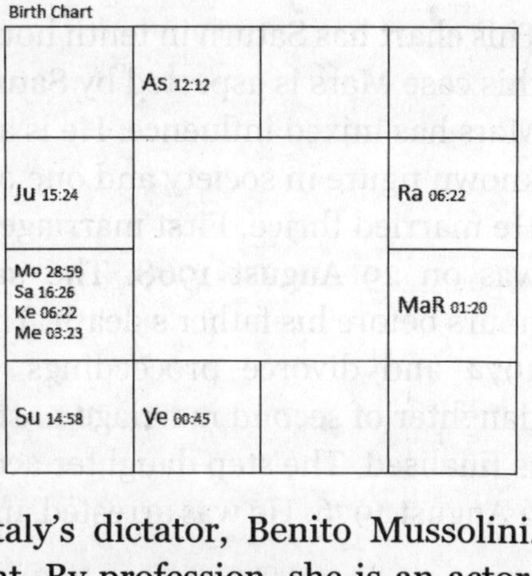

She is the granddaughter of Italy's dictator, Benito Mussolini. Actress Sophia Loren is her aunt. By profession, she is an actor, model and a politician. She was member of European Parliament and Italian senate in 2013 - 2014. She was member of Chamber of deputies from 2008 to 2013. As an actress, she won Golden Globe Award in 1977. She appeared on the cover page of Playboy magazine in two editions of the book. She married in 1989 and have 3 children. The aspect of Mars has given marriage. Mars is having aspect of Jupiter and Mars is a benefic. In the previous chart, Mars is aspected by Saturn and is no longer a benefic and denied marriage.

Example T Cullen Davis DOB 22 September 1933 TOB 20.22 POB Fort Worth Texas

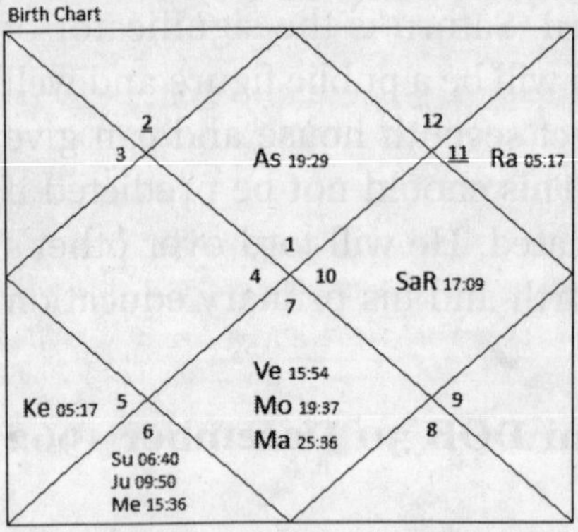

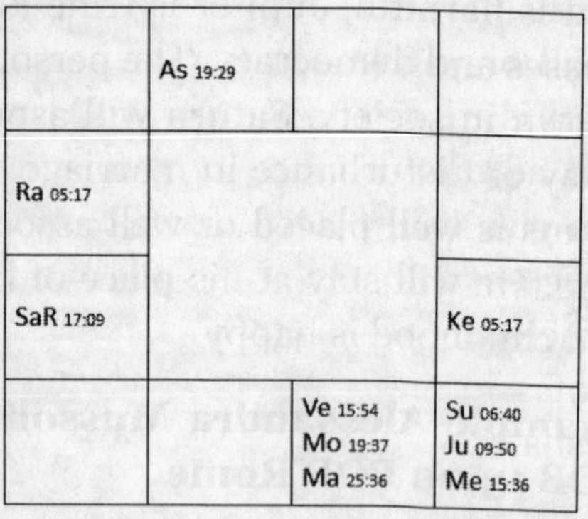

This chart has Saturn in tenth house. Venus is in seventh house. In this case Mars is aspected by Saturn and is with Moon and Venus. Mars has mixed influence. He is an heir of oil wealth. He is a well-known figure in society and one of the richest persons of his days. He married thrice. First marriage was on 29 August 1962. Second was on 29 August 1968. The marriage rituals were performed hours before his father's death. This marriage ended in September 1974 and divorce proceedings were on. He allowed the step daughter of second marriage to stay in Fort Worth till the divorce is finalised. The step daughter accused him of murder attempt on 2 August 1976. He was arrested and was tried. He was not found to be guilty. The trial was again opened. He was again acquitted. He married for third time on 5 June 1979. With all troubles, he lost his wealth and declared bankruptcy in 1980.

Aspect of Jupiter on Saturn gave yoga but the condition of lagna lord ruined him because of Venus and aspect of Saturn. Now Mars gave more effects of eighth lord.

TAURUS

Ruchaka

Saral - Mars in seventh house. Twelfth lord is placed in seventh house and gives problems in marriage. The person will not marry at all or will be separated from spouse. This is almost certain if Mars is afflicted. This Mars can take the person to a foreign country and he gains popularity abroad. Mars will aspect tenth house and can give change of jobs or early retirement. One should work in police, as arm trader, fire department or as a chemist, if Mars is not afflicted. When it is afflicted then he should avoid these professions. Mars is a maraca for Taurus and can cause death in its dasha.

Example Greta Garbo DOB 18 September 1905 TOB 19.30 POB Stockholm Sweden

Birth Chart

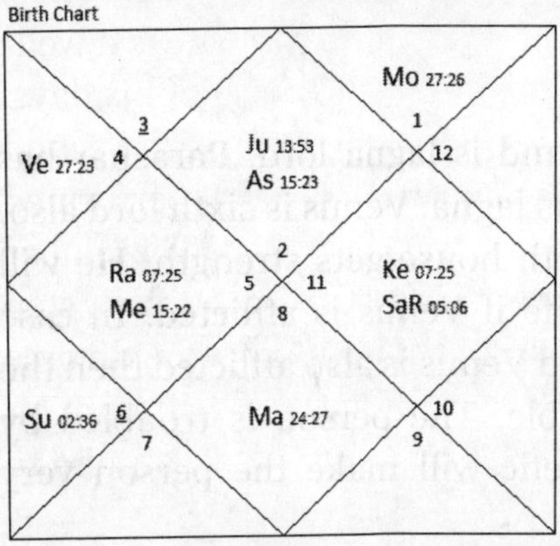

Birth Chart

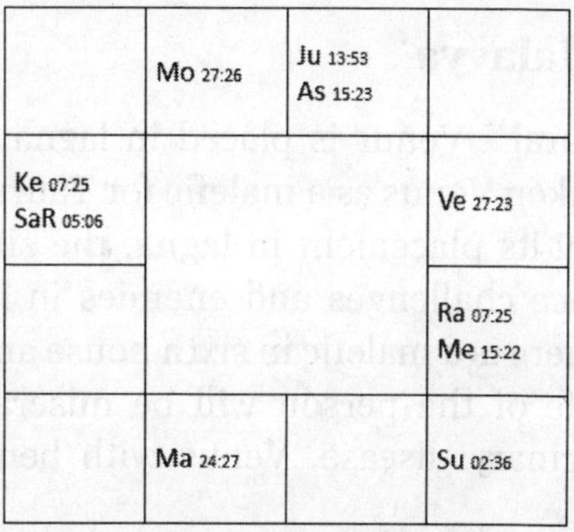

D9 Navamsha (spouse)

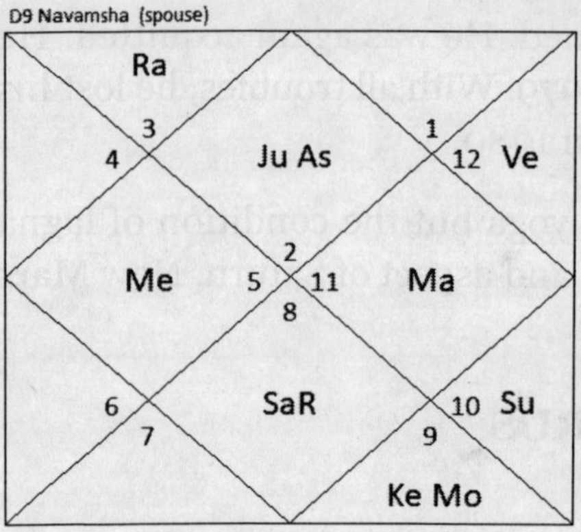

D9 Navamsha (spouse)

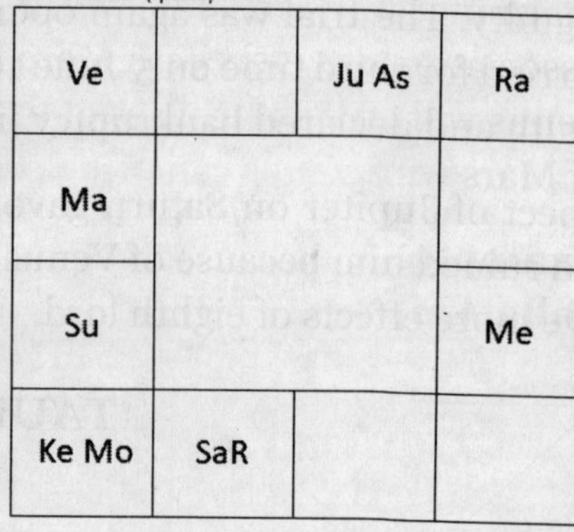

She was a famous actress of silent era of films and of sound movies. She was born in Sweden but settled in USA. She never married but had many affairs. Jupiter is placed in lagna of Navamsha and is under malefic influence. Jupiter is karaka of marriage for female. This is Karko bhava Nasaya in Navamsha. The affairs started in 1926 and continued past 1950. The lagna lord of Navamsha is exalted. Dasha of Mars started in 1921. She retired from films in 1941 after failure of her films. The dasha was Rahu/ Mercury. Rahu is in fifth house of D 10 and Mercury is fifth lord. She had cancer in 1984 and died of renal failure and pneumonia on 15 April 1990 at the age of 84 years in Mercury/ Mars.

She has a beautiful exchange of fifth and fourth lords. Her Saturn is yoga karaka and is placed in tenth house causing Sasha yoga.

Malavya

Saral - Venus is placed in lagna and is lagna lord. Parashar has taken Venus as a malefic for Taurus lagna. Venus is sixth lord also. By its placement in lagna, the sixth house gets strength. He will face challenges and enemies in life if Venus is afflicted. In case there is a malefic in sixth house and Venus is also afflicted then the life of the person will be miserable. The person is troubled by urinary disease. Venus with benefic will make the person very charming in looks and he will have impressive personality. Association of Venus with Mercury is a raj yoga and a Dhana yoga. Venus will give all luxuries of life which are ruled by him. Relation of Mars with Venus can bring problems in marriage or in affairs.

Example Gregory Peck DOB 5 April 1916 TOB 8.0 POB La Jolla Amago CA

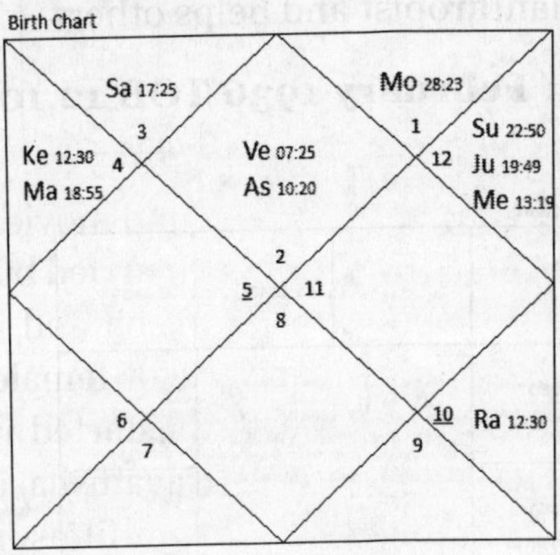

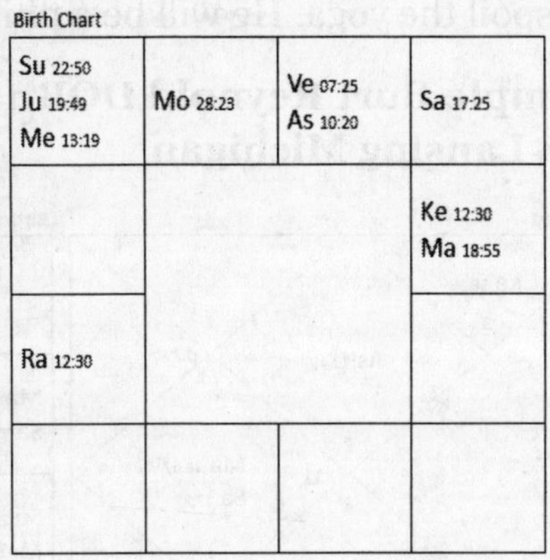

He was adjusted the best actor in 1962. He was an actor and a politician. He started acting in films in 1940 and remained at the peak of his career for 20 years during the dasha of Rahu and Jupiter. He had many romances but had two marriages. He had five children. Fifth lord Mercury is aspecting fifth house. Lagna lord of Saptamsha, Saturn, is exalted in Saptamsha. His parents were divorced when he was five years old. He was looked after by his maternal grandmother. When she died, he came to live with his father. He was considered as a challenge to Nixon in the presidential race. He died in sleep on 12 June 2003 due to broncho pneumonia in dasha of Mercury/ Rahu.

Venus is not afflicted and is exalted in Navamsha making him an impressive personality. His tenth lord Saturn is in second house and gives wealth and fame.

Sasha yoga

Saral - Saturn is in tenth house. Saturn is a yoga karaka and placement in own sign in tenth house is excellent. He will give high status in society. If Saturn is having any relation with other trine or Kendra's lord then the potency of Saturn increases many times. Saturn should not have any relation with trishadaya lords as this will spoil the yoga. He will be a philanthropist and helps others.

Example Burt Reynold DOB 11 February 1936 TOB 12.10 POB Lansing Michigan

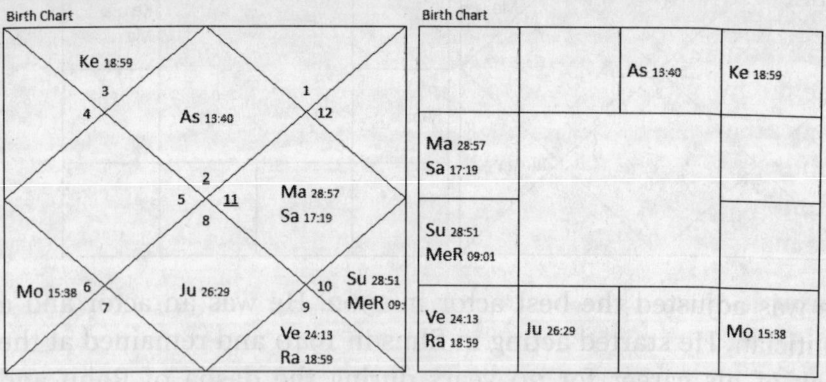

He was an actor, director, producer of films and TV serials. He owned a restaurant and training school. He had multiple activities. His tenth lord of Dashamsha is in third house. He started his career in 1962 in dasha of Rahu. He remained world's number one box office star for five years from 1978 to 1982 in dasha of Jupiter.

He was married twice and had many other relations. Eighth lord Jupiter is placed in seventh house and is aspected by Saturn. He did not have a child and he adopted a son. This can be clearly seen in Saptamsha. His father was long lived till the age of 96 years.

He underwent bypass surgery in February 2010 in Mercury/ Moon. He died on 6 September 2018 in Mercury/ Saturn.

Sun and Mercury are making an excellent yoga in ninth house. Mars and Saturn in tenth house is also a good yoga and gives many occupations and hard work. Saturn is not having any relation with trishadaya lords.

GEMINI

Bhadra yoga

Saral – Mercury is in lagna. Association of trine lords will give yoga. Mercury is fourth lord also and will promote the effects of fourth house. Any relation with trishadaya lords is not welcome since it can give unexpected events in life. Mercury alone in lagna is very auspicious. He will have healthy body, wealth, able speaker, honourable, intelligence but obstinate. He will be fond of arguments and is learned. He will be proficient in work and will have many sons and friends.

Example John Nash DOB 13 June 1928 TOB 7.00 POB Bluefield West Virginia

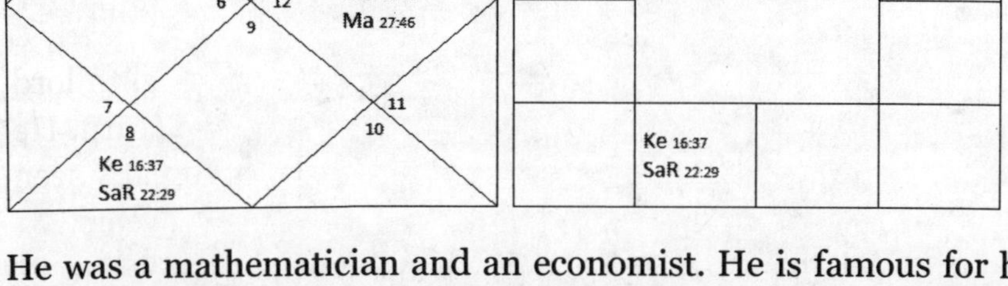

He was a mathematician and an economist. He is famous for his researches on game theory, differential geometry and partial differential equations. He was honoured with Noble prize and Able prize for economic sciences in 1994 in dasha of Rahu/ Sun. He is the only person to have received both these prizes. He suffered from mental illness in 1961 and remained under treatment for nine years. In 1970, he refused to go to hospital and never visited a hospital again. This was in dasha of Moon. He married twice. He died in a car accident with his wife on 23 May 2015. Sudden events are seen in his D 8 chart.

His Mercury is aspected by Digbali Mars. Lord of eighth house, Saturn is in sixth house in Vipreet yoga and is aspecting eighth house of research. Lords of tenth and eleventh house are in exchange giving reward for his work.

Hansa yoga

Saral – Jupiter is in seventh house. The person will be charming and will get a beautiful wife. He will be greater than his father or preceptor. He will be a good speaker and famous. Jupiter in Sagittarius is strong but is not Digbali. If Jupiter is retrograde or afflicted by malefic then he faces disgrace due to relations with females. Jupiter alone and without any other relation will give liking for solitary life and independent profession. Jupiter is tenth lord also and is strongly placed in its mooltrikona and in tenth from tenth house will give high status to the person in his dasha. Jupiter is a strong maraca and can give death in his dasha.

Example Jaya Lalitha DOB 24 February 1948 TOB 15.00 POB Melukote Kerala

Birth Chart

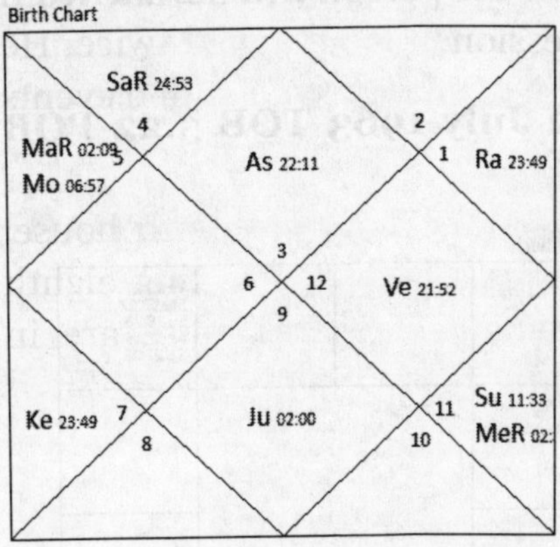

Birth Chart

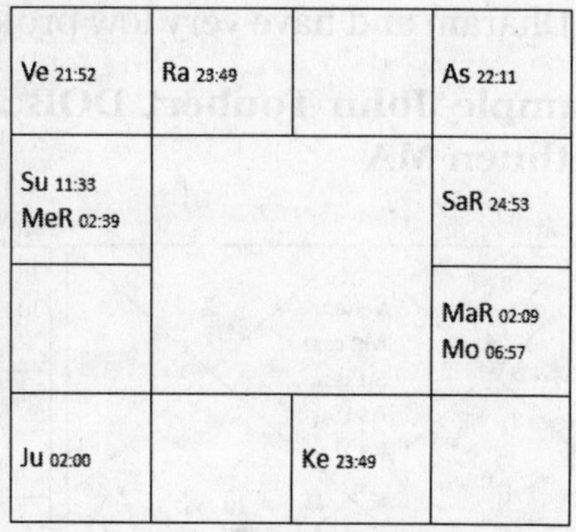

She was a famous actress and was Chief Minister of Tamil Nadu for six times. She was born in a rich family. Her father did not support the family and her mother asked her to join film to earn for the family. She joined films in mid-sixties and acted in more than 140 films. She joined MGR, the then CM and founder of AIADMK party. She joined politics in 1982 and her rise in politics was also very rapid. MGR died in 1987 and she became the chief of the party. She became CM in 1991 and remained in that chair, off and on, till her death on 5 December 2016 in Jupiter dasha.

The trishadaya houses and lords are closely related and tenth house is occupied. This has given a good Upchaya house effect and a successful but hard life.

Hansa yoga

Saral - Jupiter is in tenth house. Jupiter alone and without any other relation is very good. He will be honoured by king and relatives. He will be proud, fearless, firm in his undertaking and be an adviser to the king. Jupiter under malefic influence is very dangerous and he becomes revengeful. He is not tolerant and wants to supress his enemy by any means. Jupiter is the karaka of religious activities. Tenth house, tenth lord and karaka are together and create a situation of Karko bhava Nasaya. If Jupiter is afflicted, without any benefic association, then the person will deviate from his Dharam and have very low profession.

Example John Toubert DOB 2 July 1963 TOB 5.22 POB Methuen MA

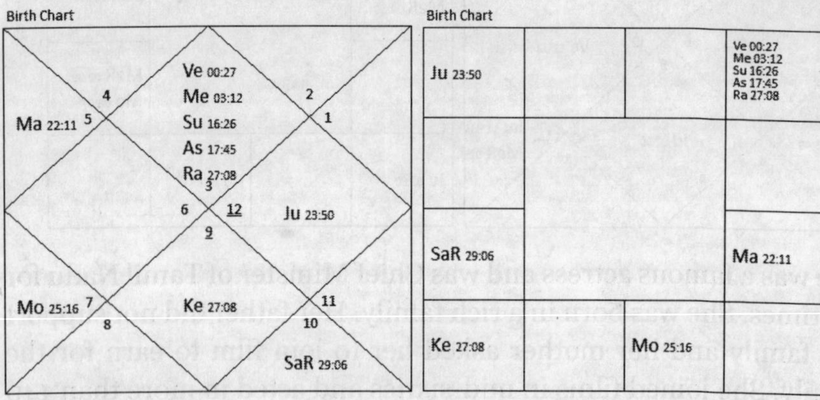

Jupiter is tenth lord. Jupiter is aspected by Saturn and Mars. The actions are very bad. He murdered three boys in the year 1982 – 83. He was arrested on 1 November 1984. He was sentenced to death by electrocution on 9 October 1985. The sentence was executed on 17 July 1996 after 11 years of mental torture in dasha of Mercury/ Venus/ Mars. Mercury is lagna lord forming Bhadra yoga and Venus is yoga karaka for Gemini lagna.

CANCER

Malavya yoga

Saral - Venus is eleventh lord also. This can deny any elder sibling and the person has to move out of his place of birth. If Venus is with malefic then it is certain. He possesses many wives, gems, will be helpful to his family and relatives, have good appearance and be the principal person of the family. Venus can be a maraca also but will give monetary gains in his dasha.

Example Raj Kapoor DOB 14 December 1924 TOB 21.20 POB Peshawar

Birth Chart

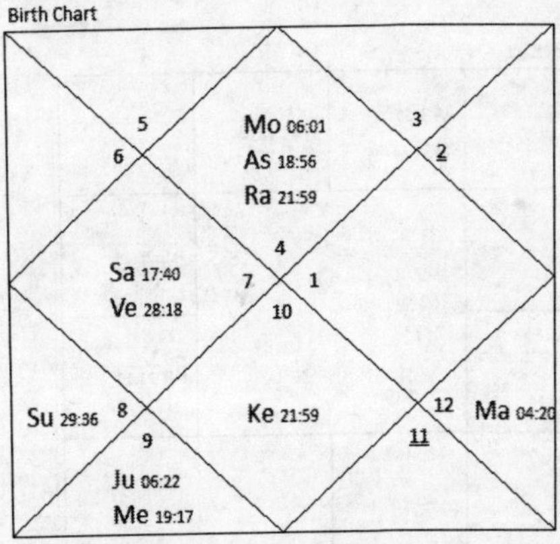

Birth Chart

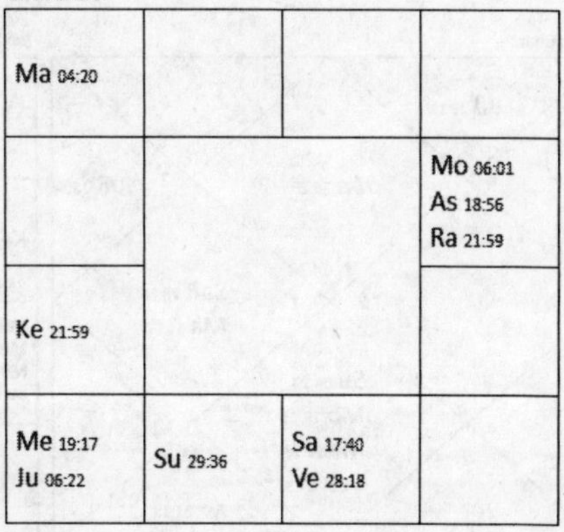

He is considered the greatest showman of Indian cinema. He is the eldest of six siblings. He started his film career as a child artist in 1935. His education was not regular and he attended several schools. His big break came in 1947 in Neelkamal movie. He was honoured with many awards including Dada Saheb Phalke award. He was honoured with Padma Bhushan by Government of India. He was married in 1946 and has five children. He has supported his family and many of them became big names in film industry. He suffered from Asthma before his death on 2 June 1988.

His tenth lord is in ninth house and ninth lord is aspecting tenth house. Lagna lord Moon is influenced by malefic only. Mercury is in Prishtodaya sign. This makes a person to work for success by any means.

Ruchaka yoga

Saral – Mars in tenth house is Digbali. Mars related with benefics will give high position, he will have power to punish and is a friend of the king. If Mars is afflicted it may give punishment from king.

Mars is a yoga karaka for Cancer lagna. He will be courageous, fond of war, have sons and have happiness. He can be army chief and win battles.

Example Mohammed Ali DOB 17 January 1942 TOB 18.35 POB Louisville Kentucky

Birth Chart

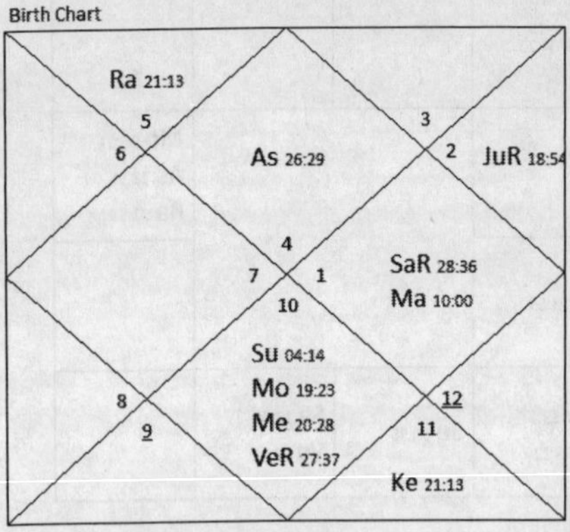

Birth Chart

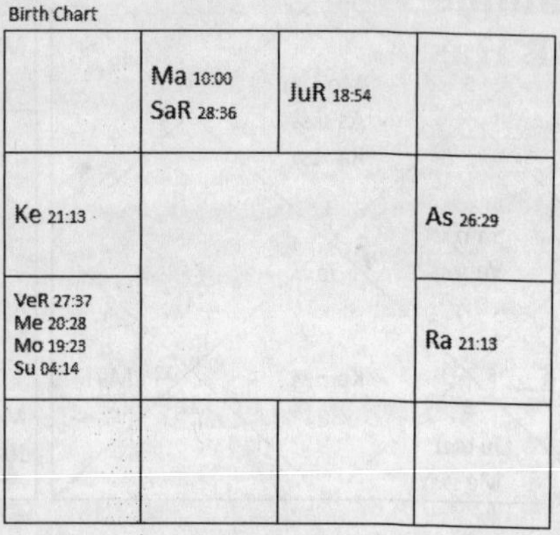

He is named the sportsman of twentieth century. He had won 57 of the 61 fights out of which 37 were won by knockout. He was worth 50 million dollars. He won his first Gold at the age of 18 years in light weight category. He was drafted for Army but refused to join and earned displeasure of the Government. He married four times and had nine children. Seventh house is very strong. He died on 3 June 2016.

His Mars is with debilitated Saturn. This made him earn Government displeasure. In the previous example Saturn is exalted as eighth lord and gives honours. His Moon is influenced by five planets and is a great yoga giving position of a king.

Sasha yoga

Saral - Saturn is in seventh house. Saturn is lord of eighth house also. When Saturn is alone then it gives position and disease to self and wife from time to time. This disease will be more problematic if Saturn is related to any planet. Saturn is a neutral planet for Cancer Ascendant. His results will depend on his other associations and aspects. Saturn aspect on ninth house is not good. He may not have any respect or regards for his preceptors or Guru. Saturn can prove maraca in his dasha.

Example H D Devegowda DOB 18 May 1933 TOB 11.00 POB Hassan

Birth Chart

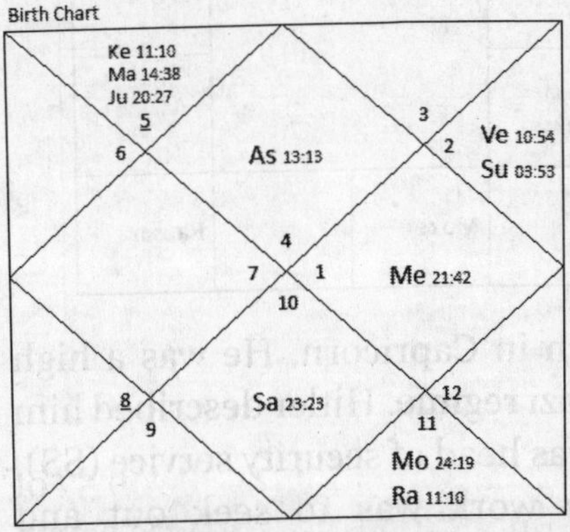

Birth Chart

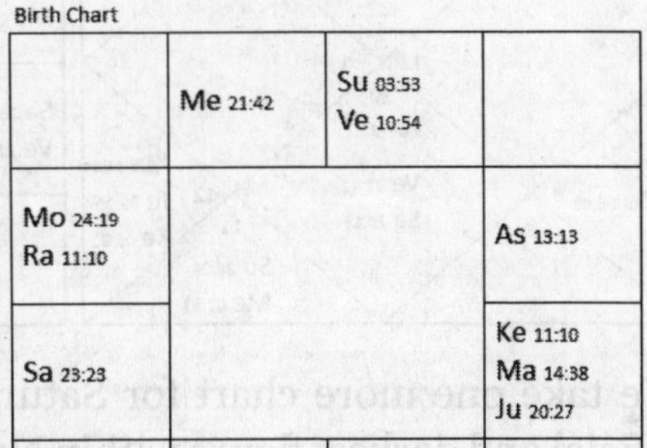

He was Prime Minister of India from 1 June 1996 to 21 April 1997. He was CM of Karnataka from 1994 to 1996. He was elected four times to Lok Sabha but lost in 2019. Even after losing he came to Rajya Sabha. He was elected MLA for six times. He is the President of JD(S).

His lagna lord Moon is with Rahu and aspected by Mars. Mercury is in Prishtodaya sign. Mars is in seventh house from Moon. Aspect of Jupiter on lagna lord and tenth house gives position. He is keen to hold office of authority by any means. Placement of Mercury in tenth house gives changes in job and no permanency.

Sasha yoga

Example Reinhard Heydrick DOB 7 March 1904 TOB 15.00 POB Halle Germany

Birth Chart

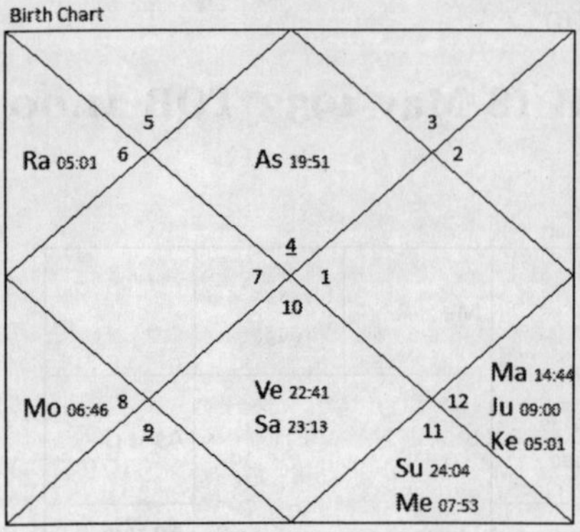

Birth Chart

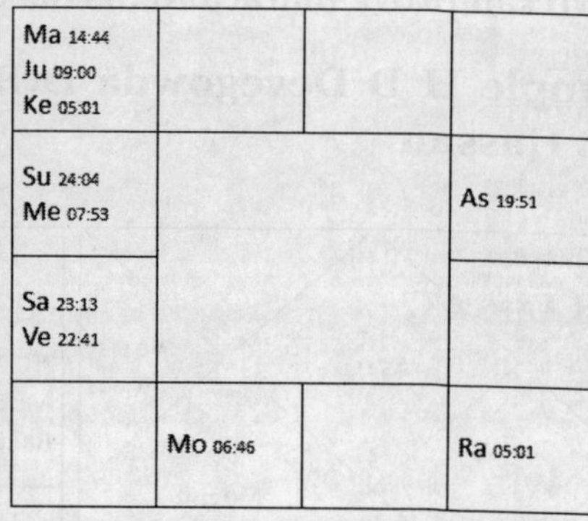

We take one more chart for Saturn in Capricorn. He was a high official and darkest figure within Nazi regime. Hitler described him as "The man with iron heart". He was head of security service (SS), an intelligence organisation. His work was to seek out and neutralise resistance to Nazi party by arrest, deportation and murder. On 9 and 10 November 1938, he organised series of attacks in Austria killing 2 million people by mass shooting. This was in dasha of Ketu/ Rahu. He was killed on 4 June 1942 in Venus/ Venus.

Venus is a lord of Kendra and is placed in maraca house. His third house is very strong. The aspect of eighth lord on ninth house and lord made him forget the Dharma.

LEO

Ruchaka yoga

Saral - Mars is yoga karaka lord of ninth and fourth house. Mars is placed in fourth house and gives all happiness, comforts, home and good relations in the family. Mars will give high position to the person. His mother and father may not keep good health but they will be fortunate and wealthy. Scorpio is sign of occult and research. If Mars is related to Jupiter, then person is inclined to do research and becomes a great person. Any relation of Mars with Mercury will give wealth. Relation with Sun will give high position. If seventh house is afflicted, then Mars can give separation from wife.

Example Dick Cheney DOB 31 January 1941 TOB 19.30 POB Lincoln Nebraska

Birth Chart

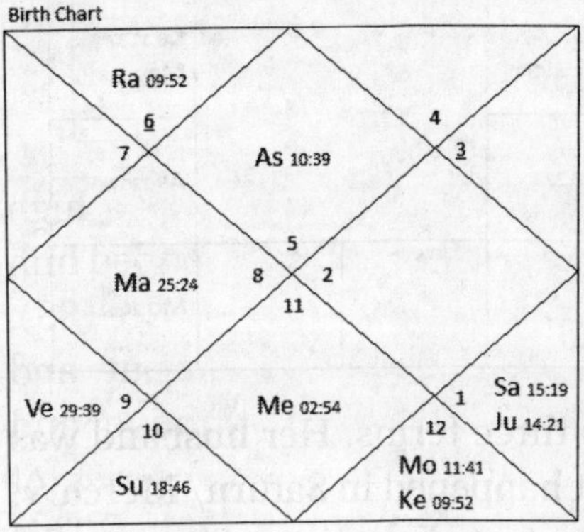

Birth Chart

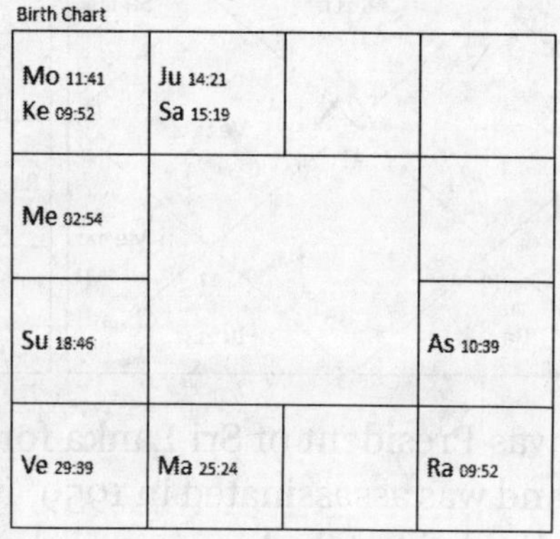

He is a politician and a businessman. He was Vice President of USA from 2001 to 09. He is considered the most powerful VP till date. He was also secretary of Défense from 1989 to 93. The dasha was Venus. He married in 1964 and has two children. He held these posts in Venus dasha. Mars is a yoga karaka and aspects tenth house. Venus is tenth lord placed in fifth and is aspected by fifth lord. Seventh and fifth lord conjoined in a trine is an excellent yoga. Mars in Kendra in own sign can give death.

Malavya yoga

Saral - Venus is third lord and his placement in tenth house will give position by showing courage. Venus in tenth house gives happiness, good sexual relations, honour, wealth, fame and wisdom. He will support his family and relations and gets respect from them. Mansagari says that the person will have royal status even when he is living in a forest. He will be the principal person of the family. Venus in Kendra in own sign can give death.

Example S. Bandarnaike DOB 17 April 1916 TOB 15.35.30 POB Balangoda Sri Lanka

Birth Chart

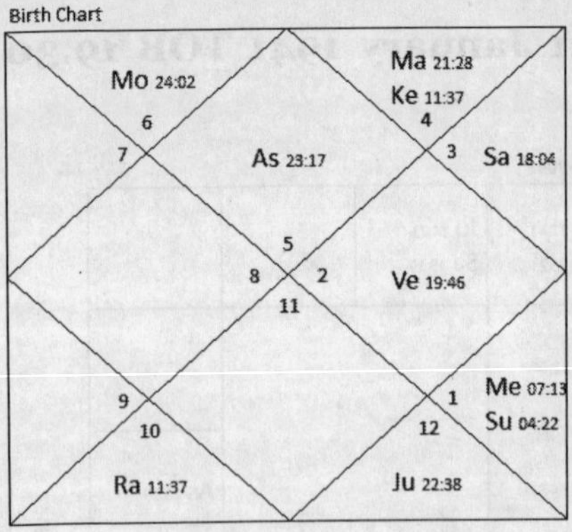

Birth Chart

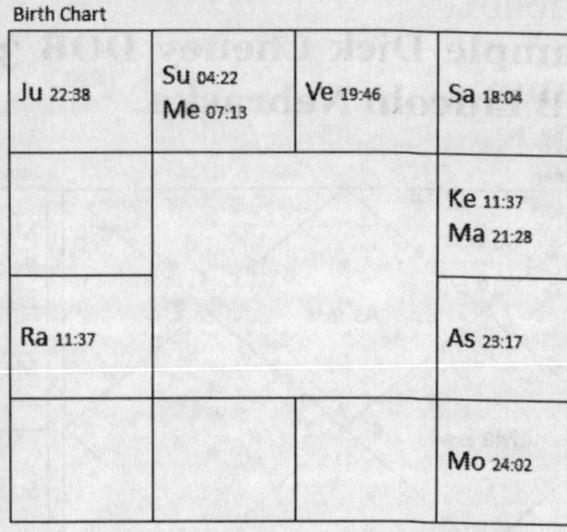

She was President of Sri Lanka for three terms. Her husband was PM and was assassinated in 1959. It happened in Saturn/ Mercury. She decided to take his place and contested elections. She won the elections and became the first woman Prime Minister in the world in 1960. The dasha was Saturn/ Mercury. Her second term was from 1970 to 1977. Third term was from 1994 to 2000. Her daughter was also PM. Her son was a minister.

She was born as Sirima in a famous family of Sri Lanka. She was married on 2 October 1940. The marriage is called the wedding of the century. She has three children. She died on 10 October 2000 in dasha of Venus/ Venus/ Moon.

Her lagna lord is exalted. Sun is with Mercury and is in Subh Kartari of Venus and Jupiter.

Sasha yoga

Saral - Saturn is lord of a Kendra and of trik and trishadaya sixth house and is a malefic for Leo lagna. Saturn placed in Aquarius will give more effects of Capricorn. The person likes competition and wins it. He will not keep good health. This Saturn will not give happiness of seventh and fourth house. He can have many relations with women. If ninth house has a malefic then person will not follow his Dharma. Saturn is a maraca.

Example Woody Allen DOB 1 December 1935 TOB 22.55 POB New York

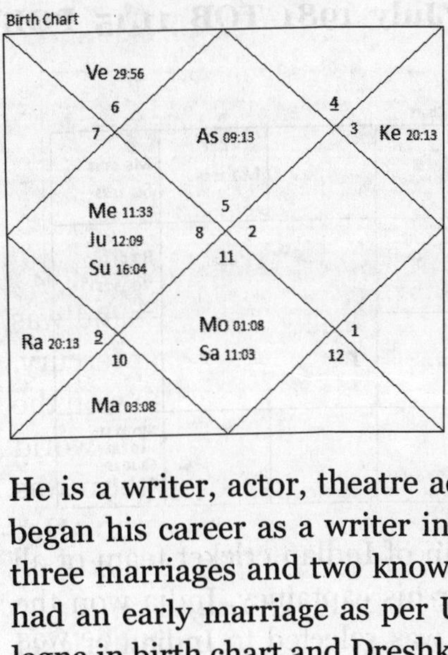

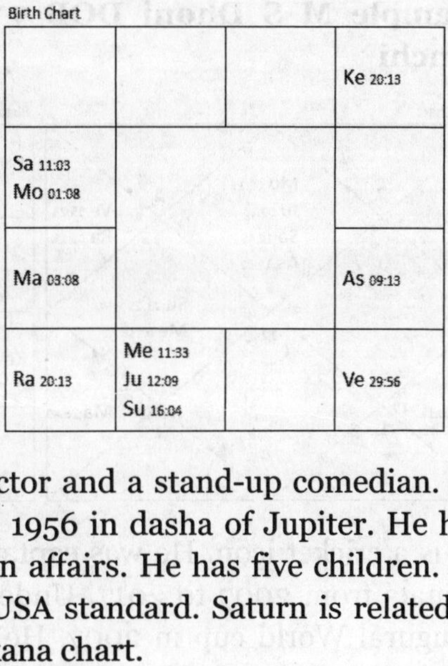

He is a writer, actor, theatre actor and a stand-up comedian. He began his career as a writer in 1956 in dasha of Jupiter. He had three marriages and two known affairs. He has five children. He had an early marriage as per USA standard. Saturn is related to lagna in birth chart and Dreshkana chart.

He is still active at the age of 86. His eighth house is aspected by Venus and eighth lord Jupiter.

VIRGO

Bhadra yoga

Saral - Mercury in tenth house in Gemini gives high position in life. The person will be wealthy and can foresee the events and earn fame. He will be wealthy and has a good family and takes care of them. He is very intelligent in his professional field. Any association with Saturn or Venus will confer raj yoga. Association of twelfth lord can cut short the professional career but the person will continue his public service.

Example M S Dhoni DOB 7 July 1981 TOB 11.15 POB Ranchi

Birth Chart

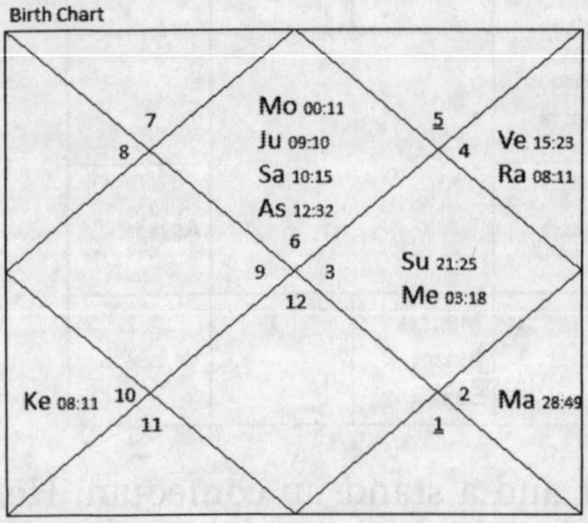

Birth Chart

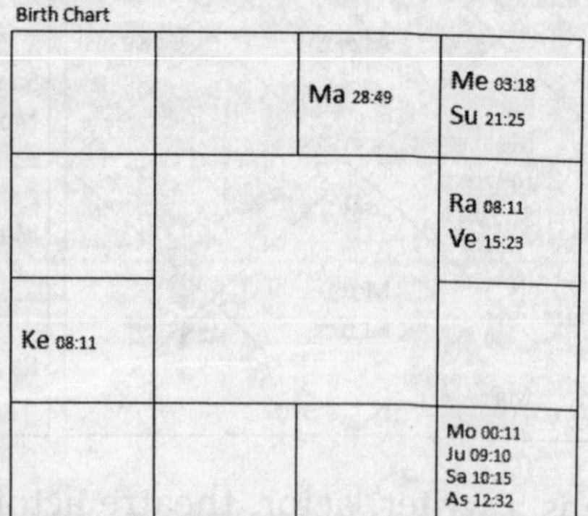

He is a cricket icon. He was captain of Indian cricket team of all formats from 2007 to 2017. Under his captaincy, India won the inaugural World cup in 2007. He was selected to Indian cricket team on 24 December 2004. He has been honoured with Padma shri in 2009 and Padma Bhushan in 2018. He retired from cricket on 15 August 2020. He is worth 130 million dollars. He married his school mate on 4 July 2010 and has a daughter born on 6 February 2015. His Rahu is in eleventh house with ninth and second lord giving him wealth and fame. Rahu dasha has proved very good.

Hansa yoga

Saral – Jupiter is in seventh house. This Jupiter will give quick rise in profession but gives problems in relationship. The problems will be more if Moon joins Jupiter. When Jupiter is retrograde then he will face insult from females. Relation of Jupiter with Venus is a good yoga and confers all happiness of life. Jupiter can be a maraca in his dasha, if it is afflicted by trishadaya lords.

Example Tatum O' Neal DOB 5. November 1963 TOB 03.38 POB Los Angeles CA

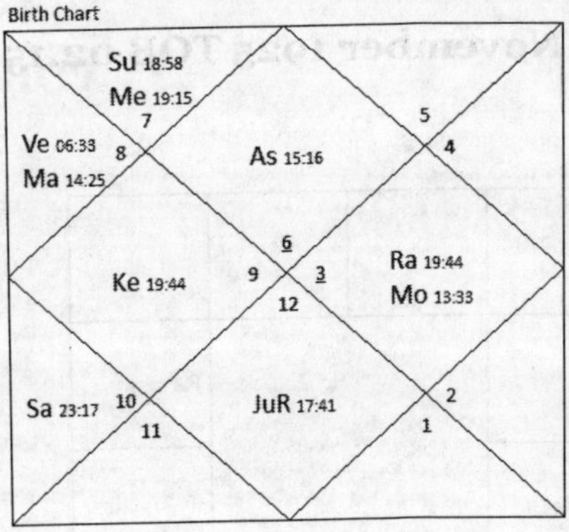

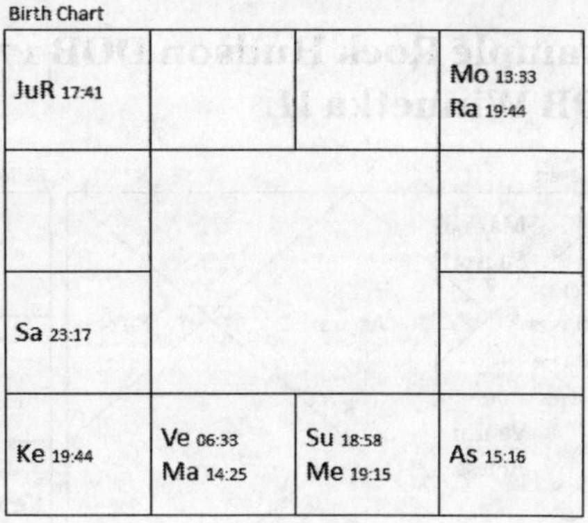

She won best supporting actress Academy award and Golden Globe award at the age of 10 years. She was the youngest actress to win two awards. Her mother was also an actress. Her early life was not good as her parents were divorced when she was three years old. She was born in Rahu dasha. She had affairs with celebrities but the affairs did not result in marriage. she was sexually misused by a friend of his father at the age of 12 years in dasha of Jupiter. She was married in 1986 in Jupiter/ Mars. She separated from the husband in 1992 and finally divorced in 1994. After this, she developed addiction to heroin. She was arrested on 1 August 2008 when she was buying cocaine. Her house was searched and more drugs were found but she was released. Ketu is in fourth house in papa kartari. Saturn is aspecting fourth lord. Saturn gives fame but has spoiled the happiness of fourth house.

Hansa yoga

Saral - Jupiter is in Kendra in his mooltrikona sign in fourth house. The person can be a preceptor conducting religious work. He will have wealth, be charitable, be friendly to his family and helps others. He likes to live alone. He has the blessings of his mother. Some classic says that he will be arrogant towards mother. Other classics hints at loss of progeny or have limited progeny with Jupiter placed in fourth house. He can have an early and fortunate marriage. Relation of trine lord with Jupiter is a good raj yoga and the person gets to a high position in life.

Example Rock Hudson DOB 17 November 1925 TOB 02.15 POB Winnetka IL

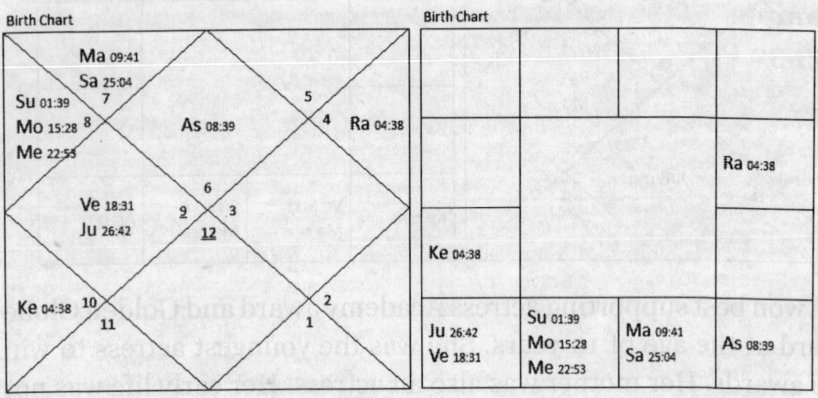

Rock Hudson is a famous film star of Hollywood. He acted in more than 70 films. He was nominated for academy award along with Elizabeth Taylor in 1956 for his movie "Soarid Giant". Jupiter is with Venus and is a good yoga for wealth and profession. His Moon Dasha started on 29 July 1977 and he was at the peak of his career which ended in 1985 during Moon Dasha itself. He died on 2 October 1985. He was suffering with AIDS detected in 1984.

Moon is trishadaya lord place in trishadaya house and is with lagna lord and twelfth lord.

LIBRA

Malavya yoga

Saral – Venus in lagna in own sign gives a charming personality and the person has attractive looks. When Venus is afflicted then he may have problems from females and he is likely to suffer venereal disease and poor eye sight. In relation with trine lord, this Venus give position, fame and wealth. Venus is eighth lord also. When eighth house is strong then it gives long and disease-free life to the person. Malefic relation will shorten the life and gives vices to the person. Eighth lord in lagna can give intuitive power when related to trine lord or sixth lord.

Example Mahatma Gandhi DOB 2 October 1869 TOB 8.35.32 POB Porbandar

Birth Chart

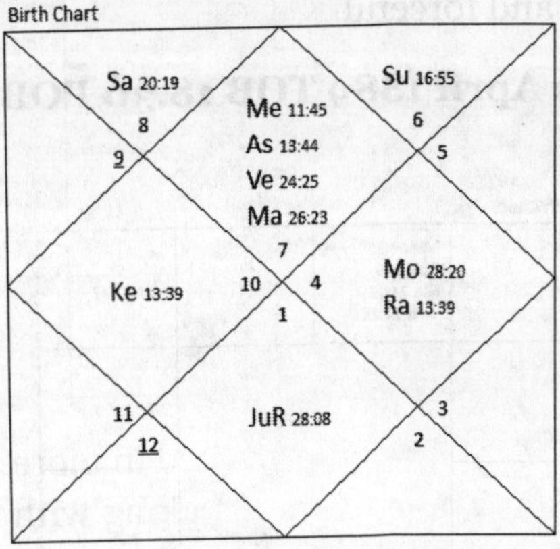

Birth Chart

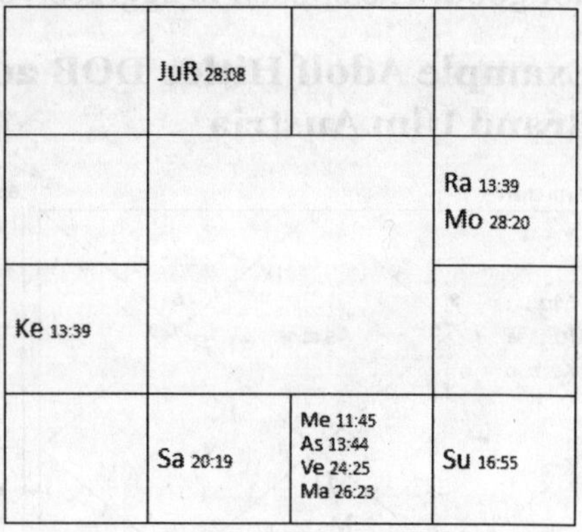

Mahatma Gandhi is the father of India. He was a lawyer and completed his study of law in UK in 1891. After a failure in India for two years, he went to South Africa and stayed there for 21 years and got the feel of racism discrimination. He returned to India in 1915 and started taking active part in civil disobedience movement. He was elected president of congress party in 1921 and the title of mahatma was added to his name. He went to jail many times and led many protests against British rule. India won freedom in 1947. He was assassinated on 30 January 1948. His major dasha of Moon started his transformation. Rahu is with tenth lord Moon and gives the results of tenth house. Venus is with Mercury and is aspected by Jupiter.

Ruchaka yoga

Saral - Mars is lord of second and seventh house and is a strong maraca. When Mars is placed in a maraca house and own sign in Kendra then it can give death in his dasha. Generally, the cause of death is in accordance to the significations of Mars or of the planet closely associated with Mars. Any relation with Mercury or Saturn will be a yoga and the person is very aggressive and never accepts defeat. Saturn is yoga Karaka and its relation with Mars gives high position to the person. He will be wealthy but his eating habits are not good. His speech is aggressive and forceful.

Example Adolf Hitler DOB 20 April 1889 TOB 18.30 POB Brand Ulm Austria

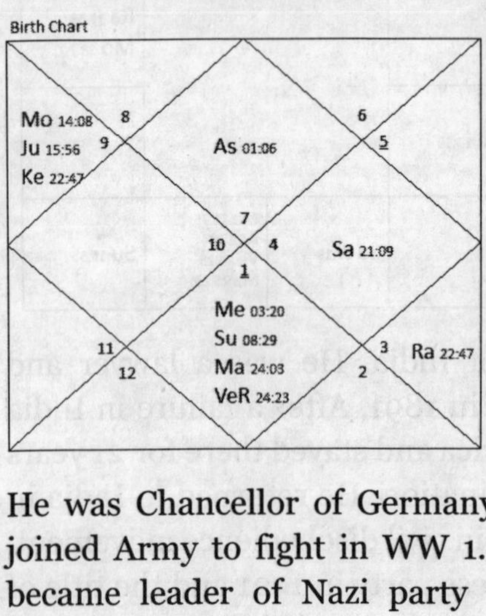

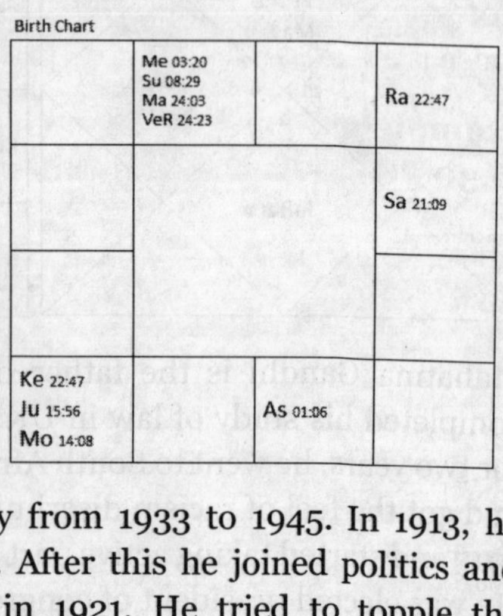

He was Chancellor of Germany from 1933 to 1945. In 1913, he joined Army to fight in WW 1. After this he joined politics and became leader of Nazi party in 1921. He tried to topple the

Government in 1923 and was sent to jail for five years but was released in 1924. He wrote 'Mein Kampf' in prison. After the election of 1932, no party had a majority but he became the Chancellor being the single largest party. He started WW 2 by invading Poland on 1 September 1939. The war ended when he committed suicide on 30 April 1945. The dasha was Rahu/ Venus/ Ketu. Mars is strong maraca and yoga Karaka. Venus is eighth lord and close to maraca Mars. Mars sent him to jail also. Mars is with Mercury and Venus giving yoga. Mercury is twelfth lord also.

His childhood was not happy as his father used to beat the children brutally.

Sasha yoga

Saral - Saturn is yoga Karaka being the lord of a Kendra and a trikona. Aspect of Saturn on lagna and tenth house gives good position if lagna lord is well placed and lagna is strong. This Saturn will give intelligence and deep thinking to the person. He likes solitude. Saturn is Karaka of masses and democracy. His profession will be related to the works involving public. If fifth house is afflicted then progeny may be denied.

Example Thomas Jermy King DOB 13 June 1933 TOB 16.30 POB Glasgow UK

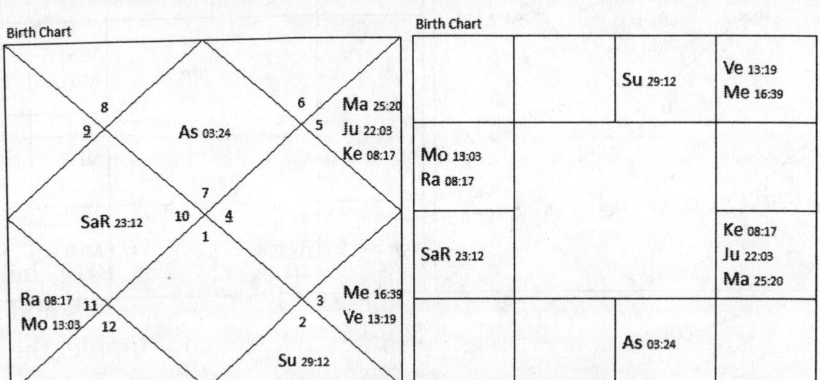

He is a politician and remained Member of Parliament from 1970 to 2001. He became MP after winning a by election in 1970. The dasha was Saturn/ Moon. Moon is tenth lord and Saturn is aspecting tenth house. He served as minister from January 1983 to April 1992. He was made the life peer of party in 2001. He has served Army also in the year 1952.

SCORPIO

Ruchaka yoga

Saral - Mars is lagna and sixth lord. Mars will give disease free and healthy physique. He will have strong opponents but he will win over them. When Saturn or Mercury are related to Mars or sixth/ eighth house then he can face accidents or sudden events. Mars is in fixed sign and is lagna lord and the person will progress at his place of birth and not shift his residence or work place very often. Mars is aspecting seventh house and can give unhappy marriage or separation in marriage since it is sixth lord also.

Example Peter Ueberroth DOB 2 September 1937 TOB 12.42 POB Evanston IL

Birth Chart

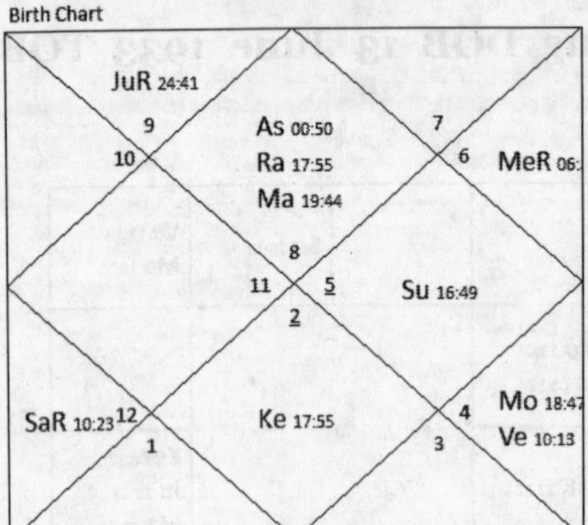

Birth Chart

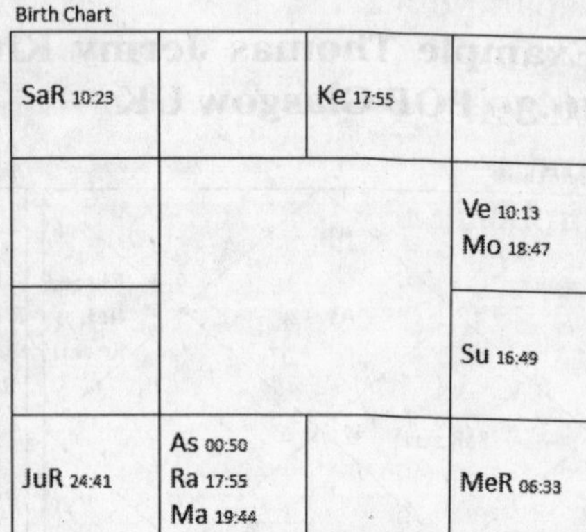

He became Vice President of Trans International Airlines at the age of 22 years and worked well. The dasha was of Venus. His ninth house is extra strong by placement of Moon and Venus in ninth house. It is the support of father. He worked with Airline till 1963 and founded his own travel company and became the second largest travel company in 1980. He was the organiser of 1984 Olympics held in Los Angeles and was named man of the year by Times Magazine in dasha of Moon.

He was baseball commissioner. He remained president of US Olympic committee from 2004 to 2008 in Rahu dasha. He also founded a school named Sage Hill School.

He is having a strong Mukut yoga. Jupiter is in Sagittarius and Moon is in Cancer. Jupiter is aspected by Saturn. This makes a leader and grants top position in any institution. **Five planets are in their own sign.**

Malavya yoga

Saral - Venus is seventh lord placed in seventh house. It gives beautiful and charming wife. But as twelfth lord, it can cause separation and give two marriages. Aspect of Venus on lagna gives good looks and impressive personality. The person will hold high office if trine lord is related to Venus. Venus is lord of maraca house and is placed in maraca house, it can give death or death like problems in his dasha.

Example Sir Ian McCarlney DOB 25 April 1951 TOB 0.15 POB Lennoxtown UK

Birth Chart

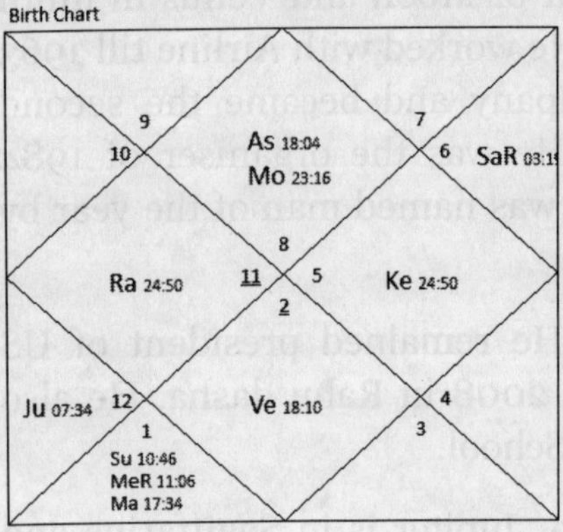

Birth Chart

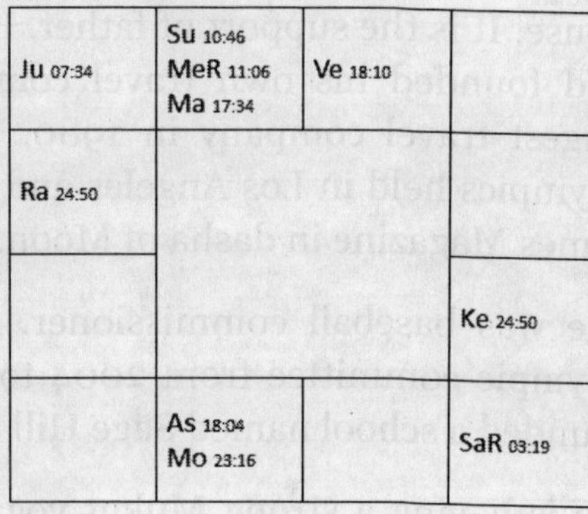

He was member of parliament from 1987 to 2010. The dasha in 1987 was of Sun. sun is tenth lord exalted in sixth house. He held ministerial post for four times. He left school at the age of 15 years. In D 24, Venus is debilitated in lagna and is with Saturn in Rahu Ketu axis. He had two marriages. Has two sons and two daughters. His eldest son died of drug overdose at the age of 23. Ninth lord Moon is in lagna and made him fortunate.

Sasha yoga

Saral - Saturn is fourth lord and is placed in fourth house. Saturn is third lord and its placement in fourth house will force the person to leave his birth place and go elsewhere. Saturn is a malefic for Scorpio lagna. Third lord in own sign in a Kendra will make him very courageous. Saturn will give more effects of third house.

Example Chandra Shekhar Azad DOB 23 July 1906 TOB 14.40 POB Jhabua MP

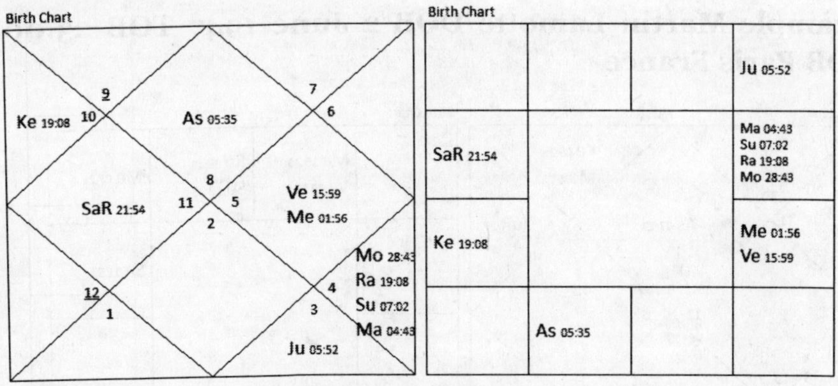

He was a great freedom fighter who was feared by the British. He joined freedom movement at the age of 14 years. The dasha was of Venus. He was an expert shooter. After the death of Ram Prasad Bismil, he headed the Hindustan Republican Association. He was involved in many revolutionary acts. These are Kakori train robbery, shooting of J P Saunders to avenge the killing of Lala Lajpat Rai and attempt to blow Viceroys train in 1929. He used to live in a forest temple in Orchha as a priest and taught children. His friend, Veer Bhadra Tiwari, played the traitor and gave the information to police. He was surrounded in a park in Allahabad. He killed three policeman and shot himself with last bullet left with him. He died on 27 February 1931. Dasha was Venus/ Saturn. Saturn is giving courage which is stronger by the aspect of Jupiter.

SAGITTARIUS

Bhadra yoga

Saral - Mercury is tenth and seventh lord placed in seventh house. Any relation of malefic with Mercury will spoil the marriage. he may not rise in his profession and not have a stable career. Benefic relation with Mercury will not give problems in profession. The significations of seventh house also gets support by benefic relation.

Example Martin Lamotte DOB 2 June 1947 TOB 23.00 POB Paris France

Birth Chart

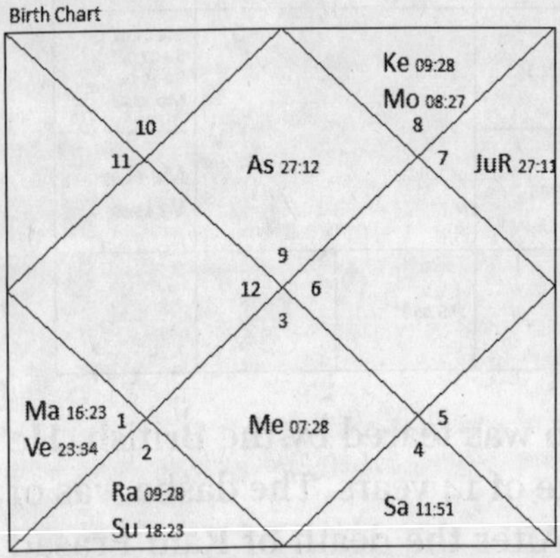

Birth Chart

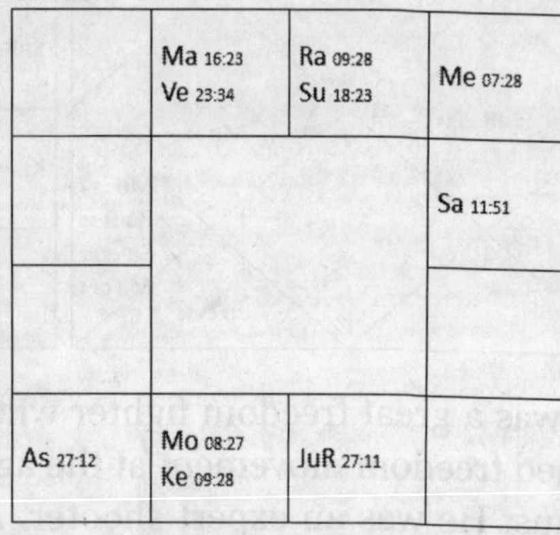

He was an actor. He made his debut in 1979 in dasha of Ketu. He used to make sketches for TV shows. He was a comedian. Mercury is in papa kartari and aspected by Jupiter. He is said to have five relationships. In Navamsha, lagna lord and seventh lords have exchanged sign and Mars is aspecting Venus placed in Scorpio. All relations were in dasha of Venus.

Hansa yoga

Saral - Jupiter is in lagna in Sagittarius. This makes a person a hard-core devotee of his Dharma and he will follow his Dharma. Malefic relation will make him a celibate. A relation with trine lord is a Raj yoga and the person will occupy high position. Generally, this Jupiter gives dispute in married life more so if seventh house has a malefic.

Example K B Hegdewar DOB 1 April 1889 TOB 01.13 POB Nagpur

Birth Chart

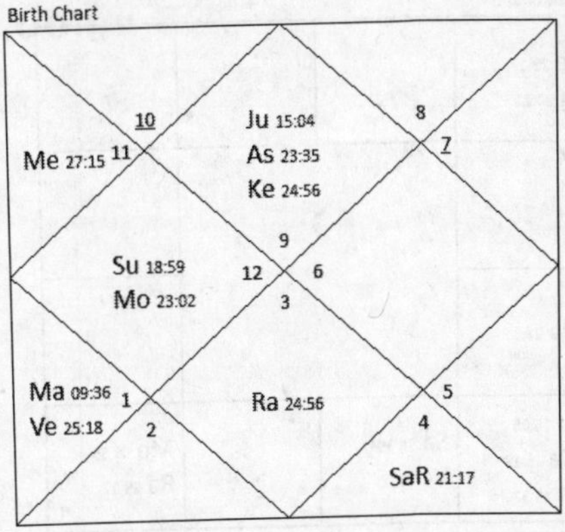

Birth Chart

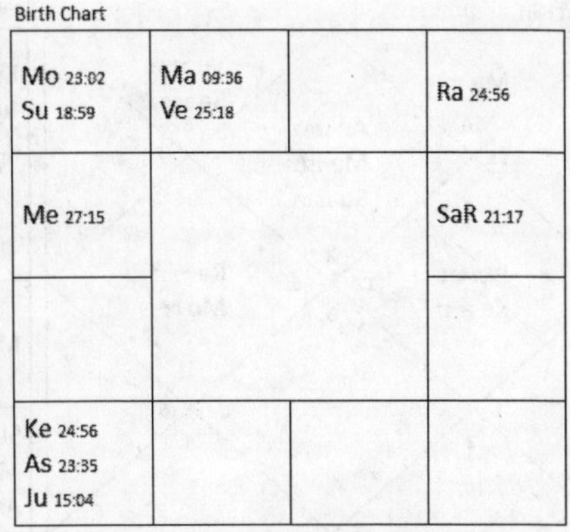

He is the founder of RSS. RSS was founded on Dussehra day of 1925. It was founded based on the ideology of Hindutva. He was born in a Telugu family. His parents died of plague when he was 13 years of age. The dasha was Ketu/ Rahu. He was taken care of by his uncle who became a father figure for him. He was expelled from school for singing Vande Matram. He however continued his study and became a physician. He never married. He died on 21 June 1940 in dasha of Moon/ Venus. Venus is a malefic and Moon is eighth lord. Eighth house has a malefic and eighth lord is with malefic. This gives short life full of miseries. Tenth house from tenth lord is aspected by its lord Mars and he created an institution.

Hansa yoga

Saral - Now Jupiter is in fourth house. Jupiter will promote happiness when associated with benefic. Jupiter will give effects of lagna lord. Relation with trine lord will give yoga. Relation with Mercury will increase the effects of tenth and seventh house in giving professional and family happiness. But relation of trishadaya lord can reduce the happiness.

Example Gladstone DOB 29 December 1809 TOB 8.15 POB Liverpool UK

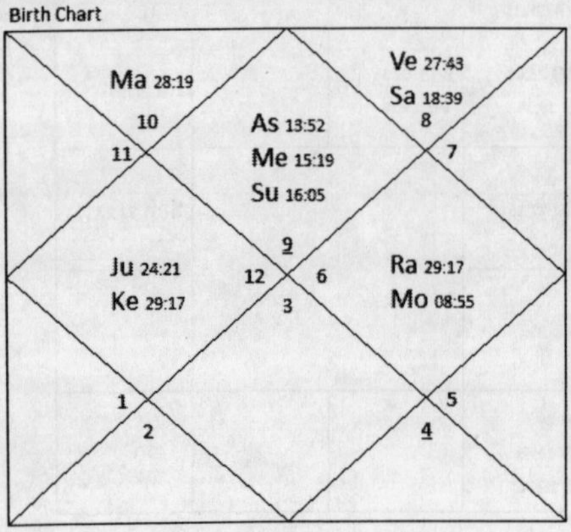

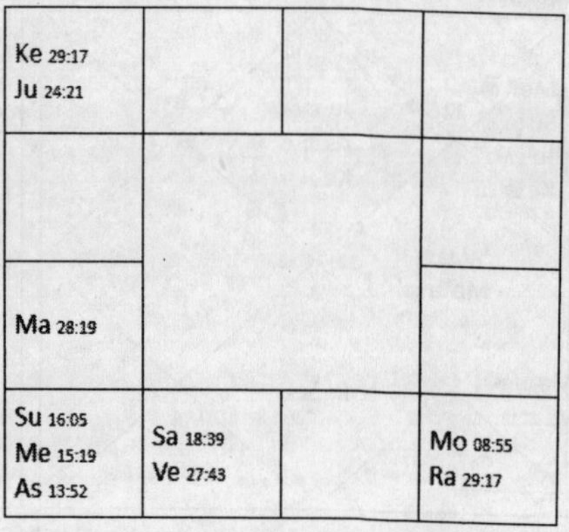

He was Prime Minister of UK for twelve years and chancellor of exchequer for twelve years. Jupiter has not denied high position.

CAPRICORN

Ruchaka yoga

Saral - Mars is lord of eleventh house and fourth house. Mars is neutral as fourth lord and becomes a malefic by ownership of eleventh house. The happiness of life is denied. The planets conjoined with or aspected by Mars will suffer. If Mars is related with trine lord, then Mars can show some good results but the trine lord will suffer and gives adverse results.

Example Mark White Jr. DOB 17 March 1940 TOB 4.15 POB Henderson Texas

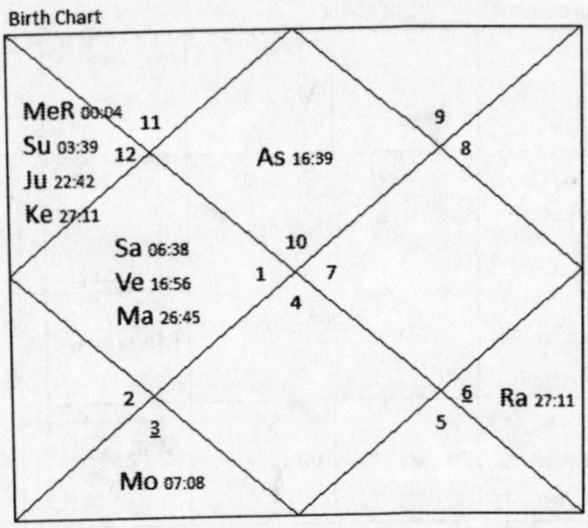

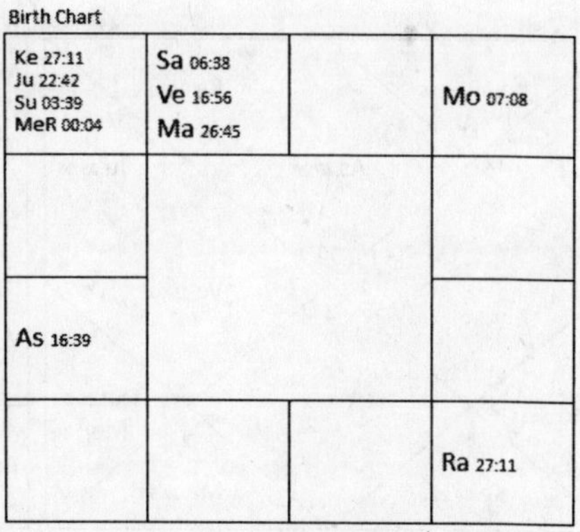

Mark is a lawyer. He held high positions in Texas. He was secretary from 1973 to 79, attorney general from 1979 to 83 and Governor of Texas from 1983 to 87. All these positions were held in the dasha of Saturn. He was married and had three children. He died of heart attack and kidney cancer on 5 August 2017 in dasha of Venus/ Mars. Mars is in own sign in Kendra.

Malavya yoga

Saral - Venus is yoga Karaka for Capricorn lagna. The person will have success in litigation and have happiness, enjoy sexual union, be honourable, have wealth, fame and is very wise. He has good relation with wife. If Saturn is in friendly Navamsha then the person will be a king. Any relation of trine lord with Venus is a raj yoga.

Example Vaclav Havel DOB 5 October 1936 TOB 15.00 POB Prague CZ

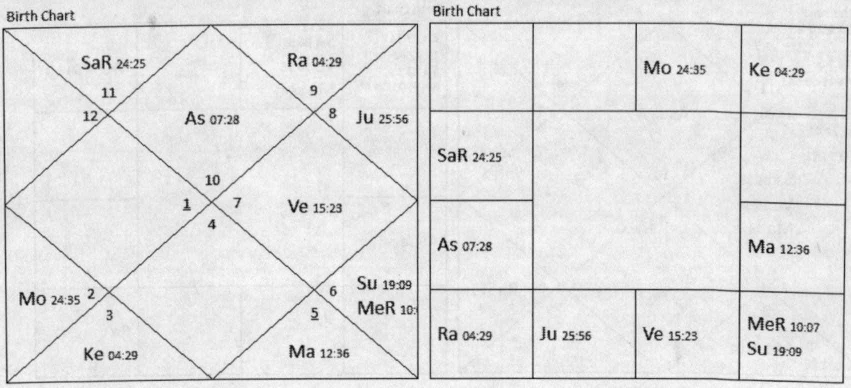

He is a politician, philosopher and writer. He is the first President of Czech Republic and was last President of Czech before it became a republic. He was last president from 1989 to 1992 and was first president of republic from 1993 to 2003. This was in Saturn dasha. His Saturn is in Taurus Navamsha. Prague airport is named after him. He married twice as her first wife died in 1996. He has received many awards including Gandhi Peace prize. He died on 18 December 2011 in dasha of Saturn/ Mercury. Saturn is second lord placed in second house.

Moon is exalted and is aspected by Jupiter. Venus is in fifth Navamsha. Saturn is in the Navamsha of Venus and Venus is in the Navamsha of Saturn.

Sasha yoga

Saral - Saturn is lord of maraca house which is the mooltrikona sign of Saturn. Saturn in Aquarius in lagna is superior to Saturn in Capricorn in lagna. Relation of Saturn with trine lord will cause a yoga. Second lord is placed in twelfth from it and gives loss of wealth or expenditure of wealth on self. Saturn is aspecting third house and gives many Coborn. Aspect of Saturn on tenth house will make the person very hard working rather a workaholic. Aspect on seventh house can spoil the marriage.

Example Nina Simone DOB 21 February 1933 TOB 6.0 POB Tryon North Carolina

Birth Chart

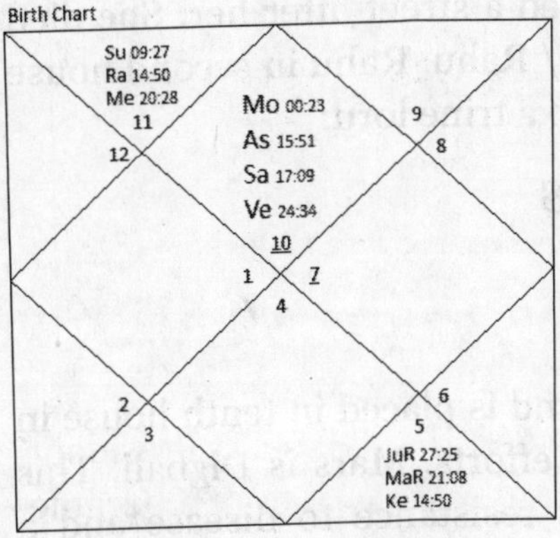

Birth Chart

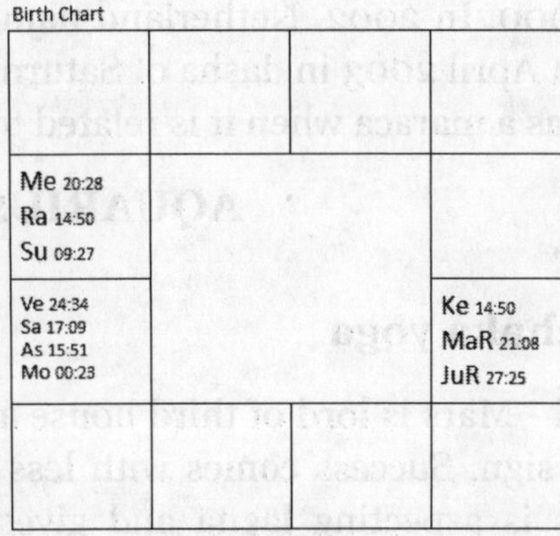

D9 Navamsha (spouse)

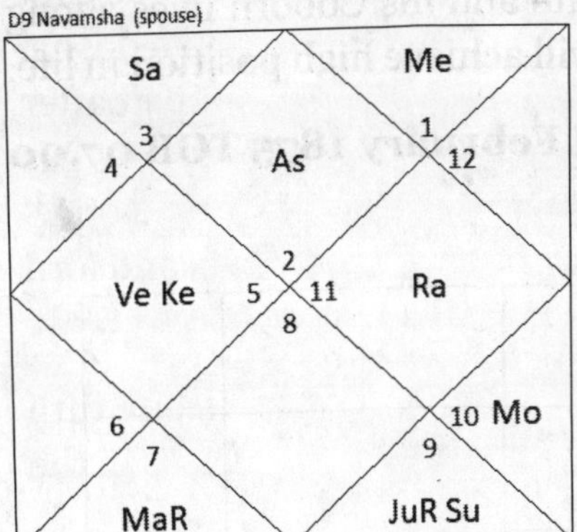

D9 Navamsha (spouse)

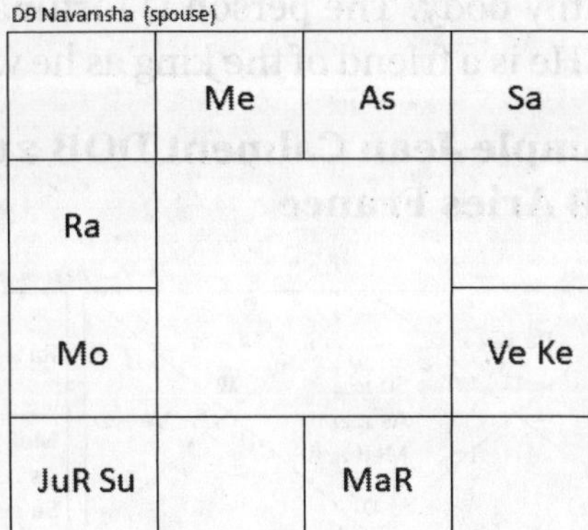

She was born in a poor family and was sixth of eight children of her parents. To make a living, she started playing piano at a night club and became a big singer. She had a wide range of singing and recorded 40 albums between 1958 to 1974. This was in Rahu dasha. She was very aggressive in temper and even fired a gun to kill an executive of recording company. Mars is aspecting second house. Her aggression came after an incident that happened in 1943. During her performance, her parents were made to vacate the seats of front row because of racism. She married twice but each marriage did not last more than 3 years. She lived as a mistress to a politician. Lagna lord of Navamsha is afflicted by Ketu. Eighth house and lord in Navamsha is also afflicted. She received many awards and honoured by granting a place in Grammy Hall of fame in 2000. In 2002, Netherland named a street after her. She died on 21 April 2003 in dasha of Saturn/ Rahu. Rahu in second house acts as a maraca when it is related to a trine lord.

AQUARIUS

Ruchaka yoga

Saral - Mars is lord of third house and is placed in tenth house in own sign. Success comes with less efforts. Mars is Digbali. This Mars is aspecting lagna and gives resistance to disease and a healthy body. The person is fortunate and his Coborn lives a long life. He is a friend of the king as he will achieve high position in life.

Example Jean Calment DOB 21 February 1875 TOB 07.00 POB Aries France

Birth Chart

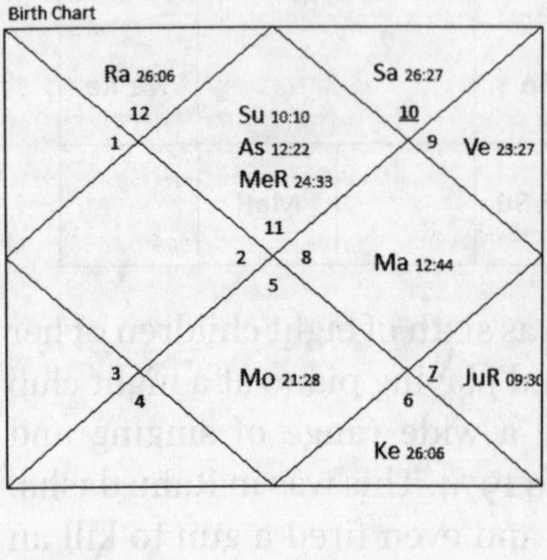

Birth Chart

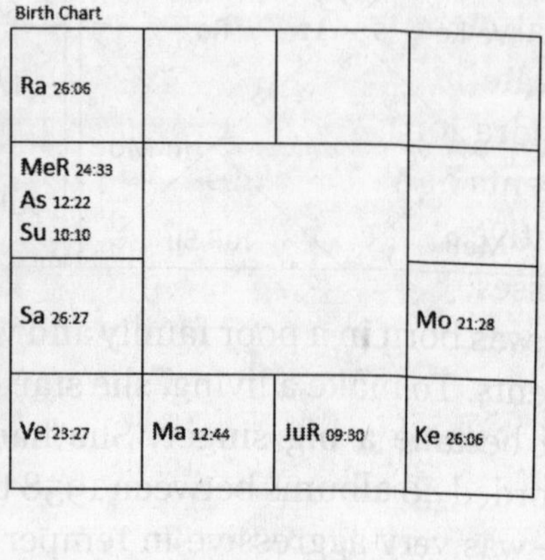

D9 Navamsha (spouse)

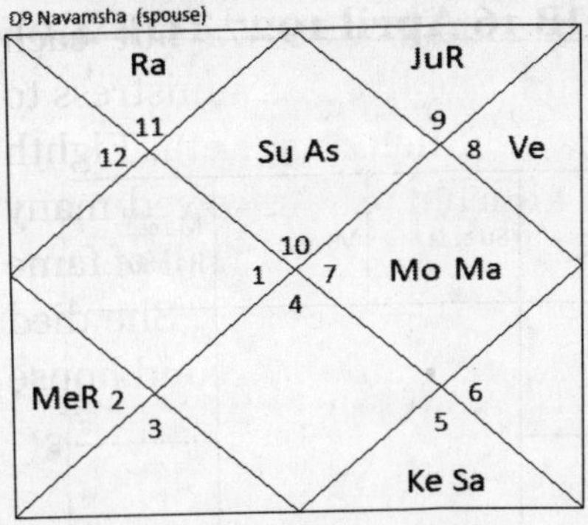

D9 Navamsha (spouse)

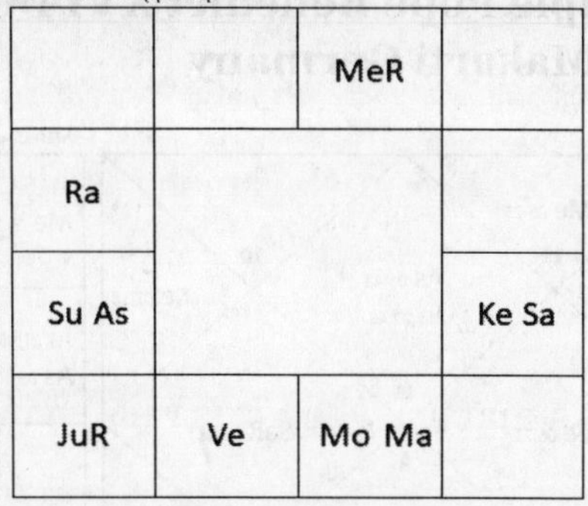

She is the longest living verified person. She lived for 122 years and 164 days. All her family members also lived more than the average age. She was married in 1896 and the wealth of her husband sustained her life. She never used any heating system for her home. She has three Karaka planets. These are Mercury, Mars and Moon. Mars is in tenth house as a Karaka from Mercury. Mercury is eighth lord. Her husband died early. Ketu and Saturn are placed in eighth house in Navamsha and indicates loss of Manglaya.

Malavya yoga

Saral - Venus is yoga karaka and its placement in fourth house will elevate a person to a high status like a king. Any relation with Kendra lord will further boost the yoga. He will have blessing of parents and of Guru. He will have good relations with family and relatives. Fourth house is the house of masses and if Karaka of masses, Saturn, also joins then he is very popular leader of the masses.

Example Pope Benedict XVI DOB 16 April 1927 TOB 4.06 POB Makarti Germany

Birth Chart

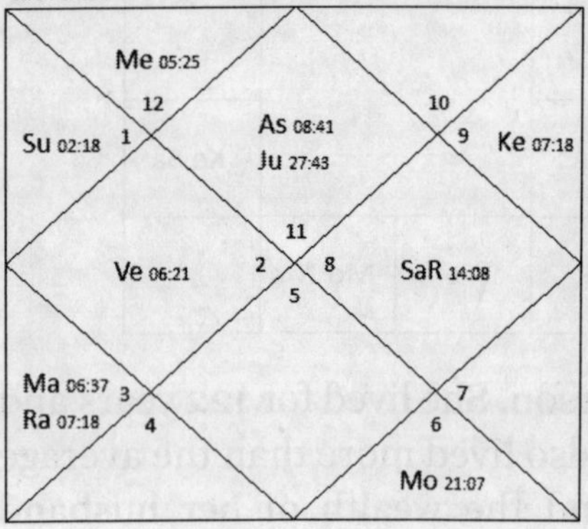

Birth Chart

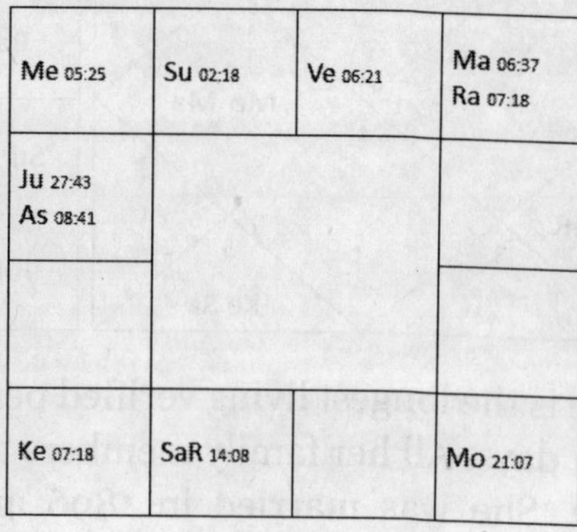

He served as Pope till his 93 years age. He became Pope in 2005 and resigned on 28 February 2013. He became a professor of Theology at the age of 31 years. He was taken as POW by allied forces during WW2.

The horoscope is having many yogas. His sixth lord is in eighth house and is aspected by Mars and Mercury. This gives fame and riches. Venus is aspected by Saturn causing a raj yoga and popularity among masses. Eighth house is aspected by eighth lord giving long life. Karaka of longevity is under benefic influence of Venus.

Sasha yoga

Saral - Saturn is in lagna in his mooltrikona sign. Saturn is a benefic for Aquarius lagna. When Saturn is under benefic influence then it will give long life. Saturn will give a kingly status. This status will improve if a trine lord is associated with Saturn by conjunction or aspect. When Saturn is under malefic influence then the person will be a liar and crafty. His marriage life can suffer especially if

Sun is also afflicted. Saturn is twelfth lord and gives fame in the outside world.

Example Phil Donahue DOB 21 December 1935 TOB 11.25 POB Cleveland Ohio

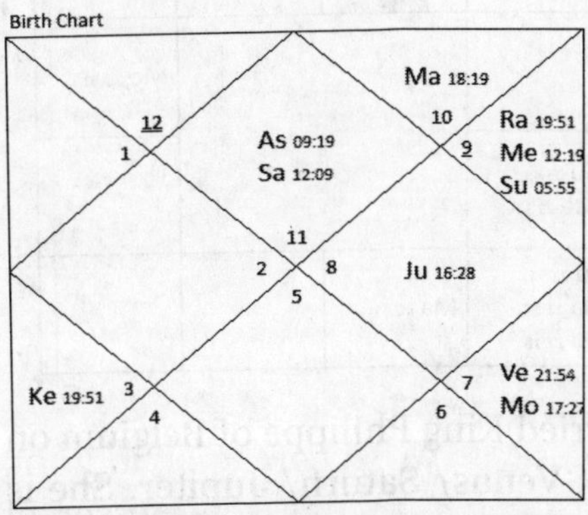

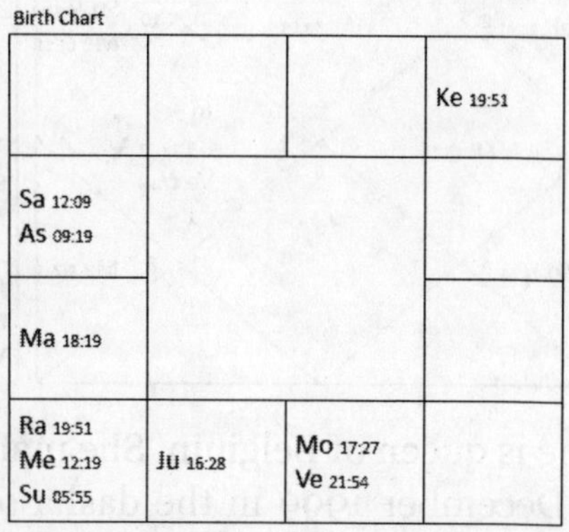

He is a media personality, writer and film producer. He is famous for his day time talk shows. His talk show ran for 29 years. He is called the king of daytime talk show. He started his career as production assistant in 1957 in the dasha of Saturn. Saturn dasha started in 1955. He has won 20 Emmy awards. He married twice and have five children from first marriage.

Twelfth lord, if well placed and strong, produces a fiction writer.

PISCES

Hansa yoga

Saral - Jupiter is in tenth house. This Jupiter will give high position and status in life. If Jupiter is afflicted it may not give a profession. In a dual sign, a planet in ninth Navamsha is in Vargottam Navamsha. Relation of Jupiter with trine lord is a raj yoga. Jupiter in tenth house in own sign gives early success in all undertakings.

Example Queen Malhilde DOB 20 January 1973 TOB 10.47 POB Uccle Belgium

Birth Chart

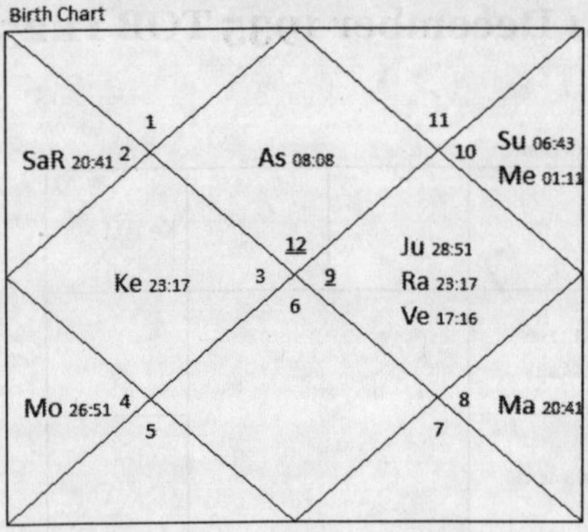

Birth Chart

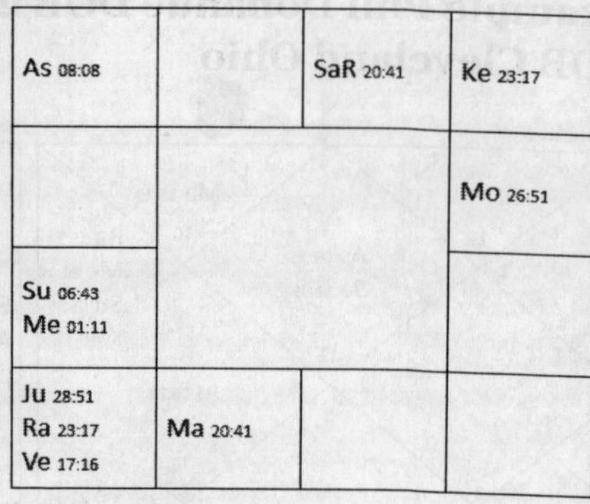

She is queen of Belgium. She married King Philippe of Belgium on 4 December 1999 in the dasha of Venus/ Saturn/ Jupiter. She is mother of four children. She holds master's degree in Psychology with honours. She is fluent in French, Dutch, English and Italian language.

The strength of horoscope is the presence of Mukut yoga. Ninth lord is in ninth house and tenth lord is in tenth house. Jupiter is Vargottam.

Hansa yoga

Saral - Jupiter in lagna as lagna lord is a great blessing. The person will be very handsome, energetic, learned and courageous. Jupiter will aspect two trine houses and will promote these houses. He will enjoy the results of his past life deeds. If Jupiter is afflicted then lagna and lagna lord are spoiled and the life becomes miserable. On the other side, if Jupiter has benefic relations only, then he will confer high position, wealth, name and fame.

Example Peter Duel DOB 24 February 1940 TOB 7.59 POB Penfield New York

Birth Chart

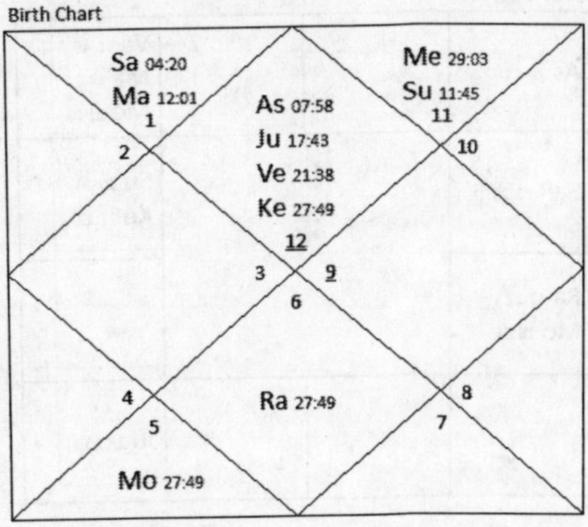

Birth Chart

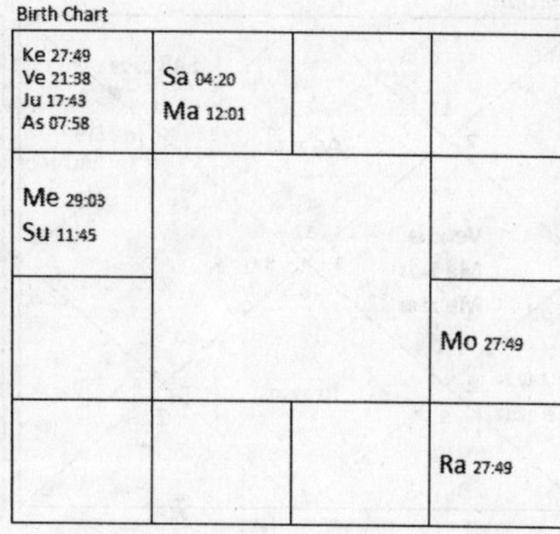

He was a stage, TV and film actor. He did his graduation in English language but left the studies for acting career. He was once arrested for drunken driving. He committed suicide on 31 December 1971. He was depressed because of heavy consumption of alcohol. The dasha was Rahu/ Mercury/ Mars. His Jupiter is with Ketu and Venus. Venus is the lord of third and eighth house. Jupiter is afflicted by Venus. In the previous chart, Jupiter is with Venus, but lagna is not afflicted.

Bhadra Yoga

Saral - Mercury is fourth and seventh lord. Mercury in fourth house and without affliction will give all luxuries, status and makes a person very intelligent. His words are honoured and he gets support of all relatives. All significations of fourth house will prosper. If Mercury is afflicted then the good effects of fourth house are reduced. His married life is not good. He can be denied progeny or have a smaller number of progenies. When Mercury is related to trine lords then Mercury can confer ministership to the person and he will have close relation with king.

Example Jean Balland DOB 26 July 1934 TOB 23.00 POB Bue France

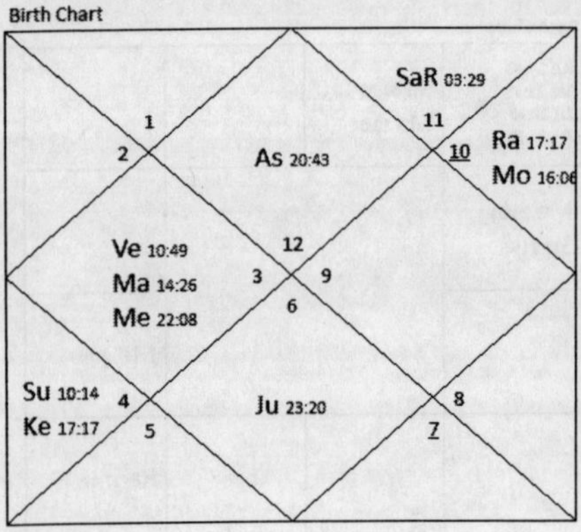

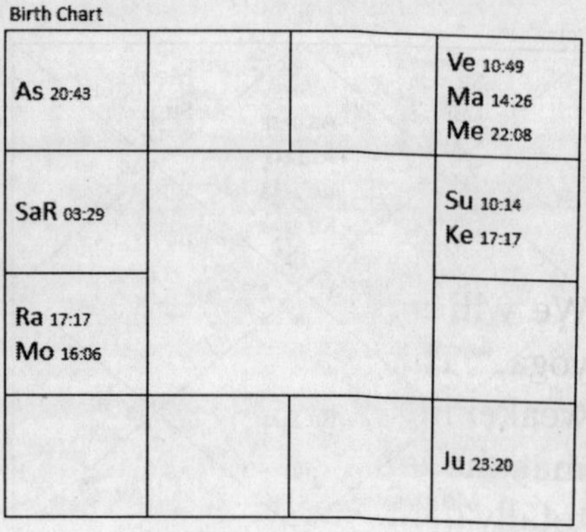

He was a priest. He holds a doctorate degree in Theology. He was Archbishop of Lyon. He was ordained as Cardinal priest on 21 February 1998 but died on 1 March 1998. The dasha was Saturn/ Jupiter/ Saturn. His Mercury is with Mars and a good yoga is formed which gave him good education and position. Association of Venus is not welcome since Venus is the lord of trishadaya houses and deprived him of family happiness but gave inner happiness.

Chapter 03

Modification of Yoga

We will now discuss the modifications of Panch Maha Purusha yoga. This modification can be cancellation or addition/ weakening of yoga. The term cancellation is bit too strong. I feel that the effects of yoga are diluted with this but the yoga is not totally defunct. We should view the cancellation in this perceptive. The yoga can gain or lose strength under some conditions.

1. **Cancellation**
2. Dev Keralam Volume 2 by Lt. Col. Raj Kumar page 5 verse 27.

In the Malavya yoga caused by exalted Venus, if Saturn is conjoined with or is aspecting Jupiter, then Malavya yoga is not effective.

This cancellation is applicable only for exalted Venus and not for Venus in own sign as stated in this verse.

Taking clue from this verse, we can extend this rule for other Panch Maha Purusha yoga which are caused by exaltation of a planet. We note that Malavya yoga is caused by Venus by its occupation in Pisces and in Kendra from lagna. Jupiter is the lord of Pisces. Jupiter is debilitated in Capricorn whose lord is Saturn. Association or aspect of Saturn on Jupiter will cancel Malavya yoga. The aspect of Jupiter on Saturn will not cancel it. Thus, we note the dispositor of exaltation of the yoga planet. Note the lord of debilitation sign of the dispositor. If this dispositor is related to the exaltation sign lord then it is the cancellation of that Panch Maha Purusha yoga. We give a table for the cancellation of each Panch Maha Purusha yoga.

Table 1 (Cancellation)

Yoga/ Planet	Exaltation sign/ Lord of Planet A	Debilitation sign/ Lord of A	Cancellation
Ruchaka/ Mars	Capricorn/ Saturn	Aries/ Mars	Mars is with or aspecting Saturn.
Bhadra/ Mercury	Virgo/ Mercury	Pisces/ Jupiter	Jupiter is with or aspecting Mercury.
Hansa/ Jupiter	Cancer/ Moon	Scorpio/ Mars	Mars is with or aspecting Moon.
Malavya/ Venus	Pisces/ Jupiter	Capricorn/ Saturn	Saturn is with or aspecting Jupiter.
Sasha/ Saturn	Libra/ Venus	Virgo/ Mercury	Mercury is with or aspecting Venus. Mercury cannot aspect Venus except in Divisional chart.

Note – Exchange of sign or Nakshatra is also a relation.

Note- We find a rule for cancellation of Panch Maha Purusha yoga cause by planet in own sign. **When Ketu is with yoga planet** then **Panch Maha Purusha yoga** is cancelled. This is discussed later in this chapter.

Stronger

1. The cancellation happens when the lord of debilitation sign of dispositor of the planet is related is related to the dispositor. If we consider the lord of exaltation sign of dispositor then will it strengthen the Panch Maha Purusha yoga? This needs more research. We give a table for this consideration which can be used for further research.

Table 2 (Stronger)

Yoga/ Planet	Exaltation sign/ Lord of Planet A	Exaltation sign/ Lord of A	Strong
Ruchaka/ Mars	Capricorn/ Saturn	Libra/ Venus	Venus is with or aspecting Saturn.
Bhadra/ Mercury	Virgo/ Mercury	Virgo/ Mercury	
Hansa/ Jupiter	Cancer/ Moon	Taurus/ Venus	Venus is with or aspecting Moon.
Malavya/ Venus	Pisces/ Jupiter	Cancer/ Moon	Moon is with or aspecting Jupiter.
Sasha/ Saturn	Libra/ Venus	Pisces/ Jupiter	Jupiter is with or aspecting Venus.

Note - The relation of planets is also there if they exchange sign or Nakshatra.

The Panch Maha Purusha yoga is formed by planet placed in a Kendra in own sign or in exaltation. Classic have praised a single planet in Kendra in this condition will lift the potential of the horoscope. The cancellation will not be of big importance. The

Panch Maha Purusha yoga is the name given for this placement. With cancellation the potential of placement will be still present. The final result is the sum total of the complete horoscope.

2. The second rule of cancellation has Ketu with a planet placed in own sign in a Kendra. Ketu will strongly act as Kendra's lord. This can give a big Raj Yoga.
3. We therefore look for the total horoscope and treat the yoga planet according to standard principles of Astrology even after cancellation of Panch Maha Purusha yoga.

We will now take few examples for cancellation.

Malavya yoga

Example 1 Anandmayi Ma DOB 1 May 1896 TOB 3.01.30 POB Kheora Bangla Desh

Birth Chart

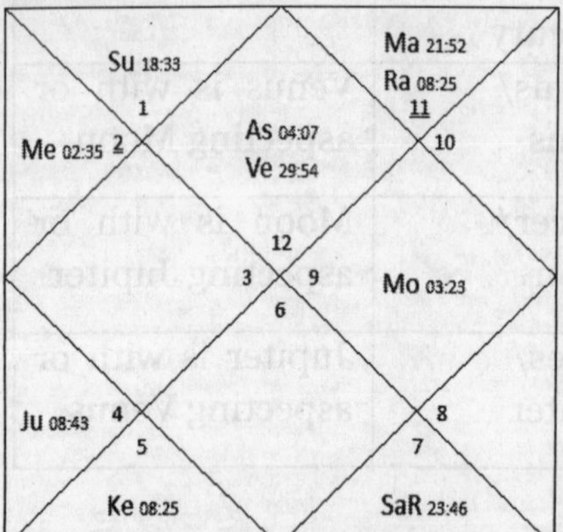

Birth Chart

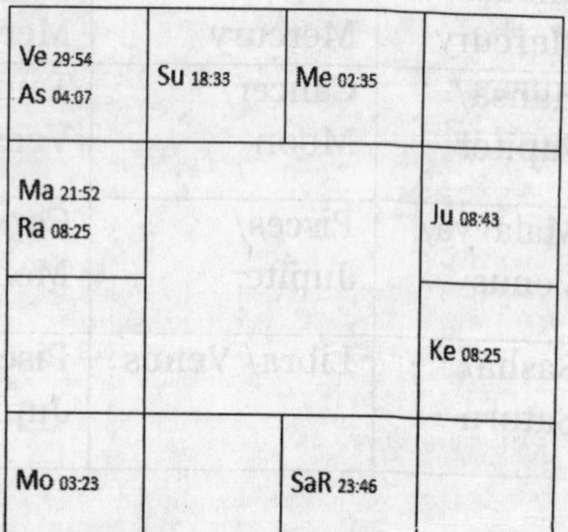

Venus is forming Malavya yoga. Saturn is aspecting Jupiter cancelling the yoga. She was a great saint and had very large number of followers. She became saint in dasha of Venus.

Example 2 Dayanand Saraswati DOB 12 February 1825 TOB 20.49 POB Morvi Gujrat

Birth Chart

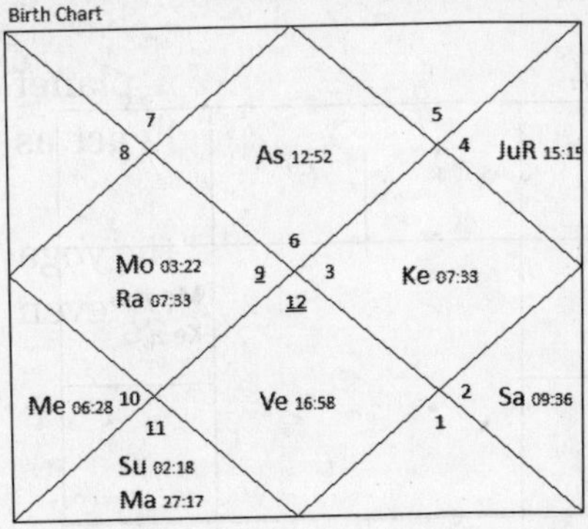

Birth Chart

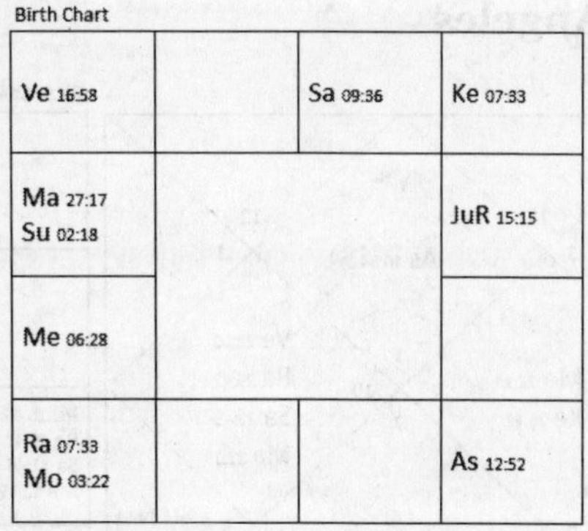

Swamiji also has Malavya yoga. This is cancelled by aspect of Saturn on Jupiter. He laid the foundation of Arya Samaj in dasha of Venus.

The Malavya yoga is supposed to give all luxuries in life. Can we say that the cancellation of Malavya yoga has not provided luxuries? The material craving was not given but they had the luxury which the material world cannot provide.

Ruchaka yoga

Example 1 Carla Hills DOB 3 January 1934 TOB 12.32 POB Los Angeles

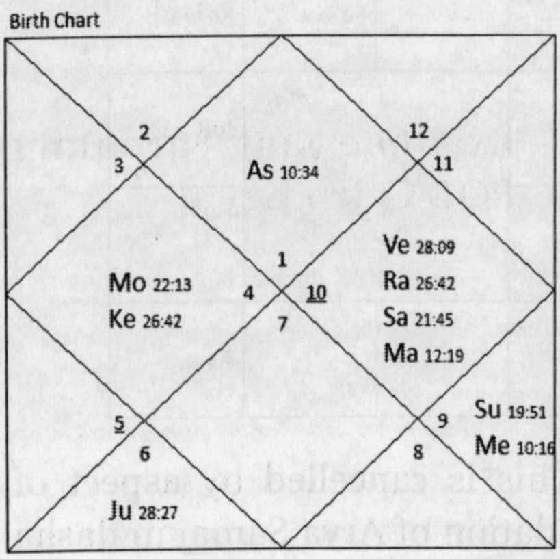

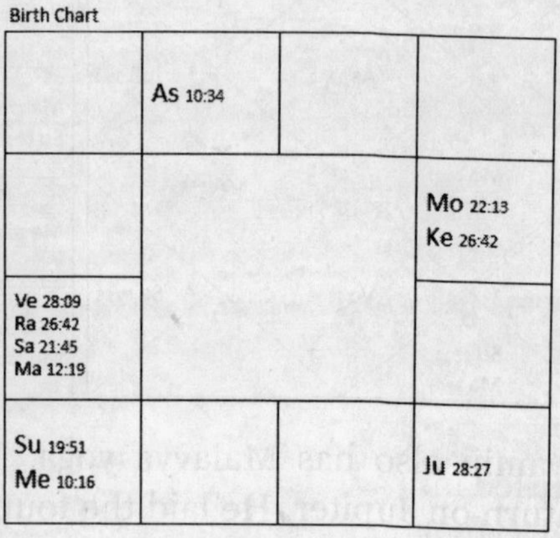

She was secretary of state for housing and urban development of USA from 1975 to 1977. She was US trade representative from 1989 to 1993. She is a lawyer by profession. She married in 1958 and her husband died in 2014. She has 4 children. Cancellation of Ruchaka yoga is there by association of Saturn with Mars. Actually, the tenth house has gained strength by presence of Saturn there. Saturn is tenth lord. Very good karaka yoga is present.

Example 2 Charles De Gaulle DOB 22 November 1890 TOB 4.02 POB Lille France

Birth Chart

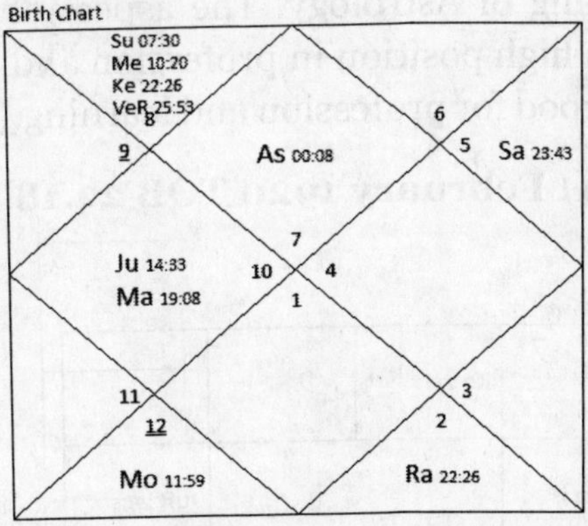

Birth Chart

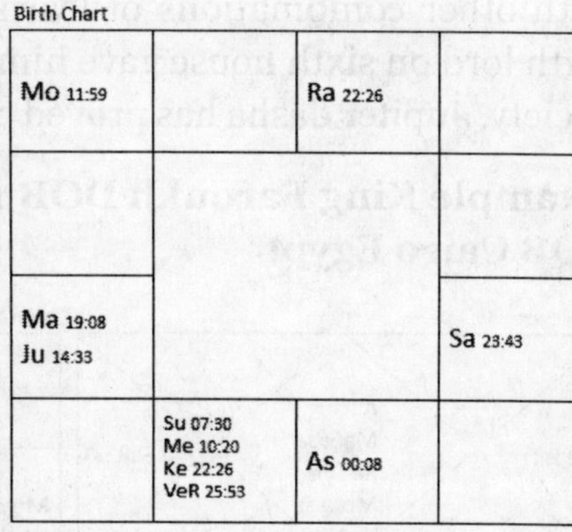

He led independent France in WW2 as the chairman of provisional government of Republic of France from 1944 to 1946. He then went into his retirement but was recalled in 1958 and appointed Prime Minister in 1958. He rewrote the constitution of France. He assumed charge of President of France in 1959 and remained in this position till his resignation in 1969. Ruchaka yoga is cancelled but he served in the Army.

Hansa yoga

Example K N Rao DOB 13 October 1931 TOB 7.53.00 POB Machlipatnam

Birth Chart

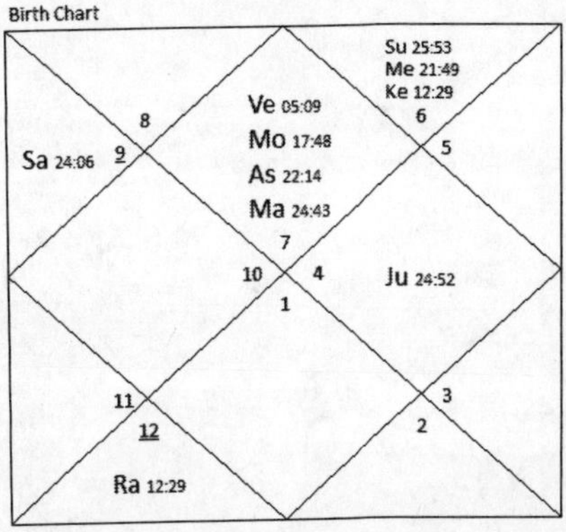

Birth Chart

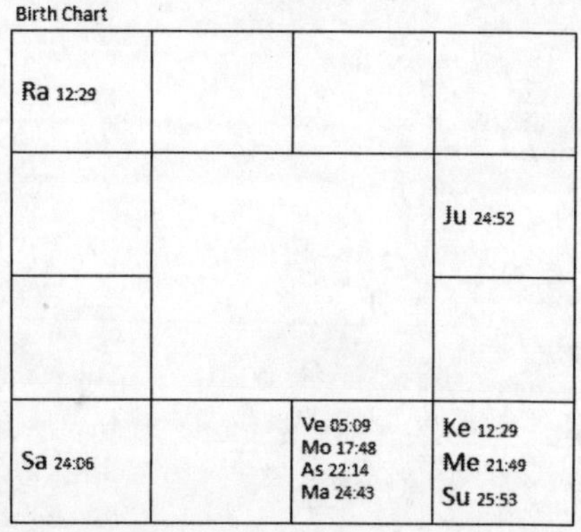

He is an eminent astrologer. Hansa yoga is cancelled by association of Moon and Mars. Jupiter has made him a good astrologer along with other combinations of learning of Astrology. The aspect of sixth lord on sixth house gave him high position in profession and society. Jupiter dasha has proved good for profession and learning.

Example King Faroukh DOB 11 February 1920 TOB 22.18 POB Cairo Egypt

Birth Chart

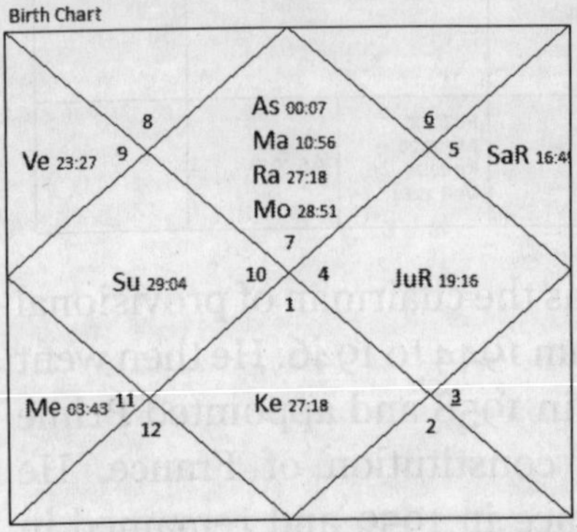

Birth Chart

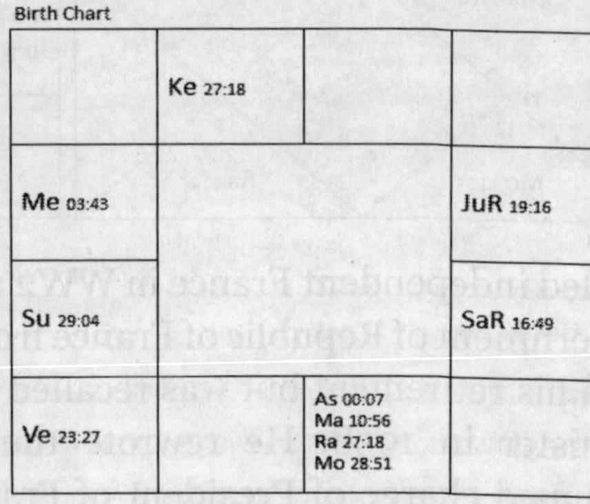

He became King of Egypt after the death of his father in 1936 in the dasha of Saturn/ Moon. He ruled for 16 years and had to go in exile due to military coup on 23 July 1952 in the dasha of Mercury/ Jupiter. He died in exile on 18 March 1965 in dasha of Ketu/ Rahu. Jupiter is retrograde and is aspected by Sun.

Bhadra Yoga

Example Marcel Kint DOB 20 September 1914 TOB 8.30 POB Zwevegem Belgium

Birth Chart

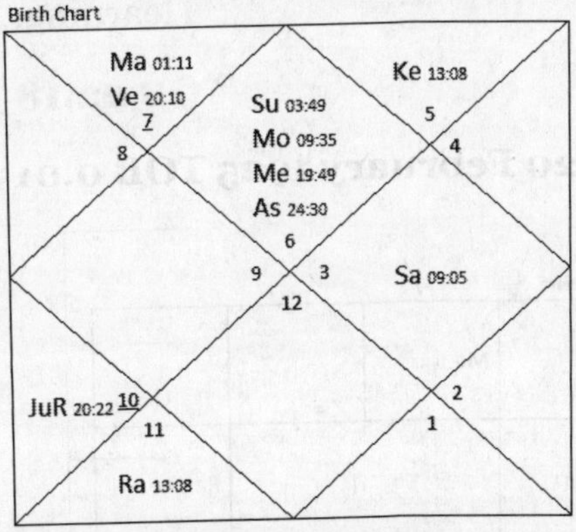

Birth Chart

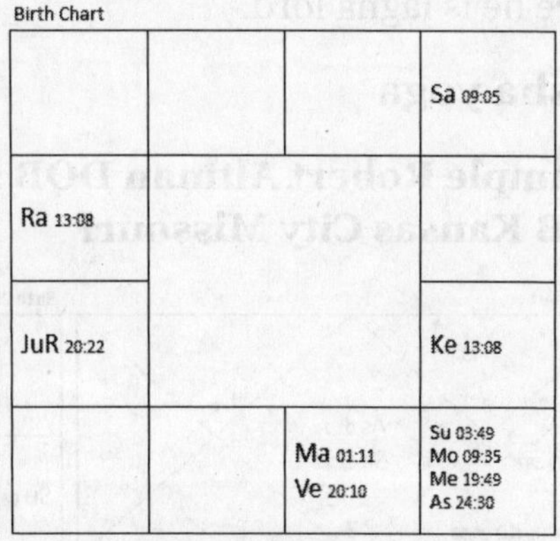

He was a bicycle racer. He won 32 racing events from 1935 to 1951. His best was in 1938 when he won the world cycle championship. The dasha was of Rahu. The cancellation of Bhadra yoga did not affect his tenth house.

Example Luigi Diberti DOB 29 September 1939 TOB 14.15 POB Turin Italy

Birth Chart

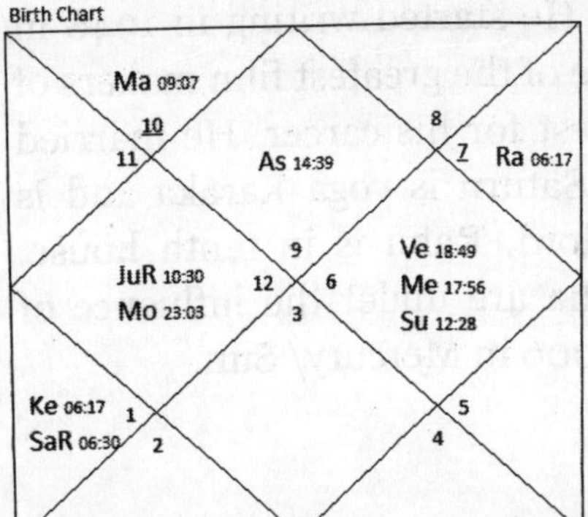

Birth Chart

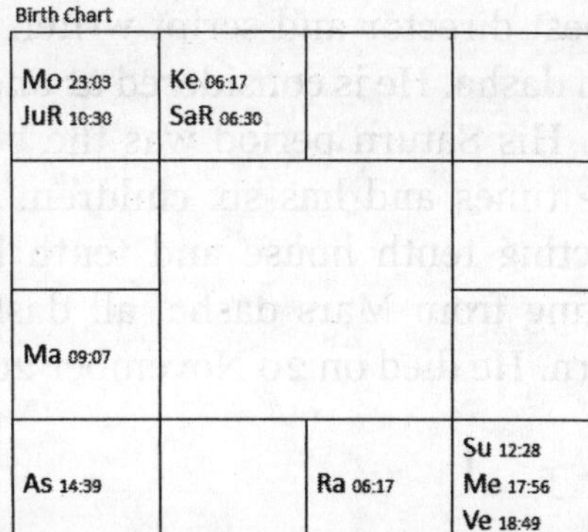

He is an actor who has acted in more than 100 films. His acting career started in 1968 in dasha of Venus/ Saturn. Venus is with tenth lord Mercury. His films have been screened in Cannes film festival. He was born in Mercury MD. Mercury is forming a good raj yoga with Sun. This yoga is not affected by cancellation of Bhadra yoga. Jupiter is giving strength to Mercury and tenth house since he is lagna lord.

Sasha yoga

Example Robert Altman DOB 20 February 1925 TOB 0.01 POB Kansas City Missouri

Birth Chart

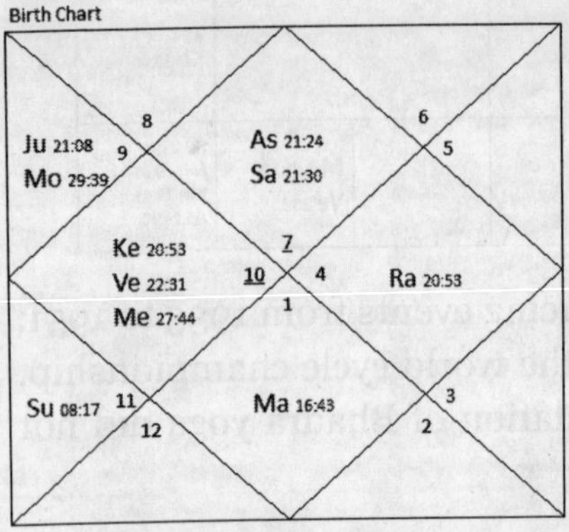

Birth Chart

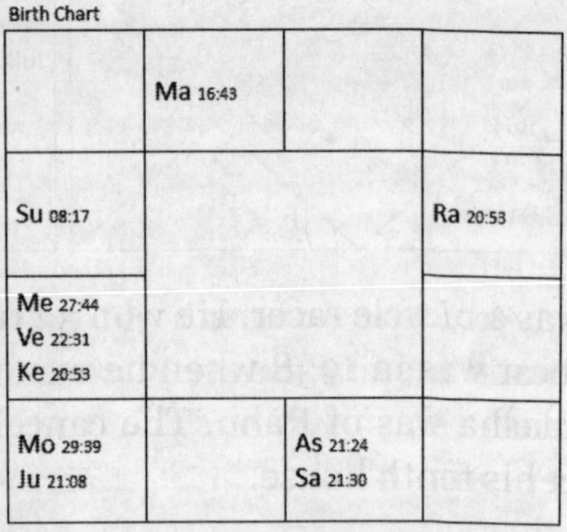

He is a film actor, director and script writer. He served in the Army during WW2 in the dasha of Mars. He was nominated five times for best director and script writer. He started writing in 1948 in Rahu dasha. He is considered as one of the greatest film makers of USA. His Saturn period was the best for his career. He married three times and has six children. Saturn is yoga Karaka and is aspecting tenth house and tenth lord. Rahu is in tenth house. Starting from Mars dasha, all dasha are under the influence of Saturn. He died on 20 November 2006 in Mercury/ Sun.

Example James Remar DOB 31 December 1953 TOB 18.52 POB Brighton Massachusetts

Birth Chart

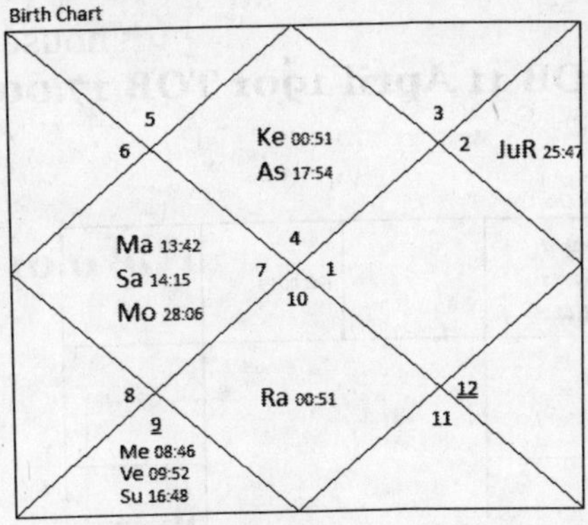

Birth Chart

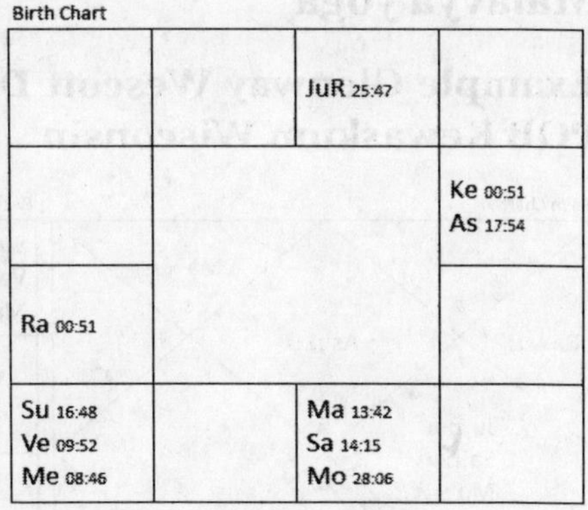

He is an American film actor. He first joined acting school and then passed his high school examination. His first film was in 1979. He mostly acted as villain in the movie. The Saturn dasha started in 1960 and his film career started in Mercury dasha. He is happily married and has two children. Saturn only delayed the start of career but groomed him for a good career. Mercury and Venus are together causing cancellation of Sasha yoga.

EXAMPLES FOR STRONGER PANCH MAHA PURUSHA YOGA

Malavya yoga

Example Glenway Wescott DOB 11 April 1901 TOB 17.00 POB Kewaskum Wisconsin

Birth Chart

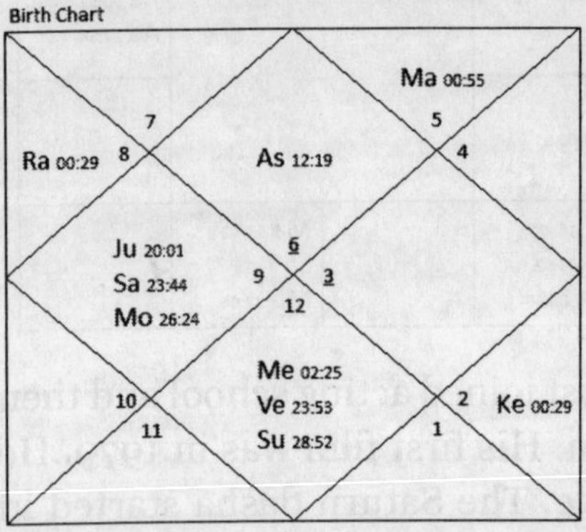

Birth Chart

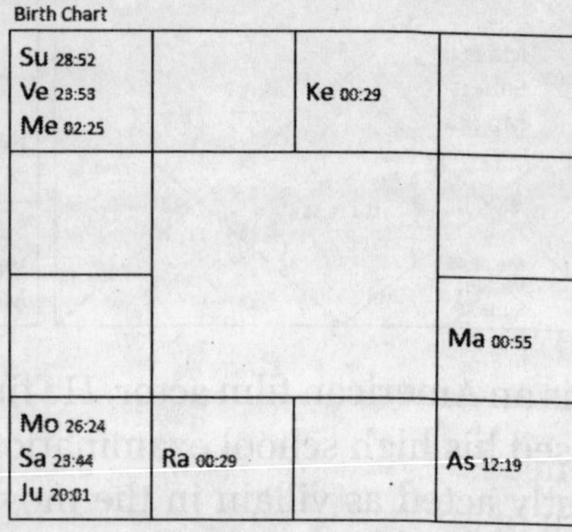

Moon and Jupiter are conjoined. Malavya yoga is strong. He was an open gay. He was a writer and was conferred Harper Noble prize. He died of heart attack on 22 February 1987 at the age of 86 years.

Ruchaka yoga

Example Guru Gobind Singh DOB 23 December 1666 TOB 01.20 POB Patna

Birth Chart

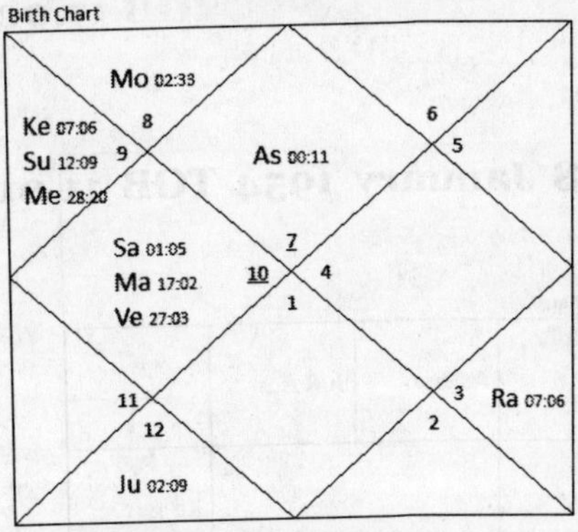

Birth Chart

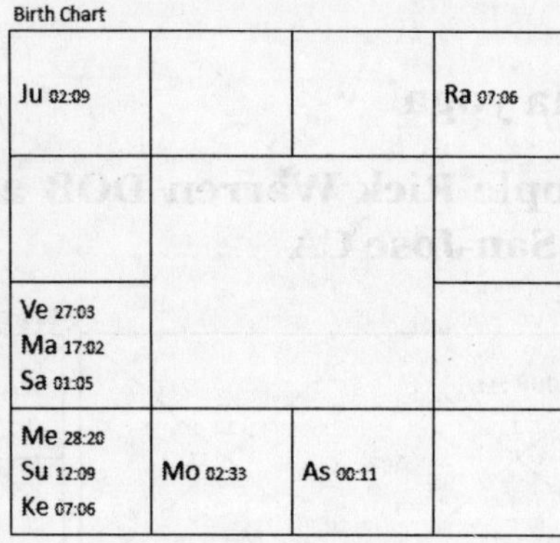

He needs no introduction as a warrior. He was the last and tenth Guru of Sikhs. He fought Mughals. His two sons were buried alive in mortar. He was also killed in sleep. Venus and Saturn are together. Ruchaka yoga is very strong.

Hansa yoga

Example Andre Pousse DOB 20 October 1919 TOB 7.30 POB Paris

Birth Chart

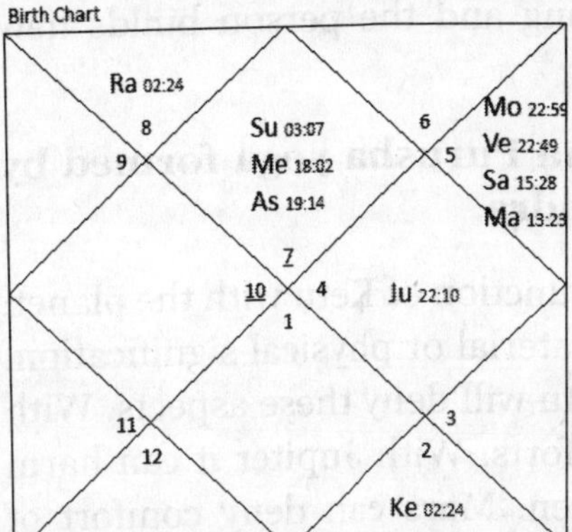

Birth Chart

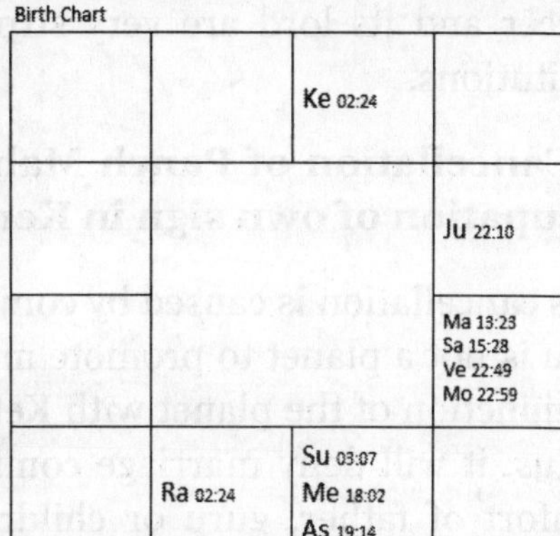

Moon and Venus are conjoined. He was a noted actor and a cyclist. He is the record holder of six days cycling. Jupiter is third and sixth lord. He died in a car accident on 9 September 2005. Jupiter is lord of third and sixth house and is very strong.

Sasha yoga

Example Rick Warren DOB 28 January 1954 TOB 11.01 POB San Jose CA

Birth Chart

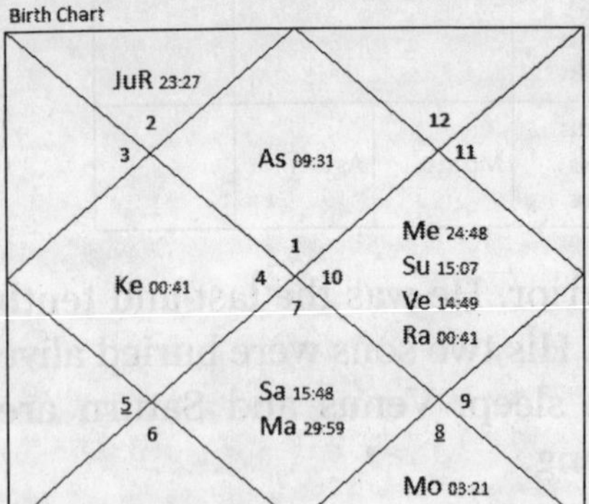

Birth Chart

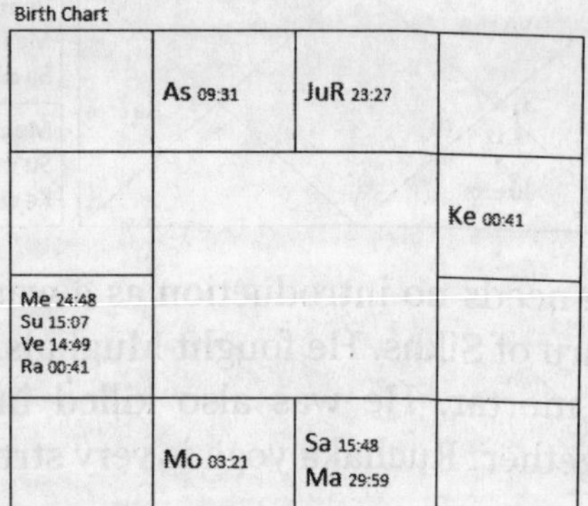

He is the founder of Saddleback Church. This is the sixth largest Church of USA. He is a writer and a Pastor. His book 'The purpose driven life' sold 30 million copies. Jupiter is aspecting Venus and gives strength to Saturn. The tenth house from tenth lord is Cancer. Cancer and its lord are very strong and the person builds new institutions.

2. Cancellation of Panch Maha Purusha yoga formed by occupation of own sign in Kendra.

This cancellation is caused by conjunction of Ketu with the planet. Ketu is not a planet to promote material or physical signification. Conjunction of the planet with Ketu will deny these aspects. With Venus, it will deny marriage comforts. With Jupiter it can harm comfort of father, guru or children. Mars can deny comfort of siblings. Mercury can deny comfort of maternal relation and Saturn deny comfort of servants. These effects are more prominent when the sign occupied by planet is the mooltrikona sign.

Ruchaka yoga

Example Max Ophuls DOB 6 May 1902 TOB 11.00 POB Saarbrucken Germany

Birth Chart

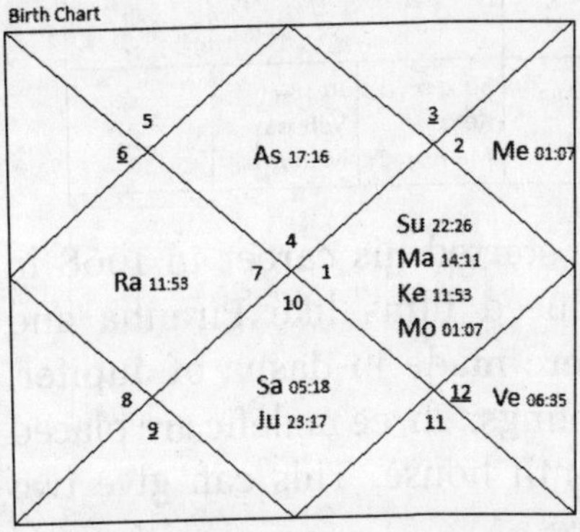

Birth Chart

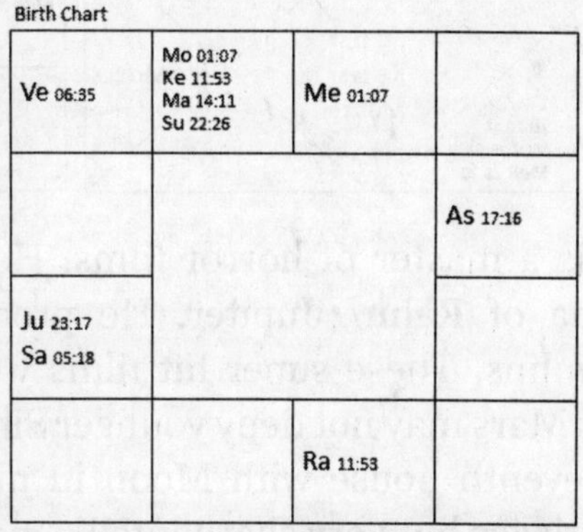

He was a film director and script writer. He wrote and produced many films in Germany, France and USA. He started films in 1929 after writing 200 plays. He directed 30 films. He worked for German films from 1931 to 1933, French films from 1933 to 1940 and from 1950 to 1957 and For US from 1947 to 1950. His dasha of exalted Sun started in 1928 and he worked till the start of Rahu dasha. He died on 25 March 1957 in dasha of Rahu/ Saturn. Saturn is in seventh house and in Capricorn which is a maraca. Association of Mars with Ketu denied younger Siblings.

Example Joe Dante DOB 28 November 1946 TOB 16.32 POB Morristown New Jersey

Birth Chart

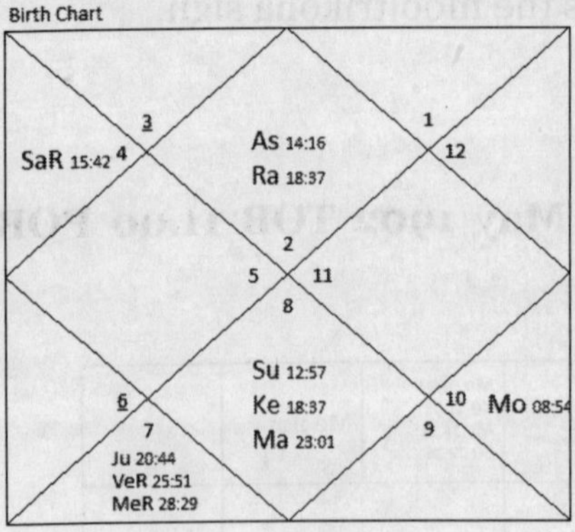

Birth Chart

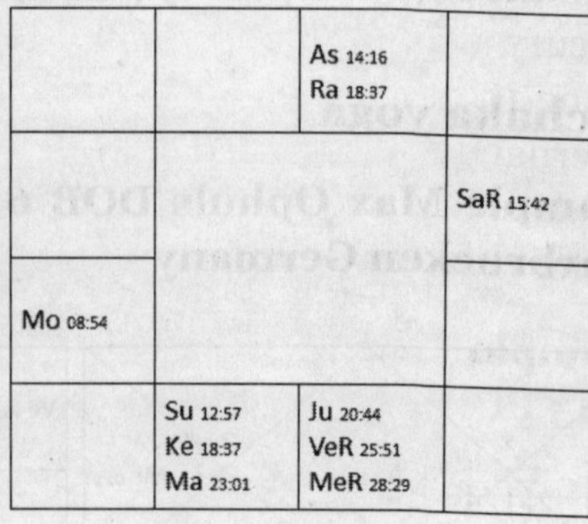

He is a master of horror films. He started his career in 1968 in dasha of Rahu/ Jupiter. He produced films like Piranha and Gremlins. These super hit films were made in dasha of Jupiter. This Mars may not deny younger Siblings. Three malefic are placed in seventh house with Moon in ninth house. This can give two marriages but very sharp intelligence.

Malavya yoga

Example Karunakaran DOB 5 July 1918 TOB 4.30 POB Trichur

Birth Chart

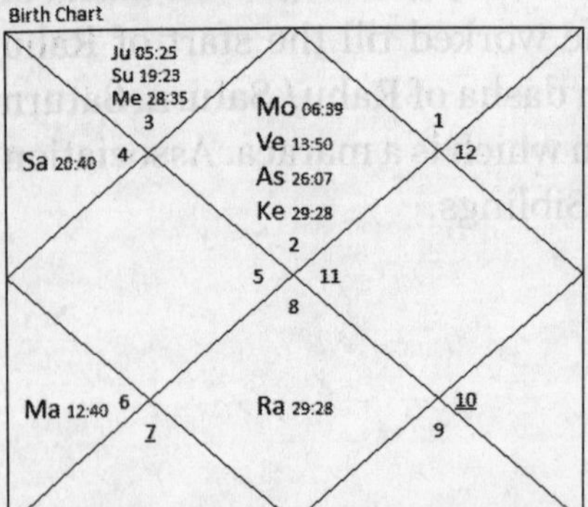

Birth Chart

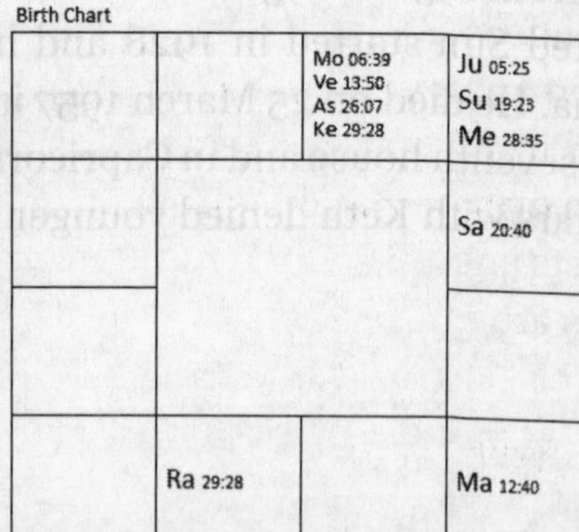

He is the founder of UDF party of Kerala. He was CM of Kerala for four times. He had two short terms of few months each and two long terms. This happened in dasha of Saturn and Mercury. Mercury also saw his downfall. He escaped a near fatal accident on 3 June 1992 in dasha of Mercury. He married the daughter of his maternal uncle. She died of heart attack. He was involved in many scandals during Venus dasha. Venus has given the marriage comfort but wife died before him.

Example Kurt Hoffman DOB 12 November 1910 TOB 22.15 POB Antwerp Belgium

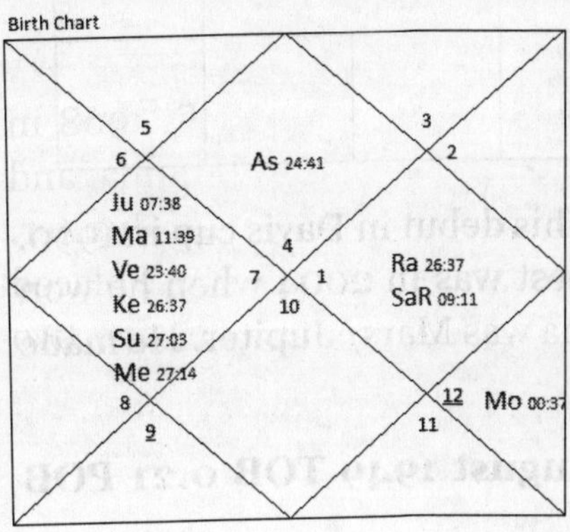

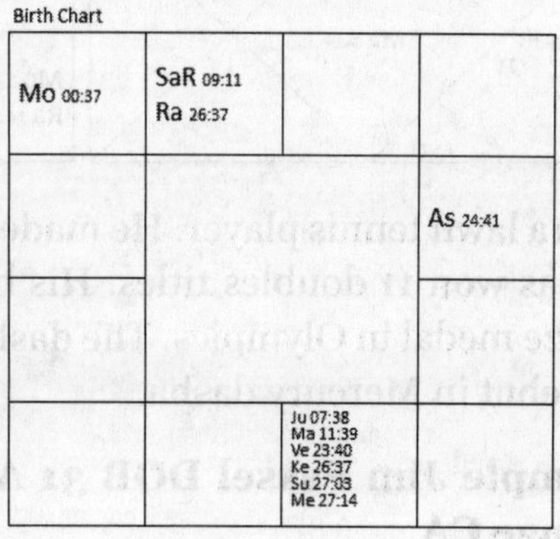

He was a film director who directed 48 films from 1938 to 1971. The dasha of Mercury started in 1933. Dasha of Venus was fruitful but ended his film career also. He married twice. His first marriage was in 1938 and ended in 1989 when his wife died. He married again in 1994 at the age of 84 years. This marriage lasted till his death on 25 June 2001 in dasha of Rahu/ Rahu. Venus is with five planets and is aspected by Saturn. Venus gains strength and many yogas are caused.

Bhadra yoga

Example Leander DOB 17 June 1973 TOB 12.00 POB Calcutta

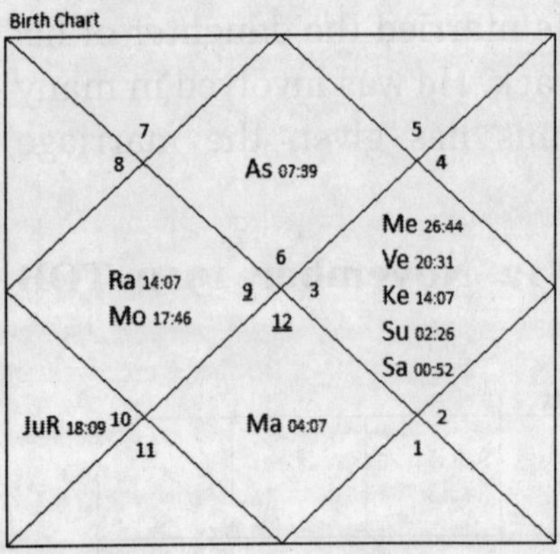

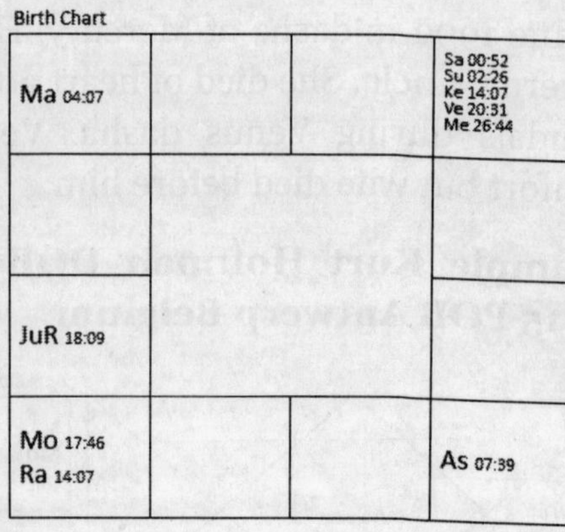

He is a lawn tennis player. He made his debut in Davis cup in 1990. He has won 11 doubles titles. His best was in 2004 when he won bronze medal in Olympics. The dasha was Mars/ Jupiter. He made his debut in Mercury dasha.

Example Jim Fassel DOB 31 August 1949 TOB 0.21 POB Orange CA

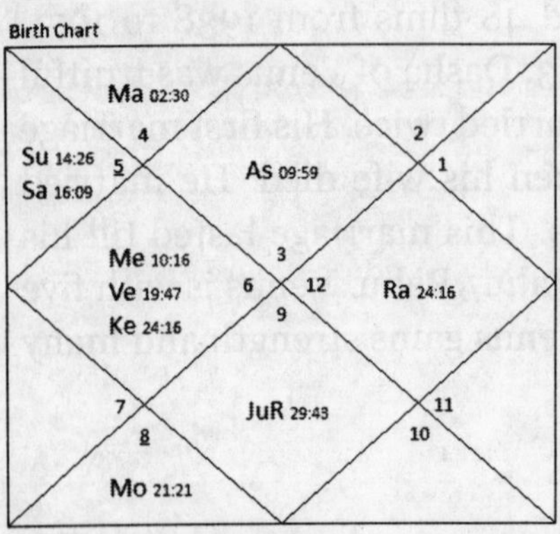

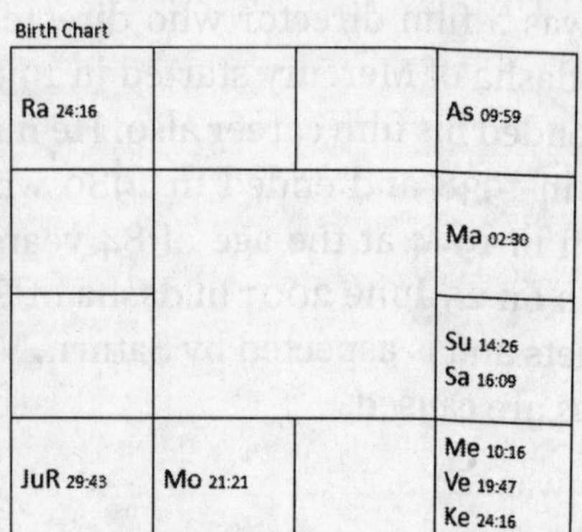

Ketu is with Mercury. He became a sportsman which is given by third and sixth house and malefic.

Hansa yoga

Example Hedgewar DOB 1 April 1889 TOB 1.13 POB Nagpur

Birth Chart

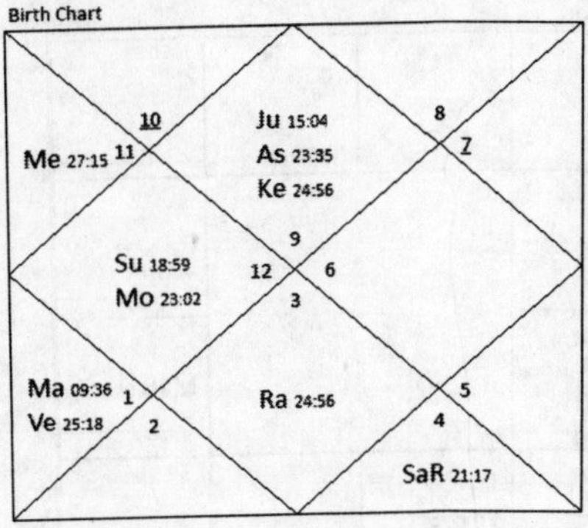

Birth Chart

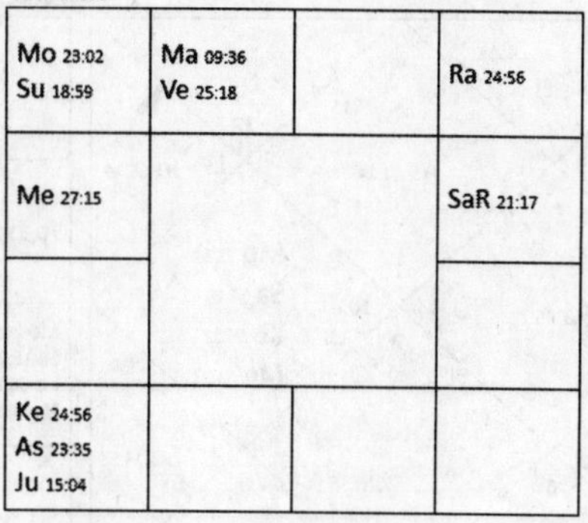

Jupiter has denied marriage and children but not the devotion to religion. Tenth house from tenth lord is very strong and he founded RSS.

Example Gladstone DOB 29 December 1809 TOB 8.15 POB Liverpool UK

Birth Chart

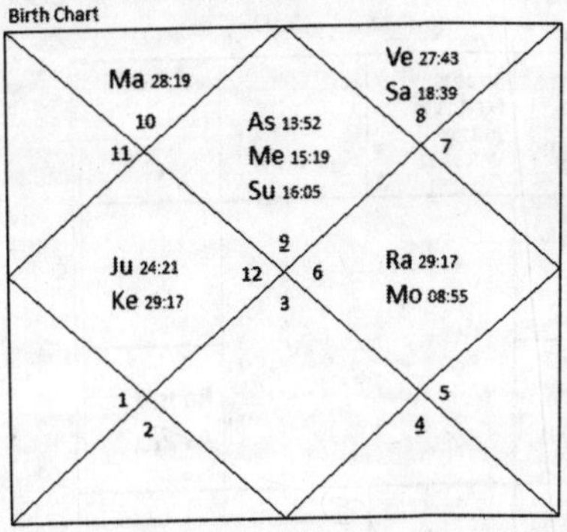

Birth Chart

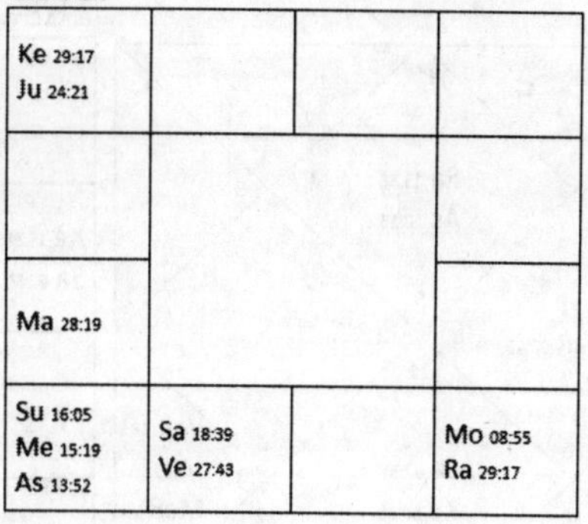

He was Prime Minister for twelve years and chancellor of exchequer for 12 years. Jupiter has not denied high position by his aspect.

Sasha yoga

Example Alessandra Mussolini DOB 30 December 1962 TOB 13.00 POB Rome

Birth Chart

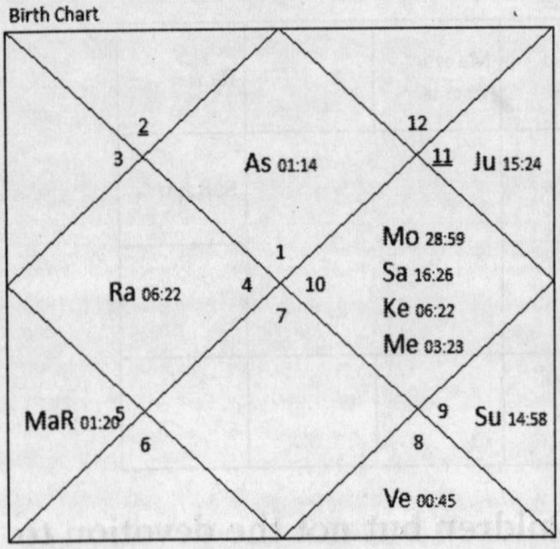

Birth Chart

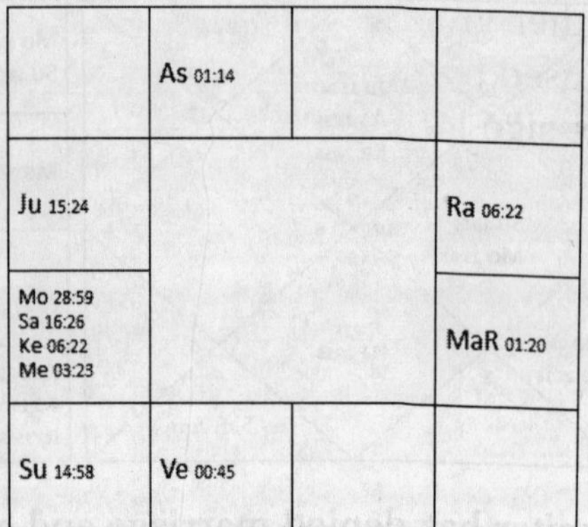

She was member of European parliament and an actress. Saturn has not spoiled the profession or position.

Example James A Mollison DOB 19 April 1905 TOB 14.45 POB Glasgow UK

Birth Chart

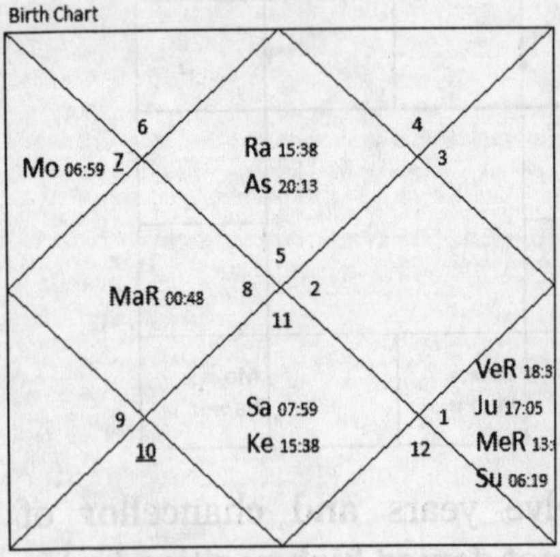

Birth Chart

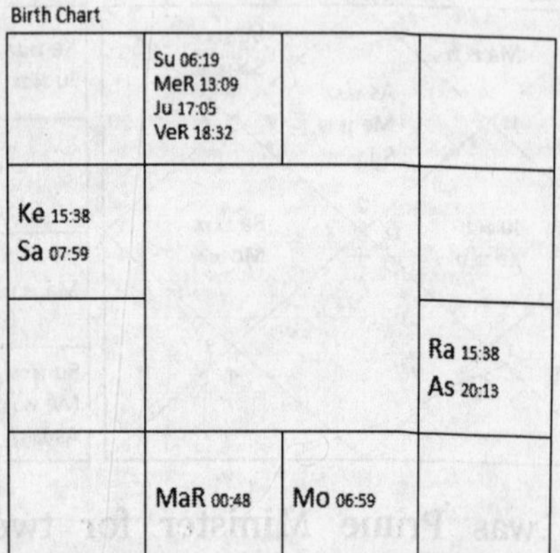

He was the youngest Airforce officer at the age of 18 years. He has a record of longest flights. First was of 8 days and 19 hours flight from Australia to England on 31 August 1931. Second is from England to Cape Town in 4 days and 17 hours in March 1932. Saturn is with Ketu in airy sign.

Note: The cancellation by association of Ketu with the planet is rather giving strength to the Panch Maha Purush Yoga which is caused by planet in Kendra and in own sign. Ketu will also act as the sign lord and boost the significations of planet.

[illegible] to England on 31 August 1927. Second is from England to Cape Town in 4 days and 17 hours in March 1932. Saturn is with Ketu in airy sign.

Note: The cancellation by association of Ketu with the planet is rather giving strength to the Panch Maha Purush Yoga which is caused by planet in Kendra and in own sign. Ketu will also act as the sign lord and boost the significations of planet.